A room without a book is like a body without a soul.

Cicero

After the basic necessities of life, nothing is more precious than books.

Pierre Simon Fournier

The Used Book Lover's Guide To The Mid-Atlantic States

New York, New Jersey, Pennsylvania & Delaware

By

David S. and Susan Siegel

Book Hunter Press
P.O. Box 193
Yorktown Heights, NY 10598

Printed and bound in the United States of America

Library of Congress Catalog Card Number 93-91597

ISBN 0-9634112-1-7

Acknowledgments

We would like to thank Frank Bequaert of Rainy Day Books, Sharon Lips of the Librarium and Warren F. Broderick for their help with the New York chapter, the Antiquarian Booksellers Association of New Jersey for its assistance with the New Jersey chapter and Andrew and Linda Winiarczyk of The Last Hurrah Bookshop for their assistance with the Pennsylvania chapter.

Last but not least, we would like to thank the over nine hundred book dealers listed in this Guide who patiently answered our questionnaire, responded to our phone calls, and chatted with us during our visits. Without their cooperation, this book would not have been possible.

Also available from Book Hunter Press:

The Used Book Lover's Guide to New England, a guide to over 600 used book dealers in Maine, Vermont, New Hampshire, Massachusetts, Rhode Island and Connecticut.

. . . and available in the near future:

The Used Book Lover's Guide to the South Atlantic States: Maryland to Florida.

If you've found this book useful in your book hunting endeavors and would like information about other titles in *The Used Book Lover* series, send your name and address to:

Book Hunter Press
P.O. Box 193
Yorktown Heights, NY 10598

(914) 245-6608

Table of Contents

List of Maps

Why ?

Why we do this.

Because David, my husband, loves to collect books and I love to drive and to explore new places.

Because, based on our own travels, and with all due respect, we know that other sources, including state guides which are seldom complete, commercial publications which are never complete, and the yellow pages, could not possibly provide the dedicated used book lover with the wealth of information we know we could.

And because we believe that the personal visits we make to the open shops listed in our guides make the guides an invaluable addition to every used book aficionado's library.

We were gratified when our first effort, *The Used Book Lover's Guide To New England*, was enthusiastically received by both professional and amateur book hunters. So pleased, in fact, that we once again postponed our trip to England and immediately began the research for this volume.

If this guide is as well received as our *New England* one, readers can look forward to a third volume in *The Used Book Lover* series covering the area from Maryland to Florida, including Washington, DC.

During the course of our travels, David and I drove over 8,000 miles and visited more than 400 open shops. I won't begin to count the number of books David bought. We met some wonderful book dealers. We argued over whether to turn left or right. We even managed to squeeze in side visits to old friends as well as to a daughter away at college. But most of all, we enjoyed doing what we enjoy most - being together.

We sincerely hope that our efforts will help enhance your quality of life - as well as the size of your book collection.

Susan Siegel
July, 1993

How To Get The Most From This Guide

This book is designed to help you find the books you are looking for, whether you travel to open shops or "browse by mail" from the comfort of your home. However, since we believe that the majority of our readers will be people who enjoy taking book hunting trips, we have organized this guide geographically by state and within each state by the three major categories of book seller:

Open shop dealers who maintain regular hours. These collections can vary in size from less than a 1,000 to more than 100,000 books and can either be a general stock with a little of everything or a specialized stock limited to one or more specialty areas.

By appointment or chance dealers who generally, but not always, have smaller collections, frequently quite specialized. Many of these dealers maintain their collections in their own home. By phoning these dealers in advance, avid book hunters can easily combine a trip to open shops and to by appointment dealers in the same region.

Mail order only dealers who issue catalogs and/or sell to people on their mailing list and frequently display their wares at book fairs.

To help the reader locate specific stores, at the beginning of each state chapter we have included an alphabetical listing of all the dealers in that state as well as a geographical listing by location.

Also, to help the reader plan itineraries to open shops and locate shops near each other, we have included a series of regional and local maps. At the beginning of each state chapter (with the exception of Delaware which is combined with Pennsylvania), a map of the entire state is divided into regional maps, along with a list of the cities included in each map. In each open shop listing, the number of the appropriate map is noted in the *Travel* section and a map identification number appears to the right of the shop name.

Within each listing, we have tried to include the kind of information about book sellers that we ourselves have found useful in our own travels.

- A description of the stock: are you likely to find the kind of book you are searching for in this shop?
- The size of the collection: if the shop has a small collection, should you go out of your way to visit it?
- Detailed travel directions: how can you get to the shop?
- Special services: does the dealer issue a catalog? Accept want lists? Have a search service?
- Payment: will the shop accept credit cards?

Perhaps the most unique feature of this guide is the *Comments* section that includes our personal observations about the shop. Based on actual visits to almost every open shop in the Mid Atlantic region, our comments are designed not to endorse or criticize any of the establishments we visited but rather to place ourselves in the position of our readers and provide useful data or insights.

If you're interested in locating books in very specific categories, you'll want to take a close look at the *Specialty Index* in the back of the book.

Note that the owner's name is included in each listing only when it is different from the name of the business. Also, in the *Special Services* section, if the dealer issues a catalog, we generally have not listed "mail order" as a separate service.

A few caveats and suggestions before you begin your book hunting safari.

Call ahead. Even when an open shop lists hours and days open, we advise a phone call ahead to be certain that the hours have not changed and that the establishment will indeed be open when you arrive.

Is there a difference between an "antiquarian" store, and a "used" book store? Yes and no. Many stores we visited call themselves antiquarian but their shelves contain a large stock of books published within the past ten or fifteen years. Likewise, we also found many older books in "used" book stores. For that reason, we have used the term "antiquarian" with great caution and only when it was clear to us that the book seller dealt primarily in truly older or rare books.

Some used book purists also make a distinction between "used" books and "out-of-print" books, a distinction which, for the most part, we have avoided. Where appropriate, however, and in order to assist the book hunter, we have tried to indicate the relative vintage of the stock and whether the collection consists of reading copies of popular works or more rare and unusual titles.

Paperbacks. The reader should also note that while we list shops that carry paperbacks, we do not list shops that are exclusively paper. Although philosophically we agree with the seasoned book dealer we met in our travels who said, "Books are books and there's a place for people who love to read all kinds of books," because we believe that most of our readers are interested in hardcover volumes, we have tried to identify "primarily paperback" shops as a caveat to those who might prefer to shop elsewhere.

Antique malls. Many used book dealers rent space in multi dealer antique malls and some malls have more than one dealer. The size and quality of these collections vary widely from a few hundred fairly common titles to interesting and unusual collections, sometimes as large as what we have seen in individual book shops. While we have listed antique malls where we knew there were used book dealers, we have not, on a systematic basis, researched every known antique mall in New York, New Jersey, Pennsylvania or Delaware. Where the information was available, we have tried to identify the name of the dealer/s who display at these shops.

Size of the collection. In almost all instances, the information regarding the size of the collection comes directly from the owner. While we did not stop to do an actual count of each collection during our visits, in the few instances where the owner's estimate seemed to be exaggerated, we made note of our observation in the *Comments* section. Readers should note, however, that the number of volumes listed may include books in storage that are not readily accessible.

Readers should also know that only dealers who responded to our questionnaire or who we were able to contact by phone are included in the guide. If the dealer did not respond to our multiple inquiries and if we could not personally confirm that the dealer was still in business, the dealer was not listed.

And now to begin your search. Good luck and happy hunting.

Delaware

Alphabetical Listing By Dealer

Alphabetical Listing By Location

Centreville

Barbara's Antiques and Books (DE1)   (302) 655-3055
5900 Kennett Pike 19807

Collection:	General stock and ephemera.
# of Volumes:	3,000-4,000
Specialties:	Regional Americana; children's; photography.
Hours:	Mon-Sat 10-5. Sun 12-5. Best to call ahead.
Travel:	Exit 7 off I-95. Proceed on Rte. 52N and Delaware Ave. Left on Delaware. Stay to left and follow Pennsylvania Ave. (Route 52) straight ahead for about 6 miles. Shop is located on the left in an accessory building behind a red brick private home with tall pine trees in front. Look for small sign on the mail box. Map 18.
Credit Cards:	No
Owner:	Barbara & Marvin Balick
Year Estab:	1979
Comments:	A modest sized collection devoted primarily to subjects of local interest, although there are books of a more general nature. The shop also sells collectibles.

New Castle

Oak Knoll Books (DE2)   (302) 328-7232
414 Delaware Street 19720   Fax: (302) 328-7274

Collection:	Specialty used and new books.
# of Volumes:	30,000
Specialties:	Books about books.
Hours:	Mon-Fri 9-5.
Services:	Appraisals, search service, catalog, accepts want lists.
Travel:	Rte. 141 exit off I-95. Proceed south on Rte. 141 to Rte. 9. Left on Rte. 9 North. At first light, stay in right lane and proceed straight onto Delaware St. Shop is on right. Map 18.
Credit Cards:	Yes
Owner:	Robert D. Fleck
Year Estab:	1976
Comments:	Don't be misled by the single speciality area listed above into thinking that this shop might not have titles in your area/s of interest. While the three story shop certainly is one of the richest sources of books dealing with publishing, paper making, printing, etc. in the region, the collection also covers books that have even the most remote connection to printing or publishing, e.g., we noted several shelves filled with mysteries which in one way or another relate to books. The shop, in our view, is

definitely worth a visit. Prices, we felt, reflected the specialty nature of the collection.

Stanton

John P. Reid (DE3)   (302) 995-6580
307 Main Street
Mailing address: PO Box 114 Bear 19701-0114

Collection:	General stock and ephemera.
# of Volumes:	5,000
Specialties:	Delaware; Maryland (eastern shore).
Hours:	Wed-Sat 11-4.
Services:	Accepts want lists, newsletter on collecting Delaware books.
Travel:	Rte. 141 exit off I-95. Proceed north on Rte. 141 to Rte. 4, then west on Rte. 4 for about 2 miles. Shop is located on Rte. 4, on the right, in a former private residence, just before intersection with Rte. 7. Map 18.
Year Estab:	1980
Comments:	A combination used book and antique shop, the owner is planning to expand the space devoted books so that he can display the non Delaware titles in his collection.

Wilmington

Around Again Books (DE4)   (302) 478-3333
1717 Marsh Road 19803

Collection:	General stock of paperback and hardcover.
Hours:	Mon-Fri 10-6, except Thu till 7. Sat 10-5.
Services:	Search service, accepts want lists.
Travel:	Exit 3 off I-95. Proceed on Marsh Rd. for about 1 mile. Shop is on right, across from shopping center. Map 18.
Credit Cards:	No
Owner:	Helen Blancard
Year Estab:	1981
Comments:	Primarily a paperback shop.

Holly Oak Book Shop (DE5)   (302) 429-0894
604 Market Street 19801

Collection:	General stock of hardcover, paperback and records.
# of Volumes:	5,000 (hardcover)
Specialties:	Mystery; science fiction.
Hours:	Mon-Fri 10-5. Sat 10-3.

Travel:	Center City/Dela exit off I-95. Take Dela to Market. Left on Market. Shop is about 3 blocks ahead in the heart of the city's downtown revitalization area. Map 18.
Credit Cards:	No
Owner:	Alexandra Rosenblatt
Year Estab:	1978
Comments:	We were impressed by the shop's shelf after shelf of older mysteries, most in their original dust jackets and most quite reasonably priced. Other hardcovers in the shop were also reasonably priced. Approximately 50% of the stock is paperback.

By Appointment Dealers

Newark

The Book Room   (302) 368-5654
PO Box 84 19715

Collection:	Specialty books and ephemera.
# of Volumes:	5,000+
Specialties:	American social history; domestic arts; cooking; trade catalogs; self-help manuals; sports and amusements; etiquette; horticulture; Delaware.
Services:	Appraisals, catalog.
Credit Cards:	No
Owner:	Nathaniel H. Puffer
Year Estab:	1991

Wilmington

Aviation Books   (302) 764-2427
705 West 38th Street 19802

Collection:	Specialty
# of Volumes:	2,000
Specialties:	Aviation, including civilian, military, biographies, technical.
Services:	Catalog
Credit Cards:	No
Owner:	M.D. Glazier
Year Estab:	1981

Mail Order Dealers

Dale A. Brandreth Books   (302) 239-4608
PO Box 151 Yorklyn 19736

Collection:	Specialty books and magazines.
# of Volumes:	40,000
Specialties:	Chess; checkers.
Services:	Appraisals, catalog, accepts want lists.
Credit Cards:	No
Year Estab:	1971

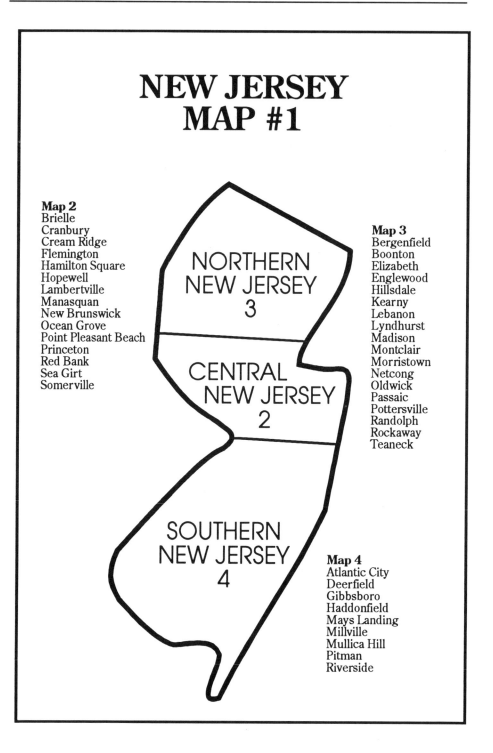

NEW JERSEY MAP #1

Map 2
Brielle
Cranbury
Cream Ridge
Flemington
Hamilton Square
Hopewell
Lambertville
Manasquan
New Brunswick
Ocean Grove
Point Pleasant Beach
Princeton
Red Bank
Sea Girt
Somerville

Map 3
Bergenfield
Boonton
Elizabeth
Englewood
Hillsdale
Kearny
Lebanon
Lyndhurst
Madison
Montclair
Morristown
Netcong
Oldwick
Passaic
Pottersville
Randolph
Rockaway
Teaneck

NORTHERN
NEW JERSEY
3

CENTRAL
NEW JERSEY
2

SOUTHERN
NEW JERSEY
4

Map 4
Atlantic City
Deerfield
Gibbsboro
Haddonfield
Mays Landing
Millville
Mullica Hill
Pitman
Riverside

New Jersey

Alphabetical Listing By Dealer

Alphabetical Listing By Location

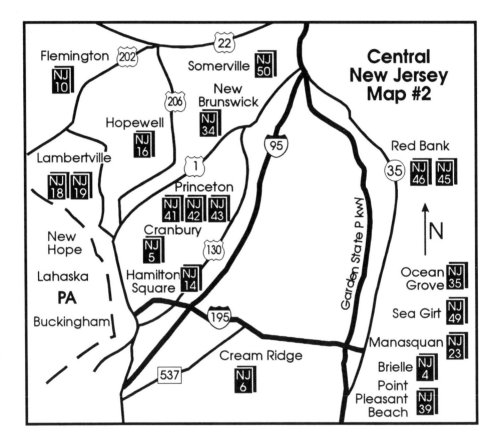

Central
New Jersey
Map #2

Flemington 202
NJ 10

22

Somerville NJ 50

New Brunswick
206
NJ 34

Hopewell
NJ 16

95

Red Bank

1

35
NJ 46   NJ 45

Lambertville
NJ 18   NJ 19

Princeton
NJ 41   NJ 42   NJ 43

N

New Hope

Cranbury
NJ 5
130

Lahaska

Hamilton Square NJ 14

Ocean Grove NJ 35

PA

Sea Girt NJ 49

Buckingham

195

Manasquan NJ 23

Cream Ridge

Brielle NJ 4

537
NJ 6

Point Pleasant Beach NJ 39

Garden State P kwy

Atlantic City

Antiquarium (NJ1)   (609) 344-6499
Merv Griffin Resorts Casino Hotel 08401

Collection:	General stock.
# of Volumes:	20,000
Hours	Daily 10-8.
Services:	Appraisals, subject printouts upon request, accepts want lists, mail order.
Travel:	Atlantic City Expy. to Pacific Ave. Left on Pacific. Proceed to North Carolina Ave. Shop is inside hotel. Map 4.
Credit Cards:	Yes
Owner:	Paul Glaser
Year Estab:	1970
Comments:	Only a few hundred books are on display in the shop. The remaining books are in a second location in the hotel and can be brought to the shop upon request. Additional books are in storage.

Bergenfield

The Book Stop (NJ2)   (201) 384-1162
52 South Washington Avenue 07621

Collection:	General stock of new, used and remainders.
# of Volumes:	30,000 (combined)
Specialties:	New Jersey.
Hours:	Mon-Sat 10-6, except Thu & Fri till 9.
Services:	Accepts want lists.
Travel:	Exit 161 off Garden State Pkwy. Proceed on Rte. 4 to Teaneck Rd/Bergenfield exit. Continue on Teaneck which becomes South Washington for about 2.6 miles. Shop is on left. Map 3.
Credit Cards:	Yes
Owner:	Jules Orkin
Year Estab:	1977
Comments:	In addition to its regular used book shelves, this storefront shop features several bargain bins offering used books for $1 each, plus a number of remainders and some recent, but still hard-to-find trade paper items that are heavily discounted. While you're not likely to find rare or antiquarian books here, you might walk away (as we did) with a few newer items that just happened to strike your fancy.

Boonton

Second Hand Prose Bookstore (NJ3)   (201) 263-3191
1021 Main Street 07005

Collection:	General stock of new and used, hardcover and paperback.
# of Volumes:	15,000
Hours:	Mon-Sat 10-5, except Wed till 8.
Services:	Accepts want lists.
Travel:	Main St/Boonton exit off I-287. Bear right at exit and make right over highway. Proceed on Main thru business district. Shop is at the end of business district on right. Map 3.
Credit Cards:	No
Owner:	Karen Sangillo
Year Estab:	1991
Comments:	A limited selection of hardcover titles are scattered throughout this mostly paperback shop.

Brielle

Escargot Books (NJ4)   (908) 528-5955
503 Route 71 08730   Fax: (908) 528-5326

Collection:	General stock.
# of Volumes:	25,000
Hours:	Mon-Sat 10-5.
Services:	Appraisals, search service, accepts want lists, mail order.
Travel:	Exit 98 off Garden State Pkwy. Proceed on Rte. 34 to Manasquan/ Sea Girt exit. At circle, proceed on Rte. 35 South and follow signs to Brielle. After "business district" sign, make sharp left on Rte. 71 North. Shop is a few blocks ahead on left. Map 2.
Credit Cards:	Yes
Owner:	Richard Weiner
Year Estab:	1979
Comments:	This very pleasant shop offers a good selection of books in most categories. Although we were particularly impressed by the humor section which had some nice titles, the entire shop is worth browsing at a leisurely pace. Moderately priced. The entrance is up a few steps.

Cranbury

Cranbury Book Worm (NJ5)   (609) 655-1063
54 North Main Street 08512

Collection:	General stock, records and magazines.

# of Volumes:	100,000
Hours:	Mon-Fri 9-8. Sat 9-5. Sun 12-5.
Travel:	Exit 8A off NJ Tpk. Follow signs into Cranbury. Map 2.
Credit Cards:	Yes
Owner:	Ralph Schremp
Year Estab:	1974
Comments:	Every room in this two story Victorian house, including the entire basement, is filled with books. While there are signs designating subject areas, there are also several bookcases, particularly on the first floor, where the books seem to be sorted with absolutely no rhyme or reason. Despite this drawback, and the fact that the condition of some of the books emulates the name of the establishment, we believe this shop is a "must see" for any true used book lover. The owner's claim to having 100,000 volumes is no exaggeration. The vast majority of the books are very reasonably priced and this includes many of the 19th century volumes we spotted.

Cream Ridge

Book Garden (NJ6)   (609) 758-7770
868 Route 537 08514

Collection	General stock and ephemera.
# of Volumes:	35,000
Specialties:	New Jersey.
Hours:	Tue-Sun 9-6, except Fri till 8.
Services:	Accepts want lists, mail order.
Travel:	Great Adventure exit (#16) off Rte. 195. Proceed west on Rte. 537 for about 7 miles. Shop is on right, about 3/4 of a mile south of junction of Rte. 539. Map 2.
Credit Cards:	Yes
Owner:	George & Joyce Engle
Year Estab:	1972
Comments:	Don't be put off by the fact that this roadside used book shop also sells flowers, comics, baseball cards and records. The used hardcover volumes, particularly in the fiction category, offer many bargains as prices are most reasonable. In addition to the shop's New Jersey specialty, we noted strong sections dealing with religion and travel and most other areas were covered quite adequately. The ephemera was especially well organized and displayed.

Deerfield

The Record-Book (NJ7)   Shop: (609) 451-2143
At Deerfield Village, Highway 77 08313   Dealer: (609) 453-2153

Collection:	General stock.
Hours:	Thu-Mon 10-6.
Travel:	Located on Rte. 77. Map 4.
Owner:	James W. Gandy
Comments:	Multi dealer antique mart.

Elizabeth

Kathy's Books (NJ8)   (908) 354-7446
544 Linden Avenue 07202

Collection:	General stock.
# of Volumes:	10,000+
Hours:	Mon-Fri 10-6. Sat 10-5.
Services:	Accepts want lists, mail order.
Travel:	Exit 137 off Garden State Pkwy. Proceed on Rte. 28 to Elizabeth. Right on Elmora then left on Linden. Shop is on right just after corner. Map 3.
Credit Cards:	No
Owner:	Kathy & Jim Reilly
Year Estab:	1989
Comments:	A small but abundantly supplied bi-level shop we would call a "sleeper." The shop stocks primarily reading copies in almost every subject category with better books stored in the owner's home. We noted a particularly nice children's section with books in excellent condition and competitively priced.

Englewood

The Book Store At Depot Square (NJ9)   (201) 568-6563
8 Depot Square 07631

Collection:	General stock.
# of Volumes:	15,000
Specialties:	Children's; folklore; Bergen County.
Hours:	Tue-Fri 11:30-5:30. Sat 10:30-5:30.
Services:	Appraisals
Travel:	From George Washington Bridge, take Rte. 4 East to Grand Ave. exit. Left on Palisade Ave, then right into municipal lot behind railroad tracks. From Rte. 80 eastbound, right on Broad

Ave, left on Palisade, then right into municipal lot. Look for a one story white building in the parking lot. Map 3.

Credit Cards: Yes
Owner: Rita Alexander
Year Estab: 1978
Comments: This attractively appointed shop offers a quality collection of moderately priced fiction and non fiction ranging from $5 to $1,000. Most of the books are in quite good condition. In addition to the specialties noted above, we saw many illustrated volumes, sets and boxed limited editions.

Flemington

The People's Bookshop (NJ10)   (908) 788-4953
160 Main Street 08822

Collection: General stock.
# of Volumes: 50,000
Specialties: Early fiction; children's.
Hours: Daily 12-5. (See Comments)
Services: Subject lists, accepts want lists, mail order.
Travel: Proceeding south on Main St, shop is an immediate left turn after the railroad tracks to the rear of the locksmith shop in a red frame building. From Rte. 202, shop is north of the traffic circle and a right turn just before railroad tracks. Map 2.
Credit Cards: No
Owner: Rosemarie Beardsley
Year Estab: 1979
Comments: When we visited, the shop was suffering from an acute case of "overload" in that the owner had just rescued several thousand volumes from imminent destruction and had not had time to reorganize her stock so that visitors could browse the collection. If and when the shop does get reorganized, from what we could see, visitors are likely to find older books, many of them library discards, and not all in the best of condition. The owner also displays a small collection at the nearby Antiques Emporium, 32 Church St, which is open daily 11-5.

Gibbsboro

Gibbsboro Book Barn and Bindery (NJ11)   (609) 435-2525
10 Washington Avenue 08026

Collection: General stock and ephemera.
# of Volumes: 12,000

Hours:	Wed & Fri 7-9:30 PM. Sat 12-6. Sun 12-5.
Services:	Bindery on premises.
Travel:	Exit 32 off I-295. Proceed toward Gibbsboro on Haddon Ave. past Golf Farm. At Shell Station, bear right. Right on Washington. Barn is on right. Map 4.
Credit Cards:	Yes
Owner:	Ray Boas, Ed Bowersock & Bill Walton
Year Estab:	1993
Comments:	This extremely well organized group shop is located on the second floor of an attractively renovated old barn. We noted some sets for sale at good prices, a large selection of first editions, signed and unsigned, and other interesting collectibles. With 10 dealers displaying their wares, at least one is likely to have something you are looking for. Future plans include expanding to the barn's first floor.

Haddonfield

Ray Boas, Bookseller (NJ12)   (609) 795-4853
407 Haddon Avenue 08033

Collection:	General stock.
# of Volumes:	15,000
Specialties:	New Jersey; business history.
Hours:	Wed-Sat 10:30-6. Mon & Tue by chance or appointment.
Services:	Catalog
Travel:	Exit 32 off I-295. Follow signs for Haddonfield. Bear left at Little League Field, then cross intersection of Haddon and Kings Hgwy. Shop is a few blocks ahead on right, just after MidLantic Bank. Map 4.
Credit Cards:	Yes
Owner:	Ray Boas
Year Estab:	1990
Comments:	The books in this immaculate, attractively decorated bi-level shop have been carefully selected for condition and uniqueness. The collection is well organized and the shop is easy to browse.

Elaine Woodford, Bookseller (NJ13)   (609) 354-9158
323 Hillside Lane
Mailing address: PO Box 68   08033

Collection:	Specialty and limited general stock.
# of Volumes:	5,000
Specialties:	Children's picture books; illustrated; nature; young adult.
Hours:	Sat & Sun 10-6. Most evenings and some weekdays by appointment.

Services:	Search service, catalog, accepts want lists.
Travel:	Exit 32 (Haddonfield) off I-295. Take Rte. 561 into Haddonfield. Right at Kings Hgwy. (Rte. 41N), then left on Grove, left on Farwood, right on Longwood and left on Hillside. Shop is in a white and gray house on right. Map 4.
Credit Cards:	No
Owner:	Elaine Woodford
Year Estab:	1991

Hamilton Square

Twice-Read Books (NJ14)   (609) 587-1960
3720 Nottingham Way 08690

Collection:	General stock of hardcover and paperback.
# of Volumes:	25,000
Hours:	Tue-Fri 12-8. Sat 10-6. Sun 12-4.
Services:	Accepts want lists.
Travel:	Quaker Bridge Rd exit off Rte. 1. Proceed south on Quaker Bridge for 4-5 miles to intersection with Nottingham Way in Mercerville. Left on Nottingham, keeping the Fire Department building on your right, and proceed for about 1.5 miles. Shop is on left, just past second left and before a cemetery. Parking is available in the rear. Map 2.
Credit Cards:	No
Owner:	J.H. Swan
Year Estab:	1990
Comments:	The entrance to this small, tightly packed shop is down a few steps. The collection consists generally of used and out of print books, many of which date back to the mid 1930's and 1940's. According to the owner, most of his stock comes from trades rather than active buying.

Hillsdale

The Book Shop (NJ15)   (201) 391-9101
430 Hillsdale Avenue 07642

Collection:	General stock of hardcover and paperback.
# of Volumes:	8,000
Specialties:	Mystery
Hours:	Tue-Sat 11-5.
Services:	Accepts want lists.
Travel:	Exit 168 off Garden State Pkwy. northbound. Right at exit and proceed to light. Left at light to Hillsdale Ave. then right on Hillsdale. Map 3.

Credit Cards:	No
Owner:	Martha Fornatale
Year Estab:	1984
Comments:	A modest sized shop with an interesting selection of mysteries and entertainment related titles. The books are in mixed condition with some book club editions on hand. The books are priced slightly higher than similar volumes found elsewhere.

Hopewell

Rising Sun Bookshop (NJ16)   (609) 466-4465
33 West Broad Street 08525

Collection:	General stock.
# of Volumes:	12,000
Specialties:	Artist monographs; art history and reference.
Hours:	Wed-Sun 11-5.
Services:	Appraisals, search service, catalog, accepts want lists, book repairs.
Travel:	From the south, Rte. 95 to Rte. 31 North to Rte. 518 East. From the north, Rte. 287 to Rte. 206 South to Rte. 518 West. West Broad St. is Rte. 518. Map 2.
Credit Cards:	No
Owner:	Roland Roberge
Year Estab:	1989
Comments:	With every purchase of a book, visitors to this neatly organized storefront shop can select a free book from a special bookcase located at the shop's entrance. The books are in good condition and are reasonably priced. The collection is especially strong in non fiction and the owner notes that his fiction section is stocked primarily with first editions.

Kearny

Collectors' Dreams (NJ17)   (201) 997-5225
580 Kearny Avenue 07032

Collection:	Specialty books and some general stock.
# of Volumes:	4,000-5,000
Specialties:	Sports; collectibles; art.
Hours:	Mon-Sat 11-6.
Services:	Appraisals and search service in sports only. Also accepts want lists and mail order.
Travel:	Exit 15W off NJ Tpk. Bear right after exit and make right at first light on Schuyler Ave. Proceed for 6 lights and make left

on Midland Ave. Kearny is at the second light. Shop is at the corner of Midland and Kearny. Map 3.

Credit Cards: Yes
Owner: Tony Sabestinas & Don Flanagan
Year Estab: 1989

Lambertville

Left Bank Books   (NJ18)   (609) 397-4966
28 North Union Street
Mailing address: PO Box 462   08530

Collection: General stock.
# of Volumes: 15,000 (See Comments)
Specialties: Modern first editions; vintage paperbacks.
Hours: Fri-Sun 12-5. Other times by appointment. (See Comments)
Services: Appraisals, search service, accepts want lists, mail order.
Travel: Trenton/Lambertville exit off Rte. 195. Following signs for Lambertville, proceed north on Rte. 29. Bear left at fork and make left on Bridge St. At second light, make right on Union. Shop is at the corner of Church St. The entrance is on Church, up two flights of stairs. Map 2.
Credit Cards: No
Owner: Reid Collins
Year Estab: 1989
Comments: Once you've caught your breath after climbing two flights of stairs, you should enjoy browsing this small but comfortable shop. The books are attractively displayed and reasonably priced. The owner is constantly adding to his stock and many of the titles we saw were not readily available elsewhere. The owner is planning to expand into an adjoining room and increase the size of the collection. Additional hours during the week are planned.

Phoenix Books (NJ19)   (609) 397-4960
49 North Union Street 08530

Collection: General stock, records and ephemera.
# of Volumes: 30,000+
Specialties: Military, art; American history; literature; film.
Hours: Mon-Thu 11-5, except Tue by chance or appointment. Fri-Sun 11-6.
Services: Accepts want lists, mail order.
Travel: See above. Map 2.
Credit Cards: Yes
Owner: Michael & Joan Ekizian and Janet & Barry Novick

Year Estab: 1988
Comments: A charming shop located in one of New Jersey's popular antique haunts. The books we saw were in good to excellent condition and priced reasonably. Book lovers are as likely to find a book they have been looking for here as in many shops twice the size. One sign of a quality used book store is the sight of several customers reading in the aisles - and we saw quite a few here.

Lebanon

Levine's Editions Bookshop (NJ20)   (908) 236-2234
Grist Mill Square (Route 22 East)
Mailing address: 148 Main Street, A-3   08833

Collection: General stock and records.
# of Volumes: 25,000+
Hours: Daily 10-6.
Travel: From east: Exit 20A off I-78. Left at light and look for "Books" sign on right. From west: Exit 18 off I-78. Shop is about 3 miles ahead on right. Map 3.
Credit Cards: Yes
Owner: Debbie & David Levine
Year Estab: 1992   (See Comments)
Comments: Located in an attractive complex of new stores on the site of a former grist mill, this shop is similar in both layout and ambience to its counterpart, Editions, in Shokan, NY. The shop is roomy, airy and very well organized with book cases clearly numbered and lettered. Most of the books are in very good condition and prices are quite reasonable. Almost every subject area is represented.

Lyndhurst

Stamps & Coins & Things (NJ21)   (201) 933-4499
306 Valley Brook Avenue 07071

Collection: General stock.
# of Volumes: 35,000
Hours: Mon-Sat 9-6.
Travel: Rte. 17 south to Valley Brook Ave. Proceed west on Valley Brook to next light. Shop is just before light on left. Map 3.
Credit Cards: No
Owner: Henry Sundvik
Year Estab: 1972
Comments: This bi-level storefront shop carries a potpourri of items in

addition to a good sized used book collection. The books are truly of an older vintage (1920's-1940's) with a smattering of "newer" volumes (1950's-1960's). The shop is relatively small but the owner makes excellent use of the space by creating a number of small alcoves. If you're looking for an unusual book, not necessarily a classic or first edition, there's a good chance that you can find it here. There are some paperbacks mixed in with the hardcover volumes. Our only misgiving about the shop is the poor lighting on the second floor.

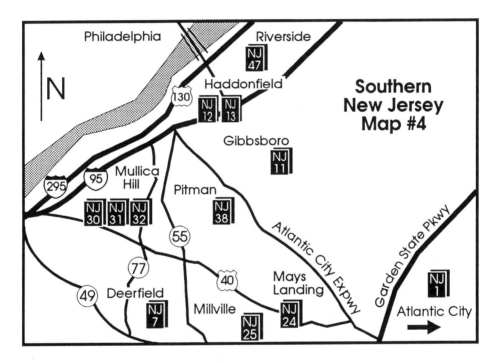

Madison

The Chatham Bookseller (NJ22)   (201) 822-1361
8 Green Village Road 07940

Collection:	General stock.
# of Volumes:	10,000
Hours:	Mon-Sat 9-5:30.
Travel:	Rte. 124 exit off Rte. 287. East on Rte. 124 for about 3 miles. After railroad underpass, right at second light on Green Village Rd. Shop is ahead on left. Parking is available in rear. Map 3.

Credit Cards:	Yes
Owner:	Frank Deodene
Year Estab:	1968
Comments:	When we visited this conveniently located storefront shop, the shelves looked "picked through" giving one the impression that at one time there were many more rare and unusual items available. The remaining books were in generally good condition and represented all categories. While some of the shelves were sparse, there were still a few unusual titles and we feel that this shop deserves a visit. The owner clearly is concerned about the quality of his collection more than the quantity. The books, we feel, were most reasonably priced. We noted an interesting section of books dealing with China.

Manasquan

Tales & Treasures (NJ23)   (908) 892-6414
At Carriage House Antique Center, 140 Main Street
Mailing address: 226 Jaehnel Parkway Point Pleasant 08742

Collection:	General stock, prints and maps.
# of Volumes:	2,000
Specialties:	New Jersey.
Hours:	Daily 10-6, except Fri & Sat till 9.
Services:	Search service, accepts want lists, mail order.
Travel:	Exit 98 off Garden State Pkwy. Proceed south on Rte. 34 to Sea Girt/Manasquan exit. Right on Atlantic Ave. and proceed for about 2.5 miles thru traffic circle. At light at Main St. make right. Shop is 4 blocks ahead on left. Map 2.
Credit Cards:	No
Owner:	Kathleen Ferris Heim
Year Estab:	1991
Comments:	A limited selection of older books in a small booth in a multi dealer antique shop. Worth a quick stop in you're in the area.

Mays Landing

Gravelly Run Antiquarians (NJ24)   (609) 625-7778
5045 Mays Landing Road 08330

Collection:	General stock, prints and photographica.
# of Volumes:	30,000
Specialties:	Americana; New Jersey; nautical; natural history; first editions; antiquarian.
Hours:	Daily 9-5. Evenings by appointment.

Services:	Appraisals, accepts want lists, mail order.
Travel:	At intersection of Rtes. 40, 50 & 559 proceed south on Rte. 559 (Mays Landing Rd) for about 2 miles. Shop is located on right in a 2 story yellow frame building. Map 4.
Credit Cards:	Yes
Owner:	Harry & Judy Reist
Year Estab:	1989
Comments:	One of the nicest shops of its kind in terms of contents and price range. Located in a former general store, the shop has a little bit of everything with an emphasis on older, scarcer and interesting titles in most fields. To say that we purchased several volumes here certainly prejudices our positive view of the establishment.

Millville

Wind Chimes Book Exchange (NJ25)   (609) 327-3714
210 North High Street 08332

Collection:	General stock of new and used, hardcover and paperback.
# of Volumes:	85,000
Hours:	Mon-Sat 11-5.
Services:	Accepts want lists.
Travel:	In center of Millville, two blocks from light at Rte. 49 and High St. Map 4.
Credit Cards:	Yes
Owner:	Dave & Diann Ewan
Year Estab:	1976
Comments:	Paperbacks (not always in the best condition) account for between 97%-98% of the shop's stock. The hardcover volumes we saw were common and most not in the best of condition.

Montclair

The Bookstore of Montclair (NJ26)   (201) 746-6212
208 Glenridge Avenue 07042

Collection:	General stock.
# of Volumes:	5,000
Hours:	Mon-Sat 11-6. Sun 1-4. Other times by appointment.
Services:	Appraisals
Travel:	Exit 148 off Garden State Pkwy. Proceed on Bloomfield Ave. for about 2 miles to Glenridge. Note: the numbering on Bloomfield changes as you pass through different communities. Map 3.
Credit Cards:	No
Owner:	Jim Harvin

Year Estab:	1992
Comments:	This modest sized shop gives the browser an overwhelming sense of overcrowding with narrow aisles, most made even narrower by unevenly stacked piles of books, and because so many of the books that are shelved are stacked sideways on top of each other rather than in the conventional vertical fashion. The books are of mixed vintage and are in mixed condition. About one third of the stock consists of paperbacks. There are no subject labels on the shelves. Because there's a combination new/used book shop across the street, the browser doesn't have to travel far to see more titles, making this shop worth a visit.

Montclair Book Center (NJ27)   (201) 783-3630
221 Glenridge Avenue 07042

Collection:	General stock of new and used hardcover and paperback.
# of Volumes:	100,000 (See Comments)
Hours:	Mon-Sat 10-8. Sun 12-6.
Services:	Search service, accepts want lists, mail order.
Travel:	See above. Map 3.
Credit Cards:	Yes
Owner:	Peter Ryby
Year Estab:	1982
Comments:	Approximately 75% of the stock in this storefront shop consists of used books, divided roughly in half between paperback and hardcover. The books are generally well displayed. However, even though ladders are available, browsing the upper shelves can be difficult. The books are moderately priced. Don't overlook the mezzanine section in the rear of the store. Although not listed as a specialty, we noted a strong humor section.

Yesterday's Books and Records (NJ28)   (201) 783-6262
559 Bloomfield Avenue 07042

Collection:	General stock.
# of Volumes:	1,500
Specialties:	Military
Hours:	Tue-Sat 12-5, except Fri till 6 or later.
Travel:	See above. Shop is about 3 blocks from Glenridge. Map 3.
Credit Cards:	No
Owner:	John G. Areson
Year Estab:	1982
Comments:	Records, mostly in the vintage category, occupy about 50% of this storefront shop while bookcases with hardcover volumes line the shop's two side walls. If you browse long enough, you

might find something of interest, although most of the sections contained a limited number of titles. The shop is worth a visit only if you happen to be in Montclair to visit either or both of the nearby used book shops.

Morristown

Old Book Shop (NJ29)   (201) 538-1210
4 John Street 07960

Collection:	General stock, magazines and ephemera.
# of Volumes:	25,000
Specialties:	New Jersey
Hours:	Mon-Sat 10-5:30.
Travel:	From Rte. 287 northbound, take exit 36B (Lafayette Ave) to first light (Ridgedale Ave). Right on Ridgedale and proceed 4/10 mile. Right on John St. From Rte. 287 southbound, take exit 36 (Ridgedale Ave) to first light, then right on Ridgedale. Proceed 2/10 mile and right on John. Map 3.
Credit Cards:	No
Owner:	Virginia Faulkner & Chris Wolff
Year Estab:	1948
Comments:	This long established shop caters to many diverse interests. Browsers should plan to spend a fair amount of time here. The aisles are comfortably wide and there are lots of stools and small ladders for the browser's comfort and convenience. The books are very moderately priced. We noted a strong humor section.

Mullica Hill

Murphy's Loft (NJ30)   (609) 478-4928
53 North Main Street 08062

Collection:	General stock, prints, records, magazines and ephemera.
# of Volumes:	50,000
Hours:	Wed-Sun 10-6. Other times by appointment or chance.
Services:	Maintains active customer "wish list", mail order.
Travel:	Exit 2 off New Jersey Tpk. Proceed east on Rte. 322, which becomes Main St. in Mullica Hill, for about 10 minutes. Shop is on the left, behind a two story cream colored house. Map 4.
Credit Cards:	Yes
Owner:	Sallie Murphy
Year Estab:	1987
Comments:	Bargains are to be had in this well organized, reasonably priced, user friendly bi-level shop. The stock consists of a good selection

of older hardcover and paperback titles. Dealers planning a trip through the area may wish to contact the owner who is planning a Bed and Breakfast for visiting colleagues in her adjoining home.

Paper Americana (B&B Antiques) (NJ31)   (609) 478-9810
At Old Mill Antique Mall, 1 South Main St. 08062   (609) 795-4216

Collection:	General stock and ephemera.
# of Volumes:	Small
Specialties:	Magazines
Hours:	Daily 11-5.
Travel:	See above. Map 4.
Credit Cards:	Yes
Owner:	Ben Solof
Year Estab:	1986
Comments:	Although the size of the book collection is limited, this modest sized shop does offer an interesting ephemera collection and is worth a stop if you're in the area.

White Papers (NJ32)   (609) 478-4992
At Wolfe's Antiques, 36 South Main Street 08062

Collection:	General stock and ephemera.
# of Volumes:	Limited
Hours:	Tue-Sat 10-4. Sun 12-5.
Travel:	See above. Located on 2nd floor of a multi dealer shop. Map 4.
Owner:	Jo White

Netcong

Books of Yesteryear (NJ33)   (201) 691-8214
39 Ledgewood Avenue 07857

Collection:	General stock.
# of Volumes:	50,000
Specialties:	Children's; children's series; history; Civil War; mystery.
Hours:	Tue-Sun 10:30-5.
Services:	Search service, occasional catalog, accepts want lists, mail order.
Travel:	Exit 27B off Rte. 80. Bear right at circle to Rte. 183 North. Shop is about 1½ blocks ahead on right. Map 3.
Credit Cards:	No
Owner:	Sandra J. Buckholtz
Year Estab:	1987
Comments:	If reading copies are your thing, this is a shop definitely worth visiting. Despite the fact that many of the books are library discards and book club editions, and some of the books are not

as well cared for as one might have wished, the shop does offer a larger than usual selection of circa 1920's-1940's titles. Most of the shelves are double stacked but because the second stack is slightly elevated, it's not all that difficult to quickly find titles one might be looking for.

New Brunswick

Old York Books (NJ34)   (908) 249-0430
122 French Street 08901

Collection:	General stock.
# of Volumes:	30,000 (See Comments)
Specialties:	Sociology; philosophy; psychology; foreign languages; music; poetry (contemporary).
Hours:	Tue-Sat 11-6.
Services:	Appraisals, search service, accepts want lists, mail order.
Travel:	New Brunswick exit off Rte. 287. Proceed south on Easton Ave. At railroad station, right on French. Shop is 3 blocks ahead on left. Map 2.
Credit Cards:	No
Owner:	E.T. Cecile Hopkins
Year Estab:	1963
Comments:	This shop is owned by a most cheerful and erudite bookseller who will, if you allow her, both charm you and disarm you. The selection of books is certainly above average, with a concentration of scholarly volumes. In addition to the books on display in the tightly packed shop, the owner estimates she has an additional 100,000 titles in storage, a considerable portion of which have been computerized for easy access.

Ocean Grove

Antic Hay Rare Books (NJ35)   (908) 774-4590
45 Pilgrim Pathway
Mailing address: PO Box 2185 Asbury Park 07712

Collection:	General stock, regional prints and autographs.
# of Volumes:	10,000
Specialties:	First editions (poetry, fiction, drama).
Hours:	Mem Day-Labor Day: Daily 10:30-6. Rest of year by appointment in Asbury Park location.
Services:	Appraisals (specialty areas only), catalog, accepts want lists, search service.
Travel:	Rte. 33 to end. Left on Rte. 71 north, then right at first light on

Main St. Left at Pilgrim Pathway. Shop is on left. Look for the singing bird in the window. Map 2.

Credit Cards: Yes
Owner: Don Stine
Year Estab: 1978
Comments: This rather small storefront shop has a limited stock with a concentration on first editions and fine bindings. Most of the books are in fine to excellent condition. Prices reflect the condition of the books and the specialty nature of the collection.

Oldwick

Marley & Scrooge (NJ36)   (908) 439-2271
Main Street
Mailing address: PO Box 419   08858

Collection: General stock.
# of Volumes: 1,500
Specialties: Fine bindings.
Hours: Tue-Sat 11-5. Other times by appointment.
Services: Restorations, accepts want lists, mail order.
Travel: Oldwick exit off Rte. 78. Proceed north on Rte. 523 for about 1 mile. Shop is in center of town, on the third floor of a building that also houses an art gallery. Map 3.
Credit Cards: Yes
Owner: William Michalski
Year Estab: 1979
Comments: If you have any kind of handicapping condition that will inhibit your climbing two flight of steep stairs, you might want to skip this establishment. When you finally reach the book shop, you are likely to find fewer than 200 volumes, which during our visit, consisted primarily of sets of histories (one authored by Theodore Roosevelt) and some older books, including some mysteries, which were by no means in the antiquarian category.

Passaic

Passaic Book Center (NJ37)   (201) 778-6646
594 Main Avenue 07055

Collection: General stock of new and used, hardcover and paperback, magazines and records.
# of Volumes: 100,000+
Specialties: Science fiction.
Hours: Mon-Sat 10-6, except Fri till 8.

Services:	Catalog, accepts want lists.
Travel:	Rte. 3 to Rte. 21 North. Exit 11A off Rte. 21. Bear right at end of exit ramp. Make first left, then right at next light. Proceed for 3 lights. Shop will be on the right. Map 3.
Credit Cards:	Yes
Owner:	Bob Lopresti
Year Estab:	1965
Comments:	If you're looking for an old fashioned used or antiquarian book shop you won't find it here. Despite its concentration on paperbacks, comics and adult material, this shop does, however, have its share of interesting older books, particularly in the fields of entertainment, science fiction and fantasy, plus some bargain priced specialty publishers and even some older pulp magazines. If you're interested in hard-to-find fantasy, the shop is worth a visit. Although ladders are available, browsing the upper shelves is difficult. Most of the bookcases are double shelved.

Pitman

Foley's Idle Hour (NJ38)   (609) 582-6253
162 South Broadway 08071

Collection:	General stock.
# of Volumes:	4,000
Specialties:	American Indian; Irish literature.
Hours:	Tue-Fri 12-6. Sat 10-6. Sun 12-3. Mon by appointment.
Services:	Search service, mail order, accepts want lists.
Travel:	Pitman exit off Rte. 55. Right on Rte. 553 toward Pitman. Right at first light and left at second light on Business District 553 (Broadway). Map 4.
Credit Cards:	No
Owner:	Jim Foley & Tom & Joan Pinkava

Point Pleasant Beach

Book Bin (NJ39)   (908) 892-3456
725 Arnold Avenue 08742

Collection:	General stock.
# of Volumes:	50,000
Specialties:	Classics; first editions; metaphysics.
Hours:	Mon-Sat 10-5.
Travel:	Exit 98 off Garden State Pkwy. Proceed on Rte. 34 to Manasquan/ Sea Girt exit. At circle, proceed on Rte. 35 South. After bridge, bear right at fork. Right at dead end on Arnold. Shop is 2 blocks ahead on right. Map 2.

Credit Cards:	No
Owner:	Gene Bramlett
Year Estab:	1981
Comments:	About 75% of the stock is paperback and most of the hardcover titles we saw were reading copies of fairly recent best sellers. Some more unusual items are to be found in glass bookcases.

Pottersville

James Cummins Bookseller (NJ40)   (908) 439-3803
Pottersville Road   Fax: (908) 439-3803
Mailing address: PO Box 232   07979

Collection:	General stock.
# of Volumes:	10,000
Specialties:	Antiquarian
Hours:	Tue-Sat 9:30-5:30. Visitors are advised to call ahead.
Services:	Catalog, accepts want lists.
Travel:	Exit 26 off Rte. 78. Proceed north on Lamington River Rd. to end. Left on Black River Rd. and proceed for about 3 miles into Pottersville. Shop is on right just after a church, in the rear of a white frame building. Map 3.
Credit Cards:	Yes
Year Estab:	1979
Comments:	Located in a former barn, this "country annex" for a New York City based antiquarian bookseller offers an excellent stock of unusual titles with a strong emphasis on art, first editions, polar exploration and travel. Prices reflect the owner's description of his stock as "antiquarian." A second shop, within walking distance, specializes in sets and fine bindings. See By Appointment Section.

Princeton

Bryn Mawr Book Shop (NJ41)   (609) 921-7479
102 Witherspoon Street 08542

Collection:	General stock.
Hours:	Tue-Sun 12-4.
Travel:	See Micawber Books below. Witherspoon St. is directly opposite Princeton University's Nassau Hall. Map 2.
Credit Cards:	No
Comments:	Owned and operated by volunteers for benefit of the college's scholarship fund. Books are donated.

Micawber Books (NJ42)   (609) 921-8454
110 Nassau Street 08542

Collection:	General stock of new and used.
# of Volumes:	3,000-5,000 (used).
Specialties:	Humanities; scholarly.
Hours:	Mon-Sat 9-8. Sun 11-5.
Services:	Appraisals, mail order.
Travel:	Princeton Business District exit off Rte. 1. Proceed on Washington Rd. (Rte. 571) to Nassau St. Left on Nassau. Shop is 2 blocks ahead on right. Map 2.
Credit Cards:	Yes
Owner:	Logan Fox
Year Estab:	1980
Comments:	This well organized shop sells primarily new books with a smattering of generally ordinary used hardcover and paperback volumes interspersed.

Witherspoon Art And Book Store (NJ43)   (609) 924-3582
12 Nassau Street 08542

Collection:	General stock.
# of Volumes:	35,000
Specialties:	Scholarly
Hours:	Mon-Sat 10-5:30.
Services:	Appraisals, accepts want lists, occasional lists, mail order.
Travel:	See above. Shop is in a red brick building at corner of Bank St. Entrance is on the side, down one flight of stairs. Map 2.
Credit Cards:	Yes
Owner:	Pat McConahay
Year Estab:	1920's
Comments:	Located in the basement vault of a former bank, this long established shop offers a largely scholarly collection along with some more general categories, e.g., cooking, art, theater, etc. We also noted many older histories, foreign language dictionaries and a section of books about books.

Randolph

Country Cottage Books & Cookies, Inc. (NJ44)   (201) 361-6777
425 Rte. 10 East 07869   Fax: (201) 989-0636

Collection:	General stock of paperback and some hardcover.
# of Volumes:	5,000-6,000
Hours:	Mon, Wed & Thu 10-5:30. Fri 10-7. Sat 10-5. Sun 11-4.
Services:	Accepts want lists.

Travel:	Rte. 10 West exit off Rte. 287. Map 3.
Credit Cards:	No
Owner:	Pat Dashosh
Year Estab:	1992
Comments:	Primarily a paperback shop with a scattering of hardcover volumes. Cookies are baked on the premises.

Red Bank

The Keith Library (NJ45)   (908) 842-7377
At Monmouth Antique Shops, 217 West Front Street 07701

Collection:	General stock, maps and prints.
# of Volumes:	2,000-3,000
Specialties:	New Jersey coast; English literature; English history; French literature; classics; fine bindings; maps; prints (17th-19th centuries).
Hours:	Daily 11-5.
Travel:	Exit 109 (Red Bank) off Garden State Pkwy. Proceed on Rte. 35 to West Front St. and Bridge Ave. Map 2.
Credit Cards:	Yes
Owner:	Col. Quentin Keith
Year Estab:	1948
Comments:	This collection is very neatly displayed in three stalls in a large multi dealer antique mall. We noted some fine collector's items along with some more run-of-the-mill titles. The prices for the more ordinary stock were, we found, a bit higher than competitive prices for the same volumes elsewhere.

Charles Lloyd, Rare Books (NJ46)   (908) 747-4277
At Red Bank Antique Center, 195B West Front Street 07701

Collection:	General stock, maps and prints.
# of Volumes:	5,000
Specialties:	Americana; American literature; English literature; maps.
Hours:	Mon-Sat 11-5. Sun 12-5.
Services:	Accepts want lists, mail order.
Travel:	Exit 109 off Garden State Pkwy. Proceed east on Newman Springs Rd, then left on Shrewsbury Ave. Right on West Front St. The collection is in the grey concrete block building marked "Building I & II." Map 2.
Credit Cards:	Yes
Year Estab:	1972
Comments:	We're pleased to report that we were delightfully surprised when we visited Charles Lloyd, Rare Books. Our experience

with booksellers located in antique malls has rarely been positive: far too often, the books found in these locations are common place and overpriced. Mr. Lloyd's books, however, are truly rare and true antiquarian book lovers would not mind going out of their way to view this collection. Indeed, if we were buying for a major university library, we would be tempted to take his entire stock. The books displayed were of historical interest, with several collections of the writings of well known statesmen, public papers, etc. There were also some very fine, one-of-a-kind works of literature.

Riverside

The Book Shop (NJ47)   (609) 461-3416
704 Bridgeboro Street 08075

Collection:	General stock of hardcover and paperback.
# of Volumes:	15,000
Specialties:	National Geographics.
Hours:	Daily 10-6, except Wed & Sun.
Services:	Search service, accepts want lists, mail order.
Travel:	Delran exit off Rte. 295. Turn in direction of Delran and proceed west on Creek Rd for about 3 miles. Right on Bridgeboro St. and follow street under Rte. 130. Shop is a corner shop, about 6 blocks ahead on left. Map 4.
Credit Cards:	No
Owner:	Arlene & Helen Phillips
Year Estab:	1957
Comments:	There are lots of bargains in this bi-level shop (especially downstairs), although the books, mostly older titles, are not all in the best condition.

Rockaway

Ray & Judy's Book Shop (NJ48)   (201) 586-9182
40 West Main Street 07866

Collection:	General stock of new and used books.
Hours:	Mon-Sat 10-6. Nov & Dec: Also, Sun 11-4.
Services:	Search service.
Travel:	Exit 37 off Rte. 80. Right off ramp and proceed down hill to Mobil station. Left on Union St. and proceed 5 streets (counting on right side). Right on Maple Ave. Proceed to end of street. Shop is on the right side of the corner. Map 3.
Credit Cards:	Yes

Owner:	Ray & Judy Sedivec
Year Estab:	1982
Comments:	A combination new and used book shop, the used collection is primarily paperback with a smattering of hardcover titles.

Sea Girt

Read It Again Books (NJ49)   (908) 974-8242
2175 Highway 35 08750

Collection:	General stock of paperback and hardcover.
# of Volumes:	10,000
Hours:	Daily 11-5:30.
Services:	Search service, accepts want lists, mail order.
Travel:	Exit 100B off Garden State Pkwy. Take Rte. 33 East to Rte. 35. Right on Rte. 35. Shop is in Sea Girt Crossroads Shopping Center, a small strip center at corner of Sea Girt Ave. Map 2.
Owner:	Bart Ritorto
Credit Cards:	Yes
Year Estab:	1993
Comments:	The stock in this recently opened bi-level shop consists of about 60% paperback with the remaining 40% mostly newer used hardcover titles. The owner makes an effort to match on opposite shelves the same subjects in paperback and hardcover. While there was a shelf or two of first editions, we saw little that we would consider out of the ordinary or rare. A good portion of the stock comes from trades. The spacious lower level is devoted exclusively to children's books.

Somerville

P.M. Bookshop (NJ50)   (908) 722-0055
59 West Main Street 08876

Collection:	General stock.
# of Volumes:	100,000
Hours:	Mon-Sat 10-5.
Services:	Accepts want lists, mail order.
Travel:	Somerville exit off Rte. 22. Follow signs for Somerville. Right at Main St. Shop is 1½ blocks ahead on left. Map 2.
Credit Cards:	No
Owner:	Judith Heir
Year Estab:	1950's
Comments:	At press time, this long established shop, formerly located in Plainfield, was in the process of relocating.

Teaneck

Chapter II Books (NJ51)   (201) 836-3863
713 Cedar Lane 07666

Collection:	General stock of paperback and hardcover.
# of Volumes:	3,000-5,000
Hours:	Mon-Fri 10-6. Sat 12-6.
Services:	Accepts want lists.
Travel:	Rte. 4 West to Teaneck Rd. Right on Teaneck, then right on Cedar Lane. Shop is on right, just before River Rd. Look for a one story stone building. Map 3.
Credit Cards:	No
Owner:	Mary Hallwachs
Year Estab:	1992
Comments:	This is a small shop with a limited stock. The hardcover volumes are mostly of recent vintage. We saw little that was unusual or out of the ordinary, but since stock turns over frequently, if you're in the neighborhood, we suggest you give this shop a try.

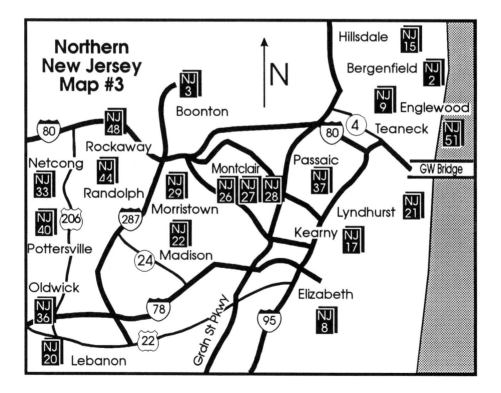

Bedminster

Baobab Books   (908) 234-9163
1555 Lamington Road 07921   Fax: (908) 781-7472

Collection:	Specialty
# of Volumes:	3,000
Specialties:	Africa, including big game hunting, military, natural history, history, conservation.
Services:	Appraisals, catalog, accepts want lists.
Credit Cards:	No
Owner:	Gitta Reist
Year Estab:	1988

Brick

Richard W. Spellman   (908) 477-2413
610 Monticello Drive 08723   Fax: (908) 920-6808

Collection:	Specialty
Specialties:	Newspapers, from 1600's to 1900's.
Services:	Catalog
Credit Cards:	No
Year Estab:	1960's

Cherry Hill

Caney Booksellers   (609) 667-7223
One Cherry Hill, Ste. 220 08002

Collection:	Specialty books and prints.
# of Volumes:	4,000
Specialties:	Modern literature; photography; press books; illustrated.
Services:	Catalog, accepts want lists.
Credit Cards:	Yes
Owner:	Rochelle & Joel Caney
Year Estab:	1988

Chester

NJ Books   (908) 879-8494
3 Parker Road 07930   Fax: (908) 879-4090

Collection:	General stock.
# of Volumes:	10,000
Specialties:	Americana; business and corporate histories; engineering; science; technology; philately and postal history; Scandinavia; first editions; military.
Services:	Search service, catalog, accepts want lists.
Credit Cards:	No

Owner:	Norman Johanson
Year Estab:	1993

Closter

Harvey W. Brewer   (201) 768-4414
Box 322 07624

Collection:	Specialty
# of Volumes:	5,000
Specialties:	Fine art; applied art; textiles; color plates; photography.
Credit Cards:	Yes
Year Estab:	1938

Denville

James R. Hogan Bookseller   (201) 586-0918
75 West Shore Road 07834

Collection:	Specialty
# of Volumes:	400
Specialties:	Theology, especially Reformed and Calvinistic literature.
Hours:	Mon-Sat only.
Services:	Appraisals, search service, catalog, accepts want lists.
Credit Cards:	No
Year Estab:	1990

Fort Lee

Vathek Books   (201) 585-1760
250 Slocum Way 07024

Collection:	General stock.
# of Volumes:	25,000
Specialties:	Gnosticism; Roman history.
Services:	Appraisals, accepts want lists, mail order.
Credit Cards:	No
Owner:	Daniel Rich
Year Estab:	1984

Haddonfield

Between The Covers Rare Books   (609) 354-7665
132 Kings Highway East 08033   Fax: (609) 354-7695

Collection:	General stock.
# of Volumes:	15,000
Specialties:	Literary first editions; mystery first editions; African American literature and history; rare; signed.
Hours:	Most days 10-7, but call beforehand recommended.

Services:	Catalog, accepts want lists.
Credit Cards:	Yes
Owner:	Thomas & Heidi Congalton
Year Estab:	1986

Hainesville

Colophon Books   (201) 948-5785
10 Ayers Road
Mailing address: PO Box 156 Layton 07851

Collection:	Specialty
# of Volumes:	5,000
Specialties:	History; science.
Services:	Appraisals, accepts want lists, mail order.
Credit Cards:	No
Owner:	John E. Tyler
Year Estab:	1988

Hopewell

On Military Matters   (609) 466-2329
55 Taylor Terrace 08525   Fax: (609) 466-4174

Collection:	Specialty
# of Volumes:	2,000+
Specialties:	Military
Services:	Appraisals, search service, catalog, accepts want lists.
Credit Cards:	No
Owner:	Dennis Shorthouse
Year Estab:	1987

Kendell Park

Richard DeVictor Books   (908) 297-0296
3 Dov Place 08824

Collection:	General stock.
# of Volumes:	3,000
Specialties:	Illustrated; N.C. Wyeth; Maxfield Parrish; Jessie W. Smith; children's; western illustrated; Brandywine artists; art.
Services:	Catalog
Year Estab:	1974

Livingston

Hammer Book Company   (201) 992-5387
308 Hillside Avenue 07039   Fax: (201) 533-1915

Collection:	Specialty

# of Volumes:	3,000-4,000
Specialties:	Bibles; Hebraica; Judaica; early printing; chemistry; biology; incuabula.
Services:	Catalog
Credit Cards:	No
Owner:	Paul Hammer
Year Estab:	1972

Matawan

Jerry Simkin, Bookseller   (908) 583-5196
10 Avalon Lane 07747

Collection:	Specialty books and related memorabilia.
# of Volumes:	2,000
Specialties:	Telegraphy; telephone; wireless, radio; television.
Services:	Search service, accepts want lists, mail order.
Credit Cards:	No
Year Estab:	1990

Millville

The Book Store   (609) 825-1615
1226 West Main Street
Mailing address: PO Box 847 Millville 08332

Collection:	General stock.
# of Volumes:	20,000
Specialties:	Southern New Jersey.
Services:	Appraisals, accepts want lists, occasional catalog.
Credit Cards:	No
Owner:	Shirley Bailey
Year Estab:	1972

Montclair

Maps of Antiquity   (201) 744-4364
160 Midland Avenue 07042

Collection:	Specialty
Specialties:	Maps
Services:	Appraisals, catalog, accepts want lists.
Credit Cards:	Yes
Owner:	Lynn Vigeant
Year Estab:	1989

Patterson Smith   (201) 744-3291
23 Prospect Terrace 07042   Fax: (201) 744-4501

Collection:	Specialty

# of Volumes:	50,000
Specialties:	Crime; criminal justice history; gambling.
Services:	Appraisals, search service, catalog, accepts want lists.
Credit Cards:	Yes
Year Estab:	1955

New Milford

Armchair Angler   (201) 261-2944
269D Faller Drive 07646

Collection:	Specialty books and ephemera.
# of Volumes:	2,500
Specialties:	Fishing
Services:	Catalog, appraisals, accepts want lists.
Credit Cards:	Yes
Owner:	Steve & Susan Starrantino
Year Estab:	1988

Parsippany

About Books   (201) 515-4591
6 Sand Hill Court
Mailing address: PO Box 5717 Parsippany 07054

Collection:	Specialty
# of Volumes:	10,000
Specialties:	Books about books; bibliography; reference books for book sellers, collectors and librarians.
Services:	Catalog, accepts want lists.
Credit Cards:	No
Owner:	Michael & Regina Winne
Year Estab:	1977

Point Pleasant

Gay Frazee   (908) 295-8611
626 Ocean Road 08742

Collection:	Specialty
Specialties:	Children's; illustrated; fishing.
Credit Cards:	No
Year Estab:	1973

Pottersville

The Mill   (908) 439-2724
Fairmount Road East 07979   Fax: (908) 439-3803

Collection:	Specialty
# of Volumes:	10,000-20,000

Specialties:	Fine bindings; sets.
Services:	Appraisals, catalog, accepts want lists.
Credit Cards:	Yes
Owner:	James & Carol Cummins
Year Estab:	1978

Princeton

Joseph J. Felcone Inc.   (609) 924-0539
PO Box 366 08542   Fax: (609) 924-9078

Collection:	Specialty
Specialties:	Rare books from 15th-20th century.
Services:	Appraisals, catalog.
Credit Cards:	No
Year Estab:	1972

River Edge

Pawprint Books   (201) 967-7306
259 Continental Avenue 07661

Collection:	Specialty
# of Volumes:	3,000
Specialties:	Photography, including monographs, histories, technical and general; 20th century art.
Services:	Appraisals, search service, catalog, accepts want lists.
Credit Cards:	No
Owner:	Perry Alan Werner
Year Estab:	1990

Short Hills

J & J Hanrahan   (201) 912-8907
320 White Oak Ridge Rd. 07078

Collection:	Specialty
Specialties:	Bibliography; military; guns; antique reference; Civil War.
Owner:	Jack Hanrahan

Somerville

D & D Galleries   (908) 874-3162
PO Box 8413 08876   Fax: (908) 874-5195

Collection:	Specialty
# of Volumes:	10,000
Specialties:	English literature; American literature; presentation/association books; sets; Lewis Carroll; Mark Twain.

Services:	Appraisals, search service, catalog, accepts want lists, book binding, restoration and repair.
Credit Cards:	Yes
Owner:	Denise & David Carlson
Year Estab:	1984

John Socia   (908) 725-8299
PO Box 90 08876

Collection:	General stock.
# of Volumes:	8,000
Specialties:	Literary criticism; biography.
Services:	Accepts want lists, mail order.
Credit Cards:	No
Year Estab:	1963

South Egg Harbor

Heinoldt Books   (609) 965-2284
1325 West Central Avenue 08215

Collection:	Specialty
# of Volumes:	6,000
Specialties:	Americana; local history; Indians; American Revolution; early travels.
Services:	Appraisals, catalog.
Credit Cards:	No
Owner:	Margaret Heinoldt
Year Estab:	1956

South Orange

Alan Angele Popular Culture   (201) 378-5822
350 Turrell Avenue 07079-2362   Fax: (201) 378-5822

Collection:	Specialty books and magazines.
# of Volumes:	5,000
Specialties:	Avant garde art; pop art; psychedelic art; beat literature; music festivals, radical movements, performing arts; communes; hippies.
Services:	Appraisals, catalog, accepts want lists.
Credit Cards:	No
Year Estab:	1992

Springfield

M. Mitterhoff   (201) 376-6291
141 Hawthorne Avenue 07081

Collection:	Specialty books, prints and ephemera.

Specialties:	Signed limited editions; Rockwell Kent; Walt Whitman; birds
Services:	Appraisals, accepts want lists.
Credit Cards:	Yes
Owner:	Murray Mitterhoff

Summit

Ernest S. Hickok-Bockus   (908) 277-1427
382 Springfield Avenue 07901

Collection:	Specialty books and related art.
# of Volumes:	1,000
Specialties:	Sports; sports reference
Services:	Accepts want lists, mail order.
Credit Cards:	No
Owner:	Sally Bockus
Year Estab:	1962

Tuckerton

Pickwick Books   (609) 296-3343
201 Cedar Street 08087

Collection:	General stock and specialty.
# of Volumes:	20,000
Specialties:	Fiction (pre 1940); biography
Hours:	Owner tries to be open weekends in the summer.
Services:	Search service, accepts want lists.
Credit Cards:	No
Owner:	William McClure
Year Estab:	1973
Comments:	The owner notes that because his display area is limited, a call ahead is recommended so that he can "unearth those books which may have some interest."

West Caldwell

Gibson Galleries   (201) 403-9377
14 Kramer Avenue 07006

Collection:	Specialty
# of Volumes:	600
Specialties:	English literature; illustrated; fine bindings.
Services:	Catalog, accepts want lists.
Credit Cards:	No
Owner:	Gordon Gibson
Year Estab:	1990

West Orange

The Book Nook   (201) 731-4054
71 Burnett Terrace 07052

Collection:	General stock of paperback and hardcover.
# of Volumes:	10,000
Specialties:	Science fiction.
Services:	Search service, accepts want lists.
Credit Cards:	No
Owner:	Roslyn Levine
Year Estab:	1990

Westwood

Bookwood Books   (201) 664-4066
Box 263 07675   Fax: (201) 664-4066

Collection:	General stock.
# of Volumes:	10,000-12,000
Specialties:	Wine; soccer.
Services:	Search service, infrequent catalog, accepts want lists, mail order.
Owner:	P.R. Goodman
Year Estab:	1972

Wycoff

Book Lady-Jane   (201) 447-1216
26 Wycoff Avenue 07481   Fax: (201) 447-1216

Collection:	General stock.
# of Volumes:	5,000
Specialties:	Children's; modern first editions; military.
Services:	Appraisals, search service, catalog, accepts want lists.
Credit Cards:	Yes
Owner:	Jane Walter Carlen
Year Estab:	1986

Bel Canto Books   (908) 548-7371
PO Box 55 Metuchen 08840

Collection:	Specialty books and ephemera.
# of Volumes:	10,000
Specialties:	Music; dance. Mostly out of print.
Services:	Search service, catalog, accepts want lists.
Credit Cards:	No
Owner:	Robert Hearn
Year Estab:	1979

Ed Bowersock   (609) 546-3060
17 Taylor Avenue Audubon 08106

Collection:	General stock.
# of Volumes:	5,000
Specialties:	Literature; early travel specializing in Africa and Egypt.
Services:	Catalog, accepts want lists.
Credit Cards:	Yes
Year Estab:	1989

Charles Canfield Brown Fine Books   (201) 451-1633
PO Box 282 Jersey City 07303

Collection:	General stock.
# of Volumes:	20,000
Specialties:	Mythology; symbolism; Jungian psychology.
Services:	Catalog, accepts want lists, bibliographic research.
Credit Cards:	No
Year Estab:	1978

Brown's Book Search   (201) 664-1120
Box 68 Hillsdale 07642

Collection:	General stock.
# of Volumes:	15,000
Services:	Search service, accepts want lists.
Credit Cards:	No
Owner:	Jill & Walt Brown
Year Estab:	1981

Carpe Librum   (609) 252-0246
PO Box 1521 Princeton 08542

Collection:	Specialty
# of Volumes:	15,000
Specialties:	Science fiction; mystery; vintage paperbacks; modern first editions; pulps.
Services:	Appraisals, search service, catalog, accepts want lists.
Credit Cards:	No

Owner: Bradford Verter
Year Estab: 1991

Cathryn Books   (215) 862-5669
PO Box 7433 West Trenton 08628

Collection: General stock.
# of Volumes: 15,000
Specialties: Medicine; children's; art; theater.
Services: Catalog, accepts want lists.
Credit Cards: No
Year Estab: 1980

The Dance Mart   (201) 833-4176
Box 994 Teaneck 07666

Collection: Specialty books and ephemera.
Specialties: Dance
Services: Catalog
Credit Cards: No
Owner: A.J. Pischl
Year Estab: 1940

John E. DeLeau   (201) 837-9638
1266 Teaneck Rd. # 4 Teaneck 07666

Collection: General stock.
# of Volumes: 1,000
Specialties: Aviation; transportation.
Services: Accepts want lists.
Credit Cards: No
Year Estab: 1988

Dionysion Arts   (201) 328-7196
PO Box 938 Dover 07802

Collection: Specialty
Specialties: Dance; cookbooks; poetry; architecture.
Services: Search service, catalog, accepts want lists.
Owner: Leo Loewenthal
Year Estab: 1920

Edison Hall Books   (908) 548-4455
5 Ventnor Drive Edison 08820   Fax: (908) 548-4455

Collection: General stock.
# of Volumes: 15,000

Specialties:	Literary first editions; children's; birds; hunting; fishing; art; illustrated; military; New York; New Jersey; witchcraft; magic; presidential; Indians; Tarzan; Edison.
Services:	Accepts want lists.
Credit Cards:	No
Owner:	George Stang
Year Estab:	1970

Editions Limited   (908) 766-1532
20 Clark Road Bernardsville 07924

Collection:	Specialty
# of Volumes:	2,000
Specialties:	Mystery; suspense.
Services:	Catalog
Credit Cards:	No
Owner:	Mavis C. Marsh
Year Estab:	1973

James Tait Goodrich, Antiquarian   (201) 567-0199
Books and Manuscripts   Fax: (201) 567-0433
214 Everett Place   Englewood 07631

Collection:	Specialty
# of Volumes:	3,000
Specialties:	Medicine (antiquarian); science; English literature (17th century); manuscripts.
Services:	Appraisals, catalog.
Credit Cards:	No
Owner:	James Goodrich
Year Estab:	1978

Angelo Iuspa   (201) 485-0151
474 North 7th Street Newark 07107

Collection:	Specialty
Specialties:	Body building; weight lifting; olympics.
Credit Cards:	No
Year Estab:	1946

Walter J. Johnson, Inc.   (201) 767-1303
355 Chestnut Street Norwood 07648   Fax: (201) 767-6717

Collection:	General stock.
Credit Cards:	Yes
Year Estab:	1942

Junius Book Distributors
(201) 868-7725

Box 85 Fairview 07022

Collection:	Specialty
# of Volumes:	400,000
Specialties:	Medicine (19th century); scholarly monographs; bibliography; sociology.
Services:	Search service, catalog.
Credit Cards:	No
Owner:	Michael V. Cordasco
Year Estab:	1975
Comments:	Stock consists of remainders and out-of-print volumes.

Brian Kathenes Autographs and Collectibles
(800) 462-1979

PO Box 77296 West Trenton 08628
Fax: (609) 530-0660

Collection:	Specialty
Specialties:	Autographs, manuscripts, letters.
Services:	Appraisals, catalog.
Credit Cards:	No
Year Estab:	1985

Louise Kumpf
(609) 894-8787

Box 1 Birmingham 08011

Collection:	General stock.
# of Volumes:	1,000
Specialties:	First editions.
Services:	Accepts want lists.
Credit Cards:	No
Year Estab:	1942

McCoy's Rare Books
(908) 722-7064

121 Choctaw Ridge Road Branchburg 08876

Collection:	Specialty new and used, hardcover and paperback.
# of Volumes:	5,000
Specialties:	Mystery; science fiction; horror; fantasy.
Services:	Catalog, search service, accepts want lists.
Credit Cards:	No
Owner:	Pat & Jamie McCoy
Year Estab:	1986

C.M.C. Myriff, Bookseller
(908) 431-1785

82 Townsend Drive Freehold 07728

Collection:	Specialty

Specialties: Military; World War II.
Services: Catalog, accepts want lists.
Credit Cards: No
Owner: Cliff M. Cheifetz
Year Estab: 1984

Harold R. Nestler (201) 444-7413
13 Pennington Avenue Waldwick 07463

Collection: Specialty books and ephemera
# of Volumes: 2,500
Specialties: Americana (early); New York State; broadsides; manuscripts.
Services: Catalog
Credit Cards: No
Year Estab: 1952
Comments: Collection can also be viewed by appointment.

Old Cookbooks - H.T. Hicks (609) 854-2844
PO Box 462 Haddonfield 08033

Collection: Specialty
# of Volumes: 500+
Specialties: Cookbooks (pre 1918).
Services: Catalog, accepts want lists, publishes *Collector's Guide To Old Cookbooks* and monographs on cookbooks.
Credit Cards: No
Owner: Harmon T. Hicks
Year Estab: 1978

Oz And Ends Book Shoppe (908) 276-8368
14 Dorset Drive Kenilworth 07033

Collection: Specialty
# of Volumes: 2,500
Specialties: Oz
Services: Appraisals, search service, irregular catalog, accepts want lists.
Credit Cards: No
Owner: Judy Bieber
Year Estab: 1982

Past History (908) 842-4545
136 Parkview Terrace Lincroft 07738

Collection: General stock.
# of Volumes: 40,000
Specialties: Americana; New Jersey.

Services:	Appraisals, search service, accepts want lists.
Credit Cards:	No
Owner:	Mike & Betty Massey
Year Estab:	1962

R & A Petrilla, Antiquarian Booksellers   (609) 426-4999
PO Box 306 Roosevelt 08555

Collection:	General stock.
# of Volumes:	Small
Specialties:	Travel (to 1900).
Services:	Appraisals
Credit Cards:	No
Owner:	Bob & Alison Petrilla
Year Estab:	1970

Princeton Antiques Bookshop   (609) 344-1943
2917 Atlantic Avenue Atlantic City 08401   Fax: (609) 344-1944

Collection:	General stock.
# of Volumes:	200,000
Services:	Appraisals, search service, accepts want lists.
Credit Cards:	No
Year Estab:	1967

Rare Book Company
Box 6957 Freehold 07728

Collection:	Specialty new and used books and related materials.
# of Volumes:	20,000 (used).
Specialties:	Christian Science.
Services:	Appraisals, search service, catalog, accepts want lists.
Credit Cards:	No
Owner:	Jerry Lupo
Year Estab:	1921

Ellen Roth Books   (908) 536-0850
47 Truman Drive Marlboro 07746   Fax: (908) 536-8073

Collection:	General stock.
# of Volumes:	80,000
Specialties:	Children's; military.
Services:	Search service, accepts want lists.
Credit Cards:	No

Rutgers Book Center   (908) 545-4344
127 Raritan Avenue Highland Park 08904

Collection:	Specialty
# of Volumes:	4,000-5,000
Specialties:	Military; firearms; armor.
Services:	Appraisals, catalog, accepts want lists.
Credit Cards:	Yes
Owner:	Mark Aziz
Year Estab:	1961

Albert Saifer: Book Auctions   (201) 731-5701
Box 51 Town Center West Orange 07052

Collection:	General stock.
# of Volumes:	45,000
Specialties:	Scholarly out of print.
Services:	Appraisals, search service, catalog, accepts want lists.
Credit Cards:	No
Year Estab:	1945

Ken Schultz   (201) 656-0966
Box M753 Hoboken 07030

Collection:	Specialty books and ephemera.
Specialties:	Ocean liner memorabilia; worlds fairs and expositions.
Services:	Catalog, accepts want lists.
Credit Cards:	No
Year Estab:	1972

Trotting Book Shop   (908) 766-6111
130 Peachcroft Drive Bernardsville 07924

Collection:	Specialty
Specialties:	Horses (trotting only).
Services:	Appraisals, catalog.
Credit Cards:	No
Owner:	Stanley Bergstein
Year Estab:	1958

Abraham Wachstein-Books   (908) 780-4187
43 Longstreet Road Manalapan 07726

Collection:	Specialty
# of Volumes:	3,000
Specialties:	Judaica (in English).
Services:	Accepts want lists.
Credit Cards:	No

Elizabeth Woodburn Books   (609) 466-0522
Booknoll Farm, PO Box 398 Hopewell 08525

Collection:	Specialty
# of Volumes:	12,000
Specialties:	Horticulture; gardening; landscape design; herbs.
Services:	Search service, catalog, accepts want lists.
Credit Cards:	No
Owner:	Bradford Lyon & Joanne Fuccello
Year Estab:	1946

Ruth Woods Oriental Books and Art   (201) 567-0149
266 Arch Road Englewood 07631   Fax: (201) 567-1419

Collection:	Specialty
# of Volumes:	2,000
Specialties:	Orient (all aspects).
Services:	Search service, catalog, accepts want lists.
Credit Cards:	No
Year Estab:	1982

The World Art Group   (609) 490-0008
1069 Washington Boulevard Robbinsville 08691   Fax: (609) 490-0009

Collection:	Specialty
# of Volumes:	3,000
Specialties:	Art; archaeology; architecture. Books are history and travel related. Imported titles only, primarily Greek, Czech, Bulgarian and Turkish books.
Services:	Search service, catalog.
Credit Cards:	No
Owner:	Pasi Mantyla
Year Estab:	1988

Timothy B. Wuchter, Used and Rare Books   (609) 599-4846
222 Mott Street Trenton 08611

Collection:	General stock and ocean liner ephemera.
# of Volumes:	10,000+
Specialties:	Americana (series); federal writers' project; rivers of America; literary first editions; signed.
Services:	Search service, catalog, accepts want lists.
Credit Cards:	No
Year Estab:	1990

New York

Alphabetical Listing By Dealer

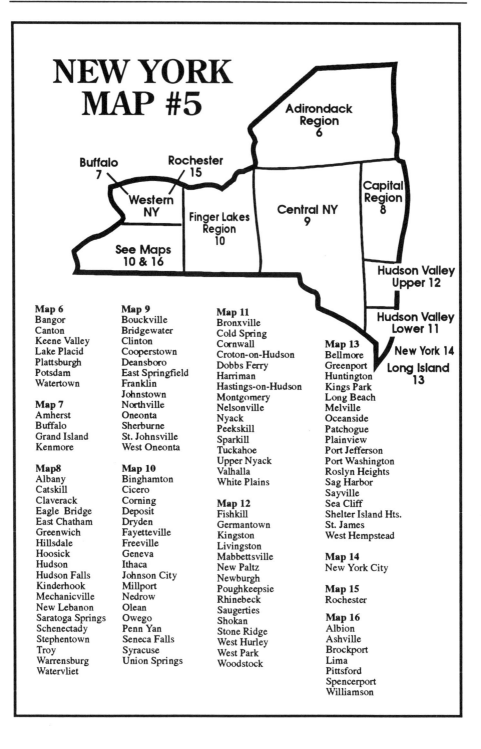

NEW YORK MAP #5

Adirondack Region 6

Buffalo 7

Rochester 15

Western NY

Finger Lakes Region 10

Central NY 9

Capital Region 8

See Maps 10 & 16

Hudson Valley Upper 12

Hudson Valley Lower 11

New York 14

Long Island 13

Map 6
Bangor
Canton
Keene Valley
Lake Placid
Plattsburgh
Potsdam
Watertown

Map 7
Amherst
Buffalo
Grand Island
Kenmore

Map8
Albany
Catskill
Claverack
Eagle Bridge
East Chatham
Greenwich
Hillsdale
Hoosick
Hudson
Hudson Falls
Kinderhook
Mechanicville
New Lebanon
Saratoga Springs
Schenectady
Stephentown
Troy
Warrensburg
Watervliet

Map 9
Bouckville
Bridgewater
Clinton
Cooperstown
Deansboro
East Springfield
Franklin
Johnstown
Northville
Oneonta
Sherburne
St. Johnsville
West Oneonta

Map 10
Binghamton
Cicero
Corning
Deposit
Dryden
Fayetteville
Freeville
Geneva
Ithaca
Johnson City
Millport
Nedrow
Olean
Owego
Penn Yan
Seneca Falls
Syracuse
Union Springs

Map 11
Bronxville
Cold Spring
Cornwall
Croton-on-Hudson
Dobbs Ferry
Harriman
Hastings-on-Hudson
Montgomery
Nelsonville
Nyack
Peekskill
Sparkill
Tuckahoe
Upper Nyack
Valhalla
White Plains

Map 12
Fishkill
Germantown
Kingston
Livingston
Mabbettsville
New Paltz
Newburgh
Poughkeepsie
Rhinebeck
Saugerties
Shokan
Stone Ridge
West Hurley
West Park
Woodstock

Map 13
Bellmore
Greenport
Huntington
Kings Park
Long Beach
Melville
Oceanside
Patchogue
Plainview
Port Jefferson
Port Washington
Roslyn Heights
Sag Harbor
Sayville
Sea Cliff
Shelter Island Hts.
St. James
West Hempstead

Map 14
New York City

Map 15
Rochester

Map 16
Albion
Ashville
Brockport
Lima
Pittsford
Spencerport
Williamson

Alphabetical Listing By Location

Albany

Bryn Mawr Bookshop (NY1)   (518) 465-8126
1 Spring Street 12210

Collection:	General stock.
Hours:	Sep-Jun: Tue-Sat 10:30-4. Jul & Aug: Tue-Thu 10:30-4, except Thu till 6.
Travel:	Three blocks from the Capitol. Map 8.
Credit Cards:	No
Comments:	Operated by volunteers for the benefit of the college's scholarship fund. All books are donated.

Capital Book Store (NY2)   (518) 434-4927
402 Broadway 12207

Collection:	General stock, magazines and records.
# of Volumes:	20,000
Hours:	Mon-Sat 11-5.
Travel:	Two blocks from Capitol between Beaver and Hudson . Map 8.
Credit Cards:	No
Owner:	William Soroka
Year Estab:	1965
Comments:	If you have the patience of a Job and are willing to spend hours searching for titles that interest you, it's conceivable that you might find something of interest in this deep but narrow storefront shop. More than likely though, you'll be frustrated (as we were) by your efforts. The store is overflowing with books of mixed vintage and condition but it's difficult to browse the shelves in a leisurely or comfortable manner as almost every aisle is overcrowded with books on the floor.

Central Station (NY3)   (518) 463-4190
260 Central Avenue 12206

Collection:	General stock and records.
# of Volumes:	2,000
Specialties:	Religion
Hours:	Mon-Sat 11-6.
Travel:	Corner of North Lake Ave. in downtown. Map 8.
Credit Cards:	Yes
Owner:	Judy & Wayne Moody
Year Estab:	1987
Comments:	Primarily a used record shop, this storefront shop stocks a modest selection of used books, most of which are in mixed condi-

tion. With the exception of some titles dealing with World War II, we saw little that was unusual.

Dove & Hudson, Old Books (NY4)   (518) 432-4518
296 Hudson Avenue 12210

Collection:	General stock.
# of Volumes:	15,000
Specialties:	Scholarly; literature; poetry; history; philosophy; architecture; art.
Hours:	Tue-Sat 11-7.
Services:	Search service; accepts want lists.
Travel:	From Rte. 787, follow signs for "Empire State Plaza." After road passes under plaza, take immediate right upon emerging from plaza on South Swan St. Proceed 4 blocks. Left on Washington and proceed one block. Left on Dove. Shop is 5 blocks ahead on the corner. Map 8.
Credit Cards:	Yes
Owner:	Dan Wedge
Year Estab:	1989
Comments:	The owner describes his shop as "more for readers than collectors." The books are carefully selected for condition and literary merit and are reasonably priced. Although the collection is well organized, browsers may be frustrated by the absence of labels on the shelves. The owner will be more than happy, however, to direct you to the books in your areas of interest.

Haven't Got A Clue Mystery Bookshop (NY5)   (518) 464-1135
1823 Western Avenue 12203

Collection:	Specialty used and new.
# of Volumes:	10,000 (combined)
Specialties:	Mystery
Hours:	Tue & Wed 10-6. Thu & Fri 10-8. Sat 10-5. Sun 12-5.
Services:	Search service, catalog, accepts want lists.
Travel:	Exit 24 off Rte. 87. Proceed to Western Ave. (Rte. 20). Right on Western. Shop is on the right at corner of Gipp & Western, approximately 1.5 miles ahead at fifth light. Map 8.
Credit Cards:	Yes
Owner:	Betsey Blaustein
Year Estab:	1989
Comments:	If you're into this field, this shop, a far cry from the typical small shops that specialize in the mystery genre, is well worth a visit. In addition to carrying the latest paperback and hardcover titles, the shop stocks a very nice sampling of older used hard-

cover titles intershelved with used paperbacks. Prices, for the most part, are quite reasonable. The shop also sells related audio tapes, puzzles, T-shirts and games.

Dennis Holzman Antiques (NY6)   (518) 449-5414
240 Washington Avenue, 2nd Fl. 12210

Collection:	General stock and ephemera.
# of Volumes:	1,500
Specialties:	Antiquarian; autographs; manuscripts; political Americana; 19th century photographs; trade catalogues, view books.
Hours:	Mon-Fri 11-5. Sat by chance or appointment.
Travel:	Downtown Albany. Map 8.
Credit Cards:	No
Owner:	Dennis Holzman
Year Estab:	1988

Nelson's Book Store (NY7)   (518) 463-1023
67 Central Avenue 12206

Collection:	General stock.
# of Volumes:	110,000
Specialties:	Beat generation.
Hours:	Daily 11-5:30, except Thu & Fri till 8.
Services:	Appraisals, search service, accepts want lists, catalog.
Travel:	Downtown Albany. Map 8.
Credit Cards:	Yes
Owner:	John Nelson
Year Estab:	1968
Comments:	The shop offers volume (on the shelves and in storage) but based on our visit, organization and quality were not among the shop's strong points. Remainders and new volumes are mixed in with older more common titles. Prices were quite reasonable.

North River Book Shop (NY8)   (518) 463-3082
386 Delaware Avenue 12209

Collection:	General stock of new and used hardcover and paperback.
# of Volumes:	8,000-10,000
Specialties:	New York State.
Hours:	Tue 10-3. Wed-Fri 10:30-6:30. Sat 10-5.
Services:	Search service, accepts want lists, mail order.
Travel:	From Capitol: Proceed west on Washington Ave. Left on Lark which becomes Delaware. Shop is on left. Map 8.
Credit Cards:	No

Owner:	Terry Tedeschi
Year Estab:	1984
Comments:	A delightful shop with newer volumes in the front of the store and used paperbacks and hardcovers in the middle and rear sections. Although the selection here is limited in terms of quantity, the books on hand are generally in good condition and prices are quite fair. A call ahead is advised as the owner may be relocating.

Strawberry Fields Bookstore (NY9)   (518) 449-8940
196 Delaware Avenue 12209

Collection:	General stock, records, prints and ephemera.
Hours:	Tue-Sat 12:30-6. Best to call ahead on Sat.
Services:	Accepts want lists.
Travel:	See North River above. Shop is between Lincoln Park and Spectrum Theater, next to pet store. Map 8.
Credit Cards:	No
Owner:	Ron Susman
Year Estab:	1992

Zeller's (NY10)   (518) 463-8221
32 Central Avenue 12210

Collection:	General stock, prints, maps and ephemera.
# of Volumes:	3,000
Specialties:	Antiques
Hours:	Mon-Sat 10-5.
Services:	Appraisals
Travel:	Downtown Albany. Map 8.
Owner:	Leslie Zeller
Year Estab:	1953
Comments:	When we visited, the shop displayed a few hundred older books, including some illustrated volumes and other titles dealing with antiques and related subjects. Most of the shop was devoted to antiques. The owner may be relocating.

Albion

Beech & Crow Books (NY11)   (716) 589-1818
14429 Ridge Road 14411

Collection:	General stock and ephemera.
# of Volumes:	30,000
Hours:	Wed-Sun 11-5. Mon & Tue by chance or appointment.
Services:	Appraisals, search service, accepts want lists, mail order.

Travel:	From NY State Twy, proceed north on Rte. 98 to Rte. 104. Right on Rte. 104 and proceed east for 1/4 mile. Map 16.
Credit Cards:	Yes
Owner:	Michael Hopkins
Year Estab:	1987
Comments:	Most of the books in this roadside shop are of an older vintage with few recent best sellers or paperbacks. We noted an interesting selection of first editions. If you enjoy browsing older book shops, you'll find yourself at home here.

Amherst

Buffalo Book Store (NY12)   (716) 835-9827
Century Mall, 3131 Sheridan Drive 14226

Collection:	General stock of new and used.
# of Volumes:	5,000-10,000 (used)
Hours:	Mon-Sat 9-9.
Services:	Search service, mail order, accepts want lists.
Travel:	Rte. 324 West exit off Rte. 290. The Century Mall is located in the larger Northtown Mall. Map 7.
Credit Cards:	Yes
Owner:	Eugene Musial
Year Estab:	1973
Comments:	The used books are located in two stores less than 100 feet apart in an indoor mall. The books we saw when we visited were in fair to poor condition and while the shelves were labeled, the books on the shelves were stacked in various stages of disarray. While it is certainly possible that browsers might locate an item or two of interest here, the discriminating book buyer can find better sources of good used and rare books in Buffalo.

Ashville

Barbara Berry Bookshop (NY13)   (716) 763-8296
Route 394
Mailing address: 231 North Maple Avenue 14710

Collection:	General stock.
# of Volumes:	85,000
Specialties:	G.S. Porter; Zane Grey; H.B.Wright; G.L.Hill; classics; modern first editions; children's; cookbooks; regional history; fine bindings.
Hours:	Sep-May: Tue-Sun 10-5. Jun-Aug: Daily 10-8.
Services:	Appraisals, search service, catalog, accepts want lists.

Travel:	Exit 8 off Rte. 17. West 2½ miles on Rte. 394. Map 16.
Credit Cards:	No
Owner:	Barbara & Warren Berry
Year Estab:	1970
Comments:	One of the very few shops in the southwestern part of the state, this shop offers a large selection of books in every category imaginable. The shop is well organized and the majority of the books are in good to excellent condition. Moderately priced with few bargains.

Bangor

The Booksmith (NY14)   (518) 481-5016
Route 11B
Mailing address: PO Box 50 12966

Collection:	General stock.
# of Volumes:	18,000
Specialties:	New England; northern New York; fishing; hunting.
Hours:	Wed-Sat 12-6 and other times by appointment or chance.
Services:	Appraisals, search service, subject lists, accepts want lists, mail order.
Travel:	In a former church building on Rte. 11B, 7 miles west of Malone. Map 6.
Credit Cards:	Yes
Owner:	Jane & Ray Smith
Year Estab:	1985

Bellmore

Booklovers' Paradise (NY15)   (516) 221-0994
2956 Merrick Road 11710

Collection:	General stock.
# of Volumes:	30,000
Specialties:	Americana; Long Island; first editions.
Hours:	Mon-Fri 11-5:30. Sat 10-5:30.
Travel:	Exit 6W off Wantagh Pkwy. Shop is 1/4 mile ahead on left. Map 13.
Credit Cards:	Yes
Owner:	Amnon Tishler
Year Estab:	1990
Comments:	The books are well organized and moderately priced. Don't overlook the New Arrivals section in the front of the store.

Binghamton

The Book Cellar (NY16)   (607) 724-6010
33 Court Street 13901

Collection:	General stock of new and used books.
# of Volumes:	75,000+
Specialties:	Literature; science fiction; history.
Hours:	Mon-Sat 10-6, except Thu till 8:30. Sun 12-5.
Travel:	Located in the heart of downtown. Exit 4 South off Rte. 17. Proceed on Rte. 363 for about 1 mile. Take the downtown exit for Rte. 11. Left on Rte. 11 which becomes Court St. Map 10.
Credit Cards:	No
Year Estab:	1987
Comments:	Like its parent company, the Syracuse based Book Warehouse, this shop offers plenty of remainders, recently published fiction and a selection of inexpensive used books that are basically reading copies of common titles. We saw little of an unusual nature in the collection. The shop offers a pleasant, browser friendly atmosphere.

Gil's Book Loft (NY17)   (607) 771-6800
82 Court Street, 2nd Floor 13901

Collection:	General stock of new and used books, signed prints, magazines and records.
# of Volumes:	30,000+
Specialties:	Literature; art; cookbooks; theatre; magazines.
Hours:	Tue-Sat 11-5:30. Also by appointment for established dealers.
Services:	Accepts want lists.
Travel:	See above. Shop is above Marine Midland Bank. Map 10.
Credit Cards:	No
Owner:	Gil & Deborah Williams
Year Estab:	1991
Comments:	Located one flight up, this is definitely a browser friendly shop with spacious aisles, a comfortable seating area and a delightful and well equipped children's corner. The owner knows his books and exercises good taste in buying. The mix of new and used hardcover titles provides something for most tastes, though we saw few if any truly rare items.

Bouckville

Bouckville Books (NY19)   (315) 893-7946
At Canal House, Route 20   (315) 682-2513
Mailing address: 21 Limestone Drive Manlius 13104

Collection:	General stock and ephemera.
# of Volumes:	3,000
Specialties:	Children's; natural history; technical; medicine; New York State.
Hours:	Apr-Jan: Daily 11-5. Evening hours by appointment.
Services:	Appraisals
Travel:	On Rte. 20. Look for a 2 story brown & white building. Map 9.
Credit Cards:	Yes
Owner:	Marvin E. Mintz
Year Estab:	1987
Comments:	Most of the books in this combination book/collectibles shop are of an older variety. The shelves are well organized and labeled and we noted some interesting titles, including a nice section of ethnic books. Prices, in our view, were a bit steep.

Bridgewater

Nineteenth Century Bookshop (NY20)   (315) 822-6745
Routes 8 & 20
Mailing address: PO Box 374   13313

Collection:	General stock.
# of Volumes:	30,000
Specialties:	Local history; New York history.
Hours:	Sat & Sun 10-5. Weekdays by chance.
Services:	Accepts want lists, mail order.
Travel:	On Rte. 20. Westbound from Utica, shop is on left. Map 9.
Credit Cards:	No
Owner:	Pablo Davis
Year Estab:	1973

Brockport

Lift Bridge Book Shop (NY21)   (716) 637-2260
71 Main Street 14420   Fax: (716) 637-7823

Collection:	Specialty
# of Volumes:	Several hundred
Specialties:	Western New York; Erie Canal.
Hours:	Mon-Fri 9:30-9. Sat 9:30-5:30. Sun 12-5.
Services:	Search service.
Travel:	Leroy exit off NY Twy. Proceed north on Rte. 19 which becomes Main St. in Brockport. Map 16.
Credit Cards:	Yes
Year Estab:	1972

Comments: Primarily a new book store, this shop offers a modest sized collection of specialty used books.

Bronxville

Recycled Ink (NY18)   (914) 961-7323
10-12 Park Place 10708

Collection:	General stock of new and used. (See Comments)
Specialties:	Mystery.
Hours:	Mon-Wed 10-9. Thu-Sat 10-10. Sun 12-6.
Travel:	Pondfield Rd. exit off Bronx River Pkwy. Proceed on Pondfield to Bronxville. Right on Park Pl. Map 11.
Credit Cards:	Yes
Owner:	Carrie & Bob Hecht
Comments:	Primarily a new book shop, the used titles are mostly paperback mysteries received in trade.

Buffalo

The Circular Word (NY22)   (716) 886-9259
799 Elmwood Avenue 14222

Collection:	General stock of paperback and hardcover.
# of Volumes:	30,000
Hours:	Mon-Sat 10-5:30.
Services:	Accepts want lists.
Travel:	Elmwood Ave. exit off Rte. 290. Map 7.
Credit Cards:	No
Owner:	Patrick Ferguson
Year Estab:	1977
Comments:	Primarily a paperback shop with a small selection of hardcover titles scattered about.

The Haunted Bookshop (NY23)   (716) 882-9273
100 Elmwood Avenue 14201

Collection:	General stock.
# of Volumes:	2,000-3,000
Specialties:	Mystery; supernatural.
Hours:	Mon-Sat 9-4, but best to call ahead.
Services:	Appraisals, search service, accepts want lists, mail order.
Travel:	See The Circular Word above. Map 7.
Credit Cards:	No
Owner:	Robert Hatch
Year Estab:	1985

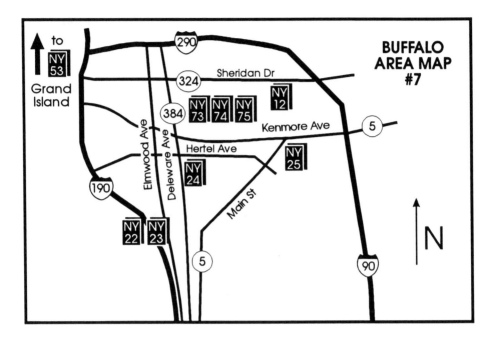

Mahoney & Weekly Booksellers (NY24)   (716) 836-5209
1419 Hertel Avenue 14216

Collection:	General stock and prints.
# of Volumes:	5,000-7,000
Specialties:	Literature; fine bindings; art.
Hours:	Tue-Sat 11-5.
Services:	Appraisals
Travel:	Main St. (Rte. 5) exit off Rte. 290. Proceed west on Main for about 1 mile to Hertel. Right on Hertel. Shop is about 6 blocks ahead, across from North Park Theatre. Map 7.
Credit Cards:	Yes
Owner:	Jon W. Weekly
Year Estab:	1972
Comments:	A spacious, browser friendly shop with a modest collection of books in good to better condition. The shop also sells some new books at discounted prices.

Old Editions Bookshop (NY25)   (716) 836-7354
3124 Main Street 14214   Fax: (716) 836-7354

Collection:	General stock.
# of Volumes:	35,000
Specialties:	Rare
Hours:	Mon-Sat 10-6. Sun by appointment. Closed major holidays.

Services:	Appraisals, accepts want lists.
Travel:	Main St. (Rte. 5) exit off Rte. 290. West on Main. Map 7.
Credit Cards:	Yes
Owner:	Ronald L. Cozzi
Year Estab:	1976
Comments:	Visiting this storefront shop is like visiting three different used book stores. While the front room contains a collection of popular paperbacks, the larger back room stocks a good sized collection of used books, many with a scholarly bent, and some first editions. A third room contains rare and collectible items, many of which are attractively displayed in glass cases. Additional used and rare volumes are located in the basement. Moderately priced.

Canton

Jenison's Fine Books & Antiques (NY26)   (315) 386-3022
23 Gouverneur Street 13617   (315) 386-4138

Collection:	General stock, ephemera and prints.
# of Volumes:	20,000
Specialties:	Civil War, northern New York State history; trade catalogs.
Hours:	Thu-Sat 12-5.
Services:	Appraisals, search service, occasional catalog, accepts want lists.
Travel:	Located on Rte. 11. Proceeding north, shop is on right, before entering town. Map 6.
Credit Cards:	Yes
Owner:	Tom Jenison
Year Estab:	1973
Comments:	This bi-level shop offers many interesting items of an older vintage, more than a few of which could legitimately be considered antiquarian and rare. Less expensive books are located in a barn behind the main shop.

Catskill

Attic Books & Records (NY27)   (203) 496-9260
473 Main Street 12414

Collection:	General stock.
# of Volumes:	10,000
Hours:	Tue-Sat 10-6.
Services:	Catalog
Travel:	Catskill exit off NY Twy. Proceed on Rte. 23B for about 3 miles into village where Rte. 23B becomes Main St. Map 8.
Credit Cards:	No

Owner:	Roger P. Steward
Year Estab:	1969
Comments:	This storefront shop, whose entrance is two steps up, offers a modest selection of books. While the shelves are appropriately labeled by subject, the actual selections in terms of both quality and quantity were lacking. We did see, however, several older volumes which might be just the ones the patient book hunter is looking for.

Books Galore and More (NY28)   (518) 943-0477
401 Main Street 12414   Fax: (518) 943-0477

Collection:	General stock of hardcover and paperback.
# of Volumes:	4,000
Specialties:	Civil War, American Revolution; local history.
Hours:	Mon-Sat 10-5.
Services:	Appraisals, occasional catalog, accepts want lists, mail order.
Travel:	See above. Map 8.
Credit Cards:	No
Owner:	Leonard Young
Year Estab:	1992
Comments:	This shop offers a modest collection of hardcover and paperback titles and a potpourri of new items. The shop's basement, if you're willing to risk descending into the depths of a dark and damp space, offers several rows of narrow bookshelves containing many older volumes. Try to get there before the mildew gets to the books, however. While the shelves upstairs are appropriately labeled, the same cannot be said for the books in the basement. The upstairs could also benefit from some general tidying up.

Cicero

The Bookshelf (NY29)   (315) 452-5672
Marketplace Mall, Circle Drive 13039

Collection:	General stock of used and some new hardcover and paperback.
# of Volumes:	4,000-5,000
Hours:	Mon-Sat 10-9. Sun 12-5.
Travel:	Rte. 11 to Circle Dr. Marketplace Mall is across from Penncan Mall. Map 10.
Credit Cards:	No
Owner:	Deborah Barber
Year Estab:	1986
Comments:	Primarily a paperback shop with some hardcover titles.

Claverack

The Lark (NY30)   (518) 851-3741
Route 23
Mailing address: PO Box 375 12513

Collection:	General stock.
# of Volumes:	3,000-5,000+
Specialties:	Art; illustrated.
Hours:	Winter: Fri 12-5 Sat 12-4. Sun 12-3. Summer: Fri & Sat 12-6. Sun 12-5.
Services:	Search service.
Travel:	Rte. 9H to light in Claverack. Turn east on Rte. 23 (towards Taconic Pkwy). Shop is the fourth house on right. Map 8.
Credit Cards:	No
Year Estab:	1992
Comments:	The owner wishes his establishment to be identified as an "open shop." However, on the Saturday afternoon we visited, the shop was closed. If you plan to visit, we strongly urge you to call ahead on the day of your visit.

Clinton

The Blue Fox (NY31)   (315) 853-6494
34 College Street 13323

Collection:	General stock and ephemera.
# of Volumes:	40,000-50,000
Specialties:	First editions; scholarly; vintage paperbacks; rare.
Hours:	Mon-Wed & Sat 10-5:30. Thu & Fri 10-9.
Services:	Appraisals, accepts want lists, irregular catalogs.
Travel:	Westmoreland exit off NY Twy. Proceed south on Rte. 233 to College St. Left on College and proceed about 5 blocks to first light. Shop is on left. Map 9.
Credit Cards:	No
Owner:	John DeForest
Year Estab:	1985
Comments:	A pleasant shop divided into several small rooms and alcoves filled with books from several different periods and generally in good condition. The collection is well labeled and moderately priced.

The Garret Gallery (NY32)   (315) 853-8145
33 Seneca Turnpike 13323

Collection:	Specialty books and prints.

# of Volumes:	3,000
Specialties:	Arctic; exploration; western Americana; Civil War; mountaineering; Custer.
Hours:	Mon-Fri 11-5 and other times by appointment.
Services:	Catalog
Travel:	Westmoreland exit off NY Twy. Proceed on Rte. 233 south to Rte. 5, then east on Rte. 5 for about 1 mile. Shop is on the left in a maroon house with white trim. Map 9.
Credit Cards:	No
Owner:	Richard Astle
Year Estab:	1985
Comments:	If your interests coincide with the shop's specialties, we feel certain you'll find several titles to your liking here. The books are in spotless condition.

Cold Spring

Antipodean Books, Maps & Prints (NY252)   (914) 265-4058
At Salmagundi Books, Ltd. 66 Main Street 10516

Collection:	General stock.
# of Volumes:	Several hundred. (See Comments).
Hours:	Daily 11-5:30.
Travel:	Rte 9 or 9D to Rte. 301. Left on 301 (Main St.) Map 11.
Credit Cards:	No
Owner:	David Lilburne
Year Estab:	1976
Comments:	This otherwise "By Appointment" dealer displays a sampling of his collection in this new book shop. The books we saw when we visited represented several areas of interest, were generally in good condition and were moderately priced. See By Appointment section.

Mrs. Hudson's (NY254)   (914) 265-4577
89 Main St. 10516

Collection:	Specialty (See Comments).
# of Volumes:	Several hundred.
Specialties:	Children's
Hours:	Mon-Fri, except Tue 12-5. Sat & Sun 11-6.
Travel:	See above. Map 11.
Credit Cards:	Yes
Owner:	Rena Hudson
Comments:	Primarily an antique and collectible shop, a brief browse will tell you all you want to know about this shop. One bookcase is

devoted to moderately priced older children's books while a second contains older books of a more general nature. The entrance is up a few steps.

Hudson Rougue Co. (NY253)   (914) 265-2211
255 Main Street Nelsonville 10516

Collection:	General stock, autographs and prints.
# of Volumes:	Several hundred.
Specialties:	Hudson River.
Hours:	Fri-Sun 12-5 and other times by appointment or chance.
Services:	Appraisals, catalog (autographs), accepts want lists, mail order.
Travel:	On Rte. 301 between Rtes. 9 and 9D. Map 11.
Credit Cards:	No
Owner:	Richard Saunders
Year Estab:	1971
Comments:	The shop offers a limited selection of mostly older books with a stronger emphasis on ephemera, prints and autographs. Most of the books deal with the Hudson Valley and/or New York State.

F. Volkmann Books (NY255)   (914) 265-9296
Fishkill Road
Mailing address: 346 Main Street Cold Spring 10516

Collection:	General stock.
# of Volumes:	10,000
Hours:	Summer: Daily 10-5. Remainder of year: TBA.
Travel:	Just off Rte. 9 about 1 mile north of Rte. 301. Proceeding north, left on Fishkill Rd. Shop is on right in a cream colored stand along building. Map 11.
Credit Cards:	No
Owner:	F. Volkmann
Year Estab:	1990
Comments:	This recently opened "open shop" offers a carefully selected collection of books, most in quite good condition, and priced to sell. We were pleased with what we saw. Don't overlook the New Arrivals and modest Antiquarian section in the front. Of the four used book dealers in Cold Spring, this is the only one that qualifies as a fully stocked used book shop.

Cooperstown

Willis Monie (NY33)   (800) 322-2995
139 Main Street 13326

Collection:	General stock and ephemera.

# of Volumes:	50,000
Specialties:	Baseball; Americana; literature; theology; fiction.
Hours:	May-Oct: Daily 10-6. Nov-Apr: Tue-Sat 9-5.
Services:	Catalog, accepts want lists.
Travel:	Rte. 28 becomes Chestnut in Cooperstown. Once in town, continue on Chestnut to light at Main St. Map 9.
Credit Cards:	Yes
Owner:	Will Monie
Year Estab:	1979
Comments:	A large, spacious, easy to browse shop with a solid collection of books in almost every category. Most of the books are in good condition and reasonably priced. The books are of mixed vintage and selected with good taste by a reader friendly owner. The ephemera is well organized in file cabinets.

Corning

Book Exchange (NY34)   (607) 936-8536
90 West Market Street 14830   Fax: (607) 936-8536

Collection:	General stock.
# of Volumes:	10,000
Specialties:	Decorative arts.
Hours:	Mon-Sat 10:30-4:30 and by appointment anytime.
Services:	Appraisals, search service, catalog.
Travel:	In downtown Corning. Map 10.
Credit Cards:	Yes
Owner:	Jim T. Iraggi
Year Estab:	1977
Comments:	A modest sized general stock with no unusual or collectible items. Most of the books are in good condition. As befits Corning, the shop carries a large selection of books dealing with glass.

Books Of Marvel (NY35)   (607) 962-6300
c/o The Glass Menagerie, 37 E. Market Street 14830   (607) 936-6610

Collection:	Specialty
# of Volumes:	5,000
Specialties:	Children's; children's series; Thorton Burgess; L. Frank Baum; Edgar Rice Burroughs; Mark Twain (including, first editions).
Hours:	May 1-June 30 & Labor Day-Oct 31st: Mon-Sat 10-5:30 & Sun 1-5. July 1-Labor Day: Daily 9:30-9:30. Nov 1-Apr 30: Mon-Sat 11-5. Other times by appointment.
Services:	Appraisals, search service (specialty areas only), mail order, accepts want lists.

Travel:	In downtown Corning, between Cedar and Pine Sts. The book room is on the second floor and access is possible only if there is a second salesperson in the shop to accompany visitors upstairs. Map 10.
Credit Cards:	Yes
Owner:	Richard L. Pope
Year Estab:	1983
Comments:	If you're heavily into this shop's specialty, you'll enjoy browsing this in depth collection. Prices, we felt, were somewhat high as we've seen similar titles available elsewhere (albeit not in such quality or quantity) for less. However, the condition of the books and the selection (particularly if you've been searching for a title or two for a long time) may well make the price worth it.

Cornwall

Firehouse Book Emporium (NY36)   (914)534-9967
263 Main Street 12518

Collection:	General stock of paperback and some hardcover.
# of Volumes:	10,000
Hours:	Mon-Fri 10-6. Sat 10-5.
Travel:	Southbound on Rte. 9W, take West Point exit. Second right on Main St. Shop is ahead about 1 mile on the left. Map 11.
Credit Cards:	No
Owner:	Susan Murphy
Year Estab:	1992
Comments:	Primarily a paperback exchange shop with a smattering of hardcover volumes.

Croton-on-Hudson

Old Book Room (NY37)   (914)271-6802
111 Grand Street 10520

Collection:	General stock.
# of Volumes:	10,000
Specialties:	New York; Hudson River Valley; 20th century American art.
Hours:	Thu-Sat 10-5.
Services:	Search service, lists (on request).
Travel:	Underhill Ave. exit off Taconic Pkwy. Proceed on Rte. 129 to Croton. Bear right at fork in village. Shop is ahead on right after traffic light. Map 11.
Credit Cards:	No
Owner:	Jane Northshield

Year Estab:	1981
Comments:	A tightly packed quaint shop that houses two distinct but related businesses: used books, and a dealer in ephemera and old prints. The books are of mixed vintage with the majority falling into the older category. The shop offers an interesting selection with a strong possibility of finding some unusual items. We saw little consistency in pricing, however: some items, we feel, were overpriced while others were priced most reasonably.

Deansboro

Berry Hill Book Shop (NY38)   (315) 821-6188
2349 State Route 12B   13328

Collection:	General stock and ephemera.
# of Volumes:	100,000+
Hours:	Mon-Sat 10-6.
Services:	Appraisals, search service, accepts want lists, mail order.
Travel:	Rte. 233 South to Rte. 12B. Proceed south on Rte. 12B for about 5 miles. Shop is on the right, behind a red two story frame house. Look for a small sign. Map 9.
Credit Cards:	No
Owner:	Doris & Doug Swarthout
Year Estab:	1968
Comments:	One of the nicest and best sources of older books in the state. The shop's three floors are packed solid with titles in almost every field one can imagine and prices are hard to beat. Plan to spend several hours here.

Deposit

Black Kettle Bookshop (NY39)   (607) 467-3182
50 Wheeler Street 13754   (607) 467-4746

Collection:	General stock.
# of Volumes:	15,000
Specialties:	American literature; music; philosophy; early civilizations; history; children's; World War I; Italian history; early Spanish and Italian literature.
Hours:	Tue-Sat 10-5. Sun by appointment or chance.
Travel:	Westbound from Rte. 17: Exit 84. Right at flashing light then first left on Wheeler. Eastbound: Exit 83. After light, left on Wheeler. Map 10.
Credit Cards:	No
Owner:	Remo Tedeschi

Year Estab:	1983
Comments:	The collection is located in an attractively decorated building located behind the owner's home. The shop concentrates on scholarly titles that have been carefully selected by the friendly and considerate proprietors. Reasonably priced.

Dobbs Ferry

The Brown Bag Bookstore (NY40)   (914) 693-2322
127A Main Street, Box 276 10522

Collection:	General stock.
# of Volumes:	40,000
Specialties:	Biography; history; art; women's studies.
Hours:	Tue-Sat 10-5. Mon by appointment.
Services:	Mail order.
Travel:	Ashford Ave. exit off Saw Mill River Pkwy. Proceed west to Broadway (Rte. 9). Right on Oak St. Main St. is one block over. Shop is across from post office. Map 11.
Credit Cards:	No
Owner:	Ruth Rosenblatt
Year Estab:	1985
Comments:	In the two years since our last visit, the collection in this delightful shop has almost doubled in size. As the square footage available for display has not increased, by necessity, the space between bookcases for browsers has become narrower. There are books in almost all categories and the titles truly reflect vintage classics in almost every field.

The Depot Attic (NY41)   (914) 693-5858
377 Ashford Avenue 10522

Collection:	Specialty books, ephemera and related items.
# of Volumes:	5,000-8,000
Specialties:	Railroads (everything and anything, including books, hardware, graphics, chinaware, etc.).
Hours:	Sat & Sun 12-5:30. By appointment during the week.
Services:	Appraisals, search service, catalog, accepts want lists.
Travel:	Ashford Ave. exit off Saw Mill River Pkwy. Shop is one block from exit. Map 11.
Owner:	Fred Arone
Year Estab:	1956

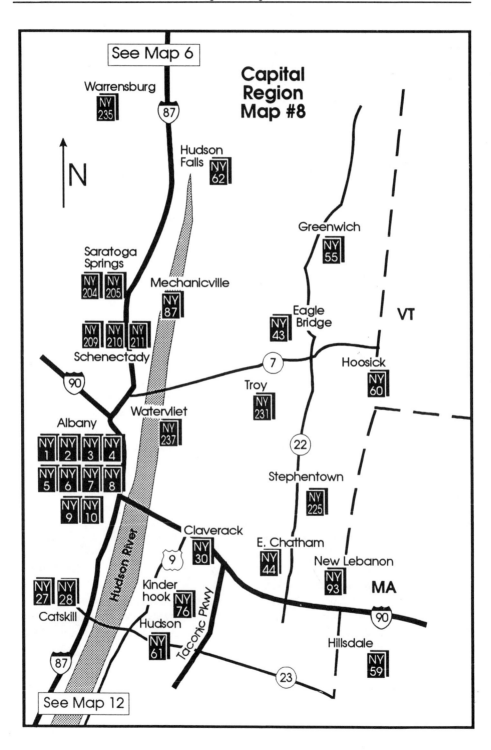

See Map 6

Warrensburg
NY 235

Capital
Region
Map #8

Hudson
Falls
NY 62

N

Greenwich
NY 55

Saratoga
Springs
NY 204 NY 205

Mechanicville
NY 87

Eagle
Bridge
NY 43

VT

NY 209 NY 210 NY 211

Schenectady

7

Hoosick
NY 60

90

Troy
NY 231

Watervliet
NY 237

Albany
NY 1 NY 2 NY 3 NY 4
NY 5 NY 6 NY 7 NY 8
NY 9 NY 10

22

Stephentown
NY 225

Claverack
NY 30

E. Chatham
NY 44

New Lebanon
NY 93

MA

Hudson River

9

Kinder
hook
NY 76

NY 27 NY 28

Catskill

Hudson
NY 61

Taconic Pkwy

90

Hillsdale
NY 59

87

23

See Map 12

Dryden

Book Barn of the Finger Lakes (NY42)   (607) 844-9365
25 Cortland Road 13053

Collection:	General stock.
# of Volumes:	50,000
Specialties:	Scholarly; art; architecture; New York State history and fiction; science; technology; landscape design; city planning; theology; labor and industrial relations; E.B. White.
Hours:	Wed-Sat 10-5:30. Sun 11:30-5. Mon & Tue by chance or appointment. Closed December 25-January 1st.
Services:	Appraisals, search service, accepts want lists, mail order.
Travel:	Proceeding north from Ithaca on Rte. 13, after intersection of Rtes. 38/392/13 and North Rd, bear left on North when Rte. 13 veers to right. Proceeding southbound on Rte. 13, right turn on North which intersects with Rte. 13 at a 45 degree angle. Once on North Rd, look for a green mailbox on the right with shop name and "198" stenciled on the box. Map 10.
Credit Cards:	Yes
Owner:	Vladimir Dragan
Year Estab:	1985
Comments:	You know you're approaching a "find" when two or three other book people are anxiously waiting for the shop to open at 10AM on a Saturday morning. Located in an attractively renovated 19th century barn that skillfully combines the ambience of the original barn with modern sheetrock and fluorescent lighting, when we visited, the owner/architect was still in the process of unpacking his stock. The collection is well organized and the books are in good condition. Prices are moderate. The barn is definitely worth a visit.

Eagle Bridge

J. Geoffrey Jones Books (NY43)   (518) 686-7974
The Inn, Main Street 12057

Collection:	General stock.
Specialties:	First editions; signed; history.
Hours:	Daily 9-9 but best to call ahead.
Services:	Appraisals, catalog, accepts want lists.
Travel:	Located in a red brick building on Rte. 67 (Main St), across from post office in heart of village. Map 8.
Owner:	Paul & Geoffrey Jones

East Chatham

Librarium (NY44)　　　　　　　　　　　　　　　　(518) 392-5209
RD 1, Box 190, Black Bridge Road 12060

Collection:	General stock and ephemera.
# of Volumes:	30,000
Hours:	Apr-Nov: Fri-Mon 10-6. Dec-Mar: Sat & Sun 10-5. Other times by appointment or chance.
Services:	Search service.
Travel:	From Berkshire extension of I-90 going east, exit at Taconic Pkwy exit. After toll booths, exit immediately at "commercial traffic" exit and follow signs to Rte. 295. Left on Rte. 295 and proceed 2 miles. Left on Black Bridge Rd and left to grey farmhouse. From Berkshire extension going west, exit at Rte. 22 exit. Proceed north on Rte. 22 to light at Rte. 295. Left on Rte. 295 and proceed 5½ miles. Right on Black Bridge and jog left to grey farmhouse. Map 8.
Credit Cards:	No
Owner:	Sharon S. Lips
Year Estab:	1979
Comments:	Located in several rooms in a wing of an old farmhouse, the shop carries a well organized and reasonably priced general stock, the majority of which date from the 1940's and upwards. Additional older less expensive books, and books in less than desirable condition, are located in a large barn about 100 feet behind the main building. The owner invites her visitors to bring lunch and picnic at tables conveniently located under the apple trees.

East Springfield

Tintagel Books (NY45)　　　　　　　　　　　　　　(607) 264-3669
CR 31, PO Box 125 13333

Collection:	General stock.
# of Volumes:	6,000
Specialties:	New York State history; antiquarian.
Hours:	Daily 10-7.
Services:	Appraisals, catalog, accepts want lists.
Travel:	Just off Rte. 20, north of Cooperstown. Look for sign on Rte. 20. Map 9.
Credit Cards:	Yes
Owner:	Ravic & Gail Shariff
Year Estab:	1984

Comments: If you're looking for quality titles in pristine condition dealing
                 with New York State, this is the place for you. Located in the
                 two front rooms of a private home elegantly decorated with
                 furniture and accessories from Kashmir, this is not a shop for
                 general browsers but specialists will love it.

Fayetteville

Book Traders (NY46)   (315) 637-5006
417 East Genesee Street 13066

Collection: General stock of paperback and some hardcover.
# of Volumes: 30,000
Hours: Mon-Fri 9:30-5:30, except Thu till 8. Sat 9-5
Services: Accepts want lists.
Travel: Exit 36A off NY Thwy (eastbound). Proceed on Rte. 481 south to
                   Dewitt/exit 3E. Proceed on Rte. 5 to Fayetteville where it be-
                   comes East Genesee. Map 10.
Credit Cards: Yes
Owner: Rosa Kurpiewski & Patricia Gaboric
Year Estab: 1992

Fishkill

Steve's Book Exchange (NY47)   (914) 896-7943
40 Elm Street 12524

Collection: General stock of paperback and hardcover.
# of Volumes: 25,000
Hours: Mon-Fri 10-6. Sat 10-5.
Services: Search service, accepts want lists, mail order.
Travel: From intersection of I-84 and Rte. 9, proceed north on Rte. 9 for
                   4 traffic lights (including light at exit). Left on Elm. Shop is 200
                   feet ahead on right. Map 12.
Credit Cards: No
Owner: Steve Ruderman
Year Estab: 1991
Comments: More than 80% of the stock consists of paperbacks. The hard-
                   cover books are mostly recent book club editions with very few,
                   if any, older volumes.

Franklin

Poor Richard's Book Barn (NY48)   (607) 829-8762
23 Center Street 13775
Mailing address: PO Box 95 13775

Collection:	General stock and ephemera.
# of Volumes:	20,000
Specialties:	History; biography; literature; poetry; children's.
Hours:	Tue-Sat 11-5 but best to call ahead. Other times by appointment or chance.
Services:	Accepts want lists, mail order.
Travel:	Exit 11 off I-88. Proceed east on Rte. 357 for about 7 miles to Franklin. Left at American Legion Hall and proceed one block to Center St. Map 9.
Credit Cards:	No
Owner:	Richard deFrances
Year Estab:	1988
Comments:	A very good general collection of well organized older books in reasonably good condition. Our only caveats are the steep flight of stairs one must climb to get to the books and caution to dress warmly in the winter as the barn is not heated.

Freeville

The Phoenix (NY49)   (607) 347-4767
1608 Dryden Road
Mailing address: PO Box 230   13068

Collection:	General stock.
# of Volumes:	50,000
Hours:	Mon-Sat 10-6. Sun 12-6.
Travel:	Located on Rte. 13 between Ithaca and Dryden. Map 10.
Credit Cards:	Yes
Owner:	A. Elizabeth Morrison
Year Estab:	1985
Comments:	When we visited this renovated book barn (which may change owners in the near future), we found it to be pleasantly fruitful in its offerings. There are many many rooms, each rich with both common and older less common (and certainly more interesting) titles. For the book lover's sake, we hope that the new owner retains the class and distinction of the shop as we saw it.

Geneva

The Book Finder (NY50)   (315) 789-9388
207 Lyons Road 14456

Collection:	General stock.
# of Volumes:	19,000
Hours:	Winter: Mon-Wed & Sat 10:30-4. Thu & Fri 10:30-8:30. Spring-Fall: Also Sun 1-4.

Services:	Appraisals, search service, accepts want lists, mail order.
Travel:	Exit 42 off NY State Twy. Proceed south on Rte. 14 for about 5 miles. If proceeding north on Rte. 14 from Geneva, note that Exchange St. becomes Lyons Rd. Map 10.
Credit Cards:	No
Owner:	Jeanne S. Busch
Year Estab:	1978
Comments:	A moderate sized shop with books representing different time periods. Worth a visit if you're in the neighborhood.

Calhoun's Books (NY51)   (315) 789-8599
1510 Routes 5 & 20 West 14456

Collection:	General stock and postcards.
# of Volumes:	60,000
Specialties:	New York State; aviation; bindings; Americana; travel; black studies; maps.
Hours:	Mid Apr-mid Nov: Daily 11-5.
Travel:	Proceeding west from Geneva, shop is on the right in a white one story building. Map 10.
Credit Cards:	Yes
Owner:	Douglas & Marlene Calhoun
Year Estab:	1981
Comments:	A traditional barn-like setting with a large collection housed in a series of rooms. Many of the non fiction shelves lacked identifying subject labels. Most of the books are older volumes, including some hard-to-find titles. If you want to browse everything the shop has to offer, allow yourself ample time. Reasonably priced.

Germantown

Main Street Books (NY52)   (518) 537-5878
Main Street
Mailing address: PO Box 274 12526

Collection:	General stock.
# of Volumes:	10,000+
Hours:	Fri- Sun 10-5. Other times by appointment.
Services:	Accepts want lists, search service.
Travel:	From Rte. 9G, turn at Germantown light and proceed to center of village. Shop is across from the telephone company building. Map 12.
Credit Cards:	Yes
Owner:	Ken Hubner

Year Estab:	1989
Comments:	This charming little book shop carries a stock of mostly recent volumes in generally good condition. While the store currently occupies only the first floor of the building, the owner has plans to expand to the second and third floors.

Grand Island

Ye Olde Book Shoppe (NY53)   (716) 773-1488
1713 Grand Island Boulevard 14072

Collection:	General stock, primarily paperback.
# of Volumes:	10,000
Hours:	Mon-Sat, except Wed, 10-5:30.
Services:	Accepts want lists.
Travel:	I-190 north. Follow signs for Niagara Falls. Take first exit off South Grand Island bridge. Map 7.
Credit Cards:	No
Owner:	Marilyn Johnson
Year Estab:	1981

Greenport

The Book Scout (NY54)   (516) 477-0256
126 Main Street
Mailing address: PO Box 184   11984

Collection:	General stock.
# of Volumes:	8,000
Specialties:	Photography; art.
Hours:	Daily 12-5. Best to call ahead in winter.
Services:	Appraisals, search service (art and photography only); accepts want lists, mail order.
Travel:	Long Island Expy (Rte. 495) to the end and proceed on Rte. 48 to Orient Point. Take ferry to Orient Point. Continue on Rte. 48 for about 10 miles to Greenport. Map 13.
Credit Cards:	No
Owner:	Peter Stevens
Year Estab:	1983

Greenwich

Owl Pen Books (NY55)   (518) 692-7039
Riddle Road
Mailing address: Rte. 2, Box 202 12834

Collection:	General stock, prints, ephemera and magazines.
# of Volumes:	75,000
Hours:	May 1-Oct 31: Wed-Sun 12-6.
Services:	Search service, accepts want lists.
Travel:	Although not difficult to find, the shop is "tucked away in the hills," and the owners suggest visitors write ahead for a map or call for specific directions once they're in the area. Map 8.
Credit Cards:	No
Owner:	Hank Howard & Edie Brown
Year Estab:	1960
Comments:	If you enjoy book barns, you're likely to walk away with a purchase or two from this rustic shop located off an unpaved country back road. The shop offers a large collection of reading copies in most categories and some surprising sections of miscellaneous items worth examining. Most of the books are in good condition and are reasonably priced. Better books are shelved in a small office in the main barn and additional volumes are located in a second smaller building.

Harriman

Harriman Book Shop (NY56)   (914) 782-4338
Harriman Square, Box 319 10926   Fax: (914) 774-8263

Collection:	General stock.
# of Volumes:	20,000
Specialties:	Hudson River Valley; military; New York State.
Hours:	Tue-Sat 10-5. Sun 12-4.
Services:	Appraisals, search service, accepts want lists, mail order.
Travel:	Exit 16 off NY Twy. or Harriman exit off Rte. 17. Proceed south on Rte. 32 for about 1 mile. Right after railroad trestle and proceed to village. Shop is on right after the stop sign. Map 11.
Credit Cards:	Yes
Owner:	Alan Hunter
Year Estab:	1985
Comments:	A good sized collection of mixed vintage books not all in the best of condition. Most subjects are represented and while the collection is generally well organized, the shelves and aisles could benefit from some tidying up.

Hastings-in-Hudson

Gordon Beckhorn - Bookperson (NY57)   (914) 478-5511
497 Warburton Avenue 10706

Collection:	Specialty

Specialties:	Modern first editions; signed limited editions; rivers and lakes of America and related series books in Americana; American folkways; trails of America.
Hours:	Mon-Sat 9-6.
Services:	Catalog
Travel:	Farragut Pkwy. exit off Saw Mill River Pkwy. Proceed 1 mile to Hastings. Bear left at first light on Main St. Left at second light on Warburton. Entrance to shop is a down flight of stairs on side of building. Map 11.
Credit Cards:	Yes
Owner:	Gordon Beckhorn
Year Estab:	1983
Comments:	Considering the wealth of books in Hastings, you can't go wrong stopping for a brief visit in this small basement shop. In addition to the specialty areas listed above, the owner has a limited selection of titles in other subject areas.

Riverrun (NY58)   (914) 478-4307
7 Washington Street 10706   Home: (914) 478-2127

Collection:	General stock.
# of Volumes:	70,000+
Specialties:	Modern literature (including first editions); science fiction; mystery; western literature in translation.
Hours:	Daily 11-6.
Services:	Accepts want lists.
Travel:	See above. Shop is around the corner. Map 11.
Credit Cards:	No
Owner:	Frank Scioscia
Year Estab:	1974
Comments:	Known as the dean of Hudson Valley rare and used book dealers, the owner of this shop has and displays books galore. Books, well labeled, in good condition and representing every category are to be found in the main shop and an annex of equal size across the street. In addition, the owner will schedule appointments with serious buyers to visit thousands of additional modern first editions stored at a third location. On occasion, the owner will even bring visitors to his home where thousands more volumes are on hand in the mystery, detective and science fiction genres. For our money, this establishment is one of the finest we have ever visited and is certainly not to be missed.

Hillsdale

Rodgers Book Barn (NY59)   (518) 325-3610
Rodman Road 12529

Collection:	General stock, records and ephemera.
# of Volumes:	50,000+
Specialties:	Literature; history; art.
Hours:	Apr-Nov: Mon,Thu & Fri 12-6. Sat & Sun 10-6 and other times by chance. Dec-Mar: Fri 12-5. Sat & Sun 10-6 and additional hours during holiday times.
Travel:	Rte. 23 to Craryville. Left at church, then left on West End Rd. and right on Rodman. Watch for small signs at intersections. Most of Rodman is an unpaved road and conditions can vary depending on the season and weather conditions. Map 8.
Credit Cards:	No
Owner:	Maureen Rodgers
Year Estab:	1972
Comments:	You should enjoy browsing through the many well appointed nooks and crannies of this "slightly out of the way" but "definitely worth a visit" shop located in a true country setting. The bi-level barn is very well organized with a generous selection of titles in almost every subject area. The books have been selected by the owner with special care and they show it. The majority of the books sell for between $3-$10, with many bargains to be found. One low ceiling "cranny" is appropriately labeled: "Underneath and Underpriced."

Hoosick

Dog Ears Book Barn (NY60)   (518) 686-9580
Route 7, Bennington-Troy Road 12089

Collection:	General stock.
# of Volumes:	30,000+
Specialties:	Children's; philosophy.
Hours:	Daily, except Tue & Wed, 10-5.
Services:	Appraisals, accepts want lists.
Travel:	One half mile east of junction of Rtes. 22 and 7. Map 8.
Credit Cards:	No
Owner:	Jeffrey & Sylvia Waite
Year Estab:	1992
Comments:	Located in an immaculate "new" barn adjacent to the owners' home, this shop offers an impressive, well organized stock that is quite reasonably priced and where book hunters may find

some bargains. The owners are still in the process of unpacking their stock and visitors are advised to ask if they don't see titles they're looking for. A second level is planned.

Hudson

Atlantis Rising (NY61)   (518) 822-0438
545 Warren Street 12534

Collection:	General stock and ephemera.
# of Volumes:	10,000
Hours:	Daily 11-4.
Travel:	Rtes 9 or 9G to Hudson. Shop is located on the main business street between Fifth & Sixth Streets. Map 8.
Credit Cards:	No
Owner:	Fred & Bernadette Timan
Year Estab:	1988
Comments:	If you like antiques and collectibles, you'll enjoy a trip to Warren Street. The rather limited used book section in this combination antique/book shop consists of fewer than a dozen bookcases (displaying considerably fewer than 10,000 titles) with older but not necessarily rare volumes.

Hudson Falls

Village Booksmith (NY62)   (518) 747-3261
223 Main Street 12839

Collection:	General stock, magazines, prints and ephemera.
# of Volumes:	40,000
Hours:	Mon-Sat 10-6. Sun 1-5.
Services:	Search service, catalog, accepts want lists.
Travel:	Main St. is Rte. 4. Shop is in center of town. Map 8.
Credit Cards:	Yes
Owner:	Clifford Bruce
Year Estab:	1976
Comments:	Each time we return to this perfectly wonderful bi-level shop we are impressed by its collection, particularly strong in mystery, cookbooks, travel and general fiction. The books here, we believe, are a true bargain and the quality of the collection is quite high.

Huntington

Book Revue (NY63)   (516) 271-1442
313 New York Avenue 11743

Collection:	General stock of new and used.
# of Volumes:	5,000-10,000 (used)
Hours:	Mon-Thu 9:30-10:30, except Fri & Sat till 11:30. Sun 10:30-10.
Services:	Appraisals
Travel:	Rte. 110 exit off I-495. Proceed north on Rte. 110 to village. Shop is just after intersection with Rte. 25A on left. Map 13.
Credit Cards:	Yes
Owner:	Richard & Robert Klein
Year Estab:	1977
Comments:	Primarily a new book shop, most of the used books are interspersed with new titles by category. There's also a separate somewhat less well organized "Clearance Section." The used collection, which the owners estimate accounts for about one fourth of the stock, ranges from remainders to older books. The store is spaciously laid out to facilitate browsing and subject categories are easy to locate. Prices are reasonable.

Oscar's Book Shop (NY64)   (516) 427-5155
389 New York Avenue 11743   (516) 421-1632

Collection:	General stock of new and used books.
# of Volumes:	50,000-60,000 (used)
Specialties:	Literature; history; modern first editions.
Hours:	Daily 9-11, except Fri and Sat till midnight.
Services:	Search service, catalog, accepts want lists, mail order.
Travel:	See above. Shop is on the left, just before intersection of Rte. 25A. Map 13.
Credit Cards:	Yes
Owner:	David Ramage. Used book manager: George Lenz
Year Estab:	1965
Comments:	Upon entering this attractive new book store, the question arises: "Where are the used books?" In effect, Oscar's is two shops in one. In addition to the large selection of new books on the main level, there's an equally large shop in the basement devoted exclusively to used books, most in quite good condition, and we're pleased to report, reasonably priced. Especially valuable first editions and signed books are located behind wire mesh in an area appropriately labeled "The Gold Mine." If you don't see a title you're looking for, ask, as the manager of the used book section also has a large stock at home (see second phone listing).

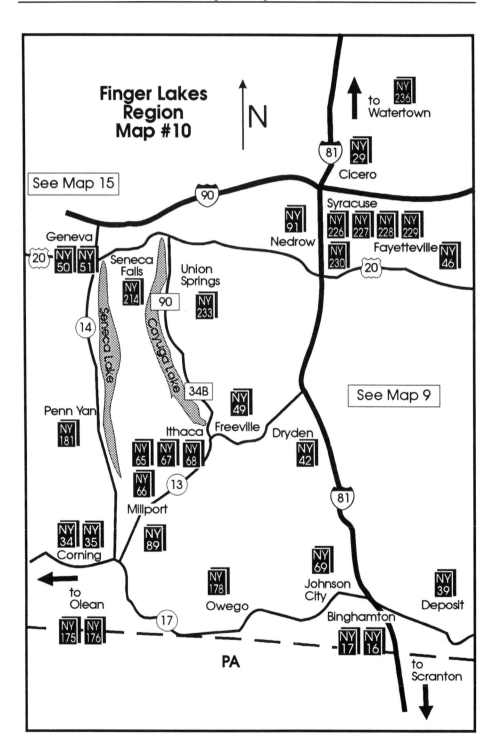

Finger Lakes
Region
Map #10

N

to
Watertown

NY
236

81   NY
      29

Cicero

90

See Map 15

Syracuse

NY
91

Nedrow

NY   NY   NY   NY
226 227 228 229

Fayetteville NY
               46

NY
230   20

20

Geneva

NY   NY
50   51

Seneca
Falls

NY
214

90

Union
Springs

NY
233

14

Seneca Lake

Cayuga Lake

34B

NY
49

See Map 9

Penn Yan

NY
181

Ithaca

Freeville

Dryden

NY   NY   NY
65   67   68

NY
66

13

NY
42

Millport

NY
89

81

NY   NY
34   35

Corning

NY
178

NY
69

Johnson
City

NY
39

Deposit

to
Olean

Owego

Binghamton

17

NY   NY
175 176

NY   NY
17   16

to
Scranton

PA

Ithaca

Autumn Leaves Used Books (NY65)   (607) 273-8239
108 The Commons 14850

Collection:	General stock of hardcover and paperback.
# of Volumes:	5,000
Specialties:	Contemporary fiction; cookbooks; children's.
Hours:	Mon-Sat 10-7, except Thu & Fri till 9. Sun 12-6.
Services:	Accepts want lists, mail order.
Travel:	In downtown Ithaca. Rte. 96 becomes State St. which leads directly to The Commons, a pedestrian mall. Map 10.
Credit Cards:	Yes
Owner:	Stephanie Marx & Joseph Wetmore
Year Estab:	1993
Comments:	This small but roomy shop offers mostly newer literature with a sprinkling of older books (located on the very top shelves). The books are in generally good condition and are reasonably priced. Some more scholarly subjects are also represented but not in any depth. If you're looking for bargain paperbacks, don't overlook the basement.

Blue Fox Books (NY66)   (607) 272-5186
104 North Aurora Street 14850

Collection:	General stock of paperbacks and hardcover.
# of Volumes:	15,000
Hours:	Mon-Sat 10-6. Sun 12-5.
Travel:	See above. Just off the east end of the Commons. Map 10.
Credit Cards:	Yes
Owner:	Bill Kehoe
Year Estab:	1979
Comments:	Located one flight up, the shop offers a mix of hardcover and paperback titles for what the owner describes as "education or relaxation." A selection of modern first editions are shelved near the owner's desk.

The Bookery (NY67)   (607) 273-5055
215 North Cayuga Street 14850

Collection:	General stock.
# of Volumes:	6,000-7,000
Hours:	Mon-Sat 10-5:30.
Services:	Appraisals, search service, accepts want lists, mail order.
Travel:	Rte. 13 to Buffalo St. East on Buffalo to Cayuga. Shop is in DeWitt Mall at corner of Buffalo and Cayuga and a few blocks from The Commons. Map 10.

Credit Cards:	Yes
Owner:	Jack Goldman
Year Estab:	1978
Comments:	Worth a visit, this shop consists of several rooms containing mostly scholarly titles, including several shelves devoted to French and German volumes in the original language. We also noted strong literature and science sections. Rare books are kept in a glass cabinet.

Shoestring Books (NY68)   (607) 277-8639
106 North Cayuga Street 14850

Collection:	General stock of hardcover and paperback.
# of Volumes:	10,000+
Hours:	Mon-Thu 10-8. Fri & Sat 10-10. Sun 12-6.
Services:	Accepts want lists.
Travel:	See above. Map 10.
Credit Cards:	No
Owner:	Stephen Cornman, Deborah Nation & Timothy Hartje
Year Estab:	1991
Comments:	Primarily a paperback shop, we spotted several hundred used hardcover volumes on the top shelves. The shop's emphasis is on popular rather than scholarly titles.

Johnson City

Fat Cat Books (NY69)   (607) 797-9111
263 Main Street 13790

Collection:	Specialty new and used.
# of Volumes:	5,000+ (combined)
Specialties:	Science fiction; fantasy; horror.
Hours:	Mon-Fri 9:30-8:30. Sat 9:30-5.
Travel:	Exit 70 off Rte. 17. Follow signs to Johnson City. Map 10.
Credit Cards:	Yes
Owner:	Brian H. Perry
Year Estab:	1976
Comments:	Typical of specialty shops of this genre, this shop carries old and new comics, and when we visited, about 200-300 used hardcover titles and 2,000-3,000 used paperbacks. Need we say more (or less).

Johnstown

K.R. Dorn Books (NY70)   (518) 762-9466
8 Walnut Street 12095-1103

Collection:	General stock.
# of Volumes:	10,000
Specialties:	New York State; natural history.
Hours:	Daily 10-7.
Travel:	Fultonville exit off New York Twy. Proceed north on Rte. 30A to Briggs. Left on Briggs. Right at end of street on N. Perry, then left on Walnut after church. Map 9.
Credit Cards:	No
Owner:	K.R. Dorn
Year Estab:	1960
Comments:	The owner's preference for books concentrating on nature are obvious as one peruses the shelves of this collection, housed in the front two rooms of the owner's home and in a separate building behind the house. While there are some books of a more general nature, the space devoted to these volumes is limited as are the number of books that do not deal with the owner's special interests. A long time dealer in the area, the owner frequently gets a first look at new collections that come on the market.

Tryon County Bookshop (NY71)   (518) 762-1060
2071 State Highway 29 12095

Collection:	General stock and related items dealing with shop's specialty areas.
# of Volumes:	8,000
Specialties:	Americana; hunting; fishing; guns; military.
Hours:	Mon-Fri 8-8. Sat & Sun by chance or appointment.
Services:	Appraisals, search service, catalog.
Travel:	On Rte. 29, 4 miles east of Johnstown. Proceeding west, the shop is just before the "Entering Johnstown" road sign. Look for a small white house with trailer in the side yard. Map 9.
Credit Cards:	Yes
Owner:	Roger S. Montgomery
Year Estab:	1960
Comments:	Located in a small former mobile home adjacent to the owner's home, space limitations and overflowing shelves make for a crowded shop that is difficult to browse. The trailer had space to display fewer than the number of volumes indicated above.

Keene Valley

Bashful Bear Bookshop (NY72)   (518) 576-4736
Main Street
Mailing address: PO Box 744   12943

Collection:	General stock of new and used.
# of Volumes:	2,000 (used)
Hours:	Mon, Thu, Fri 11-6. Sat & Sun 10-6. Jun 1-Oct 15: Daily, except Tue, 10-6.
Services:	Accepts want lists, mail order.
Travel:	On Rte. 73 in a white frame house with a porch. Map 6.
Credit Cards:	Yes
Owner:	George & Laurie Daniels
Year Estab:	1993
Comments:	This fledgling shop carries mostly new books with one room devoted to used hardcover titles. The owners advise us that they are in a buying mode and plan to expand their used collection.

Kenmore

Marilyn Bissell Books (NY73)   Home: (716) 876-0459
2828 Delaware Avenue
Mailing address: PO Box 343 Buffalo 14223

Collection:	Specialty
# of Volumes:	5,000
Specialties:	Illustrated children's.
Hours:	Mon-Fri 10-6, except Wed till 8. Sat 9-5. Sun 11-4.
Services:	Search service, catalog, accepts want lists (all in specialty area only).
Travel:	See Oracle Junction Bookshop below. Map 7.
Credit Cards:	Yes
Owner:	Marilyn Bissell
Year Estab:	1984
Comments:	The collection is displayed in the Oracle Junction Bookshop.

Browsers' Used Book Store (aka Buffaloon Books) (NY74)
2840 Delaware Avenue 14217   (716) 874-8286

Collection:	General stock.
# of Volumes:	40,000
Specialties:	Ancient history; medieval history; philosophy; history of science.
Hours:	Mon-Sat 10-7. Sun 12-6.
Travel:	Delaware Ave. South exit off I-290 or Delaware Ave. North exit off Scajaquapa Expressway. Map 7.
Credit Cards:	Yes
Owner:	Mike McIntyre
Year Estab:	1991
Comments:	An extremely well organized collection with an abundance of

browser friendly labels on the shelves. Many of the titles have a scholarly bent. The books are in good to excellent condition and are reasonably priced. A shop well worth a visit.

Oracle Junction Bookshop (NY75)   (716) 877-9244
2828 Delaware Avenue 14217

Collection:	General stock and ephemera.
# of Volumes:	70,000
Specialties:	Medicine; technology; first editions; children's.
Hours:	Mon-Fri 10-6, except Wed till 8. Sat 9-5. Sun 11-4.
Services:	Appraisals, search service, catalog, accepts want lists.
Travel:	See Browsers' Used Book Store above. Map 7.
Credit Cards:	Yes
Owner:	Richard Antonik & Patrick Lally
Year Estab:	1984
Comments:	An interesting shop with reasonably priced books in all areas of interest. The basement level contains bargain books ($1-$5). If you don't see what you're looking for, ask, as many of the shop's better books are not on display. The shop is definitely worth a visit, especially as there is another fine book shop a few doors away.

Kinderhook

The Hourglass (NY76)   (518) 758-7939
Kinderhook Antiques Center, Route 9H 12106

Collection:	General stock.
Hours:	Daily 10-4.
Travel:	Map 8.
Owner:	Sheila Coyle
Comments:	Located in multi dealer antique mall.

Kings Park

Fisher of Books (NY77)   (516) 269-4935
26 Main Street 11754

Collection:	General stock and ephemera.
# of Volumes:	3,000-5,000
Specialties:	Long Island history.
Hours:	Daily 11-6.
Services:	Appraisals, accepts want lists, mail order.
Travel:	Exit 53 north off I-495. East on Rte. 25A for about 3 miles. Rte. 25A becomes Main St. in Kings Park. Shop is on right. Map 13.

Credit Cards:	No
Owner:	Bill Fisher
Year Estab:	1982
Comments:	A small storefront shop with a modest collection. According to the owner, the shop's strengths are in non fiction. We also noted a good sports section.

Kingston

Pages Past (NY78)   (914) 339-6484
103 Tammany Street 12401

Collection:	General stock and ephemera.
# of Volumes:	7,500
Specialties:	Illustrated; decorative arts; children's; local history; New York State.
Hours:	Wed-Sat 11-5.
Services:	Search service, accepts want lists, mail order.
Travel:	One fourth mile from intersection of Rtes. 32 and 9W. From Kingston exit off NY Twy. follow signs for Rte. 32 North. Continue on Rte. 32, making right turn at gas station. After passing the railroad tracks, Tammany is a right turn just before the light at Rte. 9W. Shop is immediately after the next intersection behind the ice cream shop. Map 12.
Credit Cards:	No
Owner:	Ann Stenson & Tom Williams
Year Estab:	1992
Comments:	The ambience in this relatively new shop is that of a private home where the owners have attractively displayed their favorite books and ephemera in easy to browse oak bookcases and display cabinets. Additional books and ephemera are displayed in two upstairs rooms. The books are in generally good condition and are reasonably priced. The owners indicate that the collection is a growing one.

Ye Old Book Shop (NY79)   (914) 338-5943
605 Broadway 12401

Collection:	General stock of paperback and hardcover.
Hours:	Tue-Fri 11-5. Sat 11-4.
Travel:	Kingston exit off NY Twy. Follow signs for Kingston/Broadway. Shop will be on left. Map 12.
Owner:	Mary Williams
Credit Cards:	No
Year Estab:	1986

Comments: The vast majority of the books are paperbacks, with a sprin-
                   kling of hardcover volumes.

Lake Placid

With Pipe And Book (NY80)   (518) 523-9096
91 Main Street 12946

Collection: General stock and prints.
# of Volumes: 15,000
Specialties: Adirondacks; tobacco; skating; skiing; olympics.
Hours: Mon-Sat 9-6.
Travel: In the center of the shopping district. Map 6.
Credit Cards: Yes
Owner: Breck & Julie Turner
Year Estab: 1977
Comments: An absolutely charming bi-level shop that combines the owners'
                   love of tobacco (especially pipe smoking) with books. The well
                   organized collection includes quite reasonably priced titles from
                   several periods. A basement room contains bargain books ($2
                   for hardcovers and $1 for paperbacks) of mixed vintage. Unlike
                   the first floor, the books in the basement are not organized by
                   subject or author.

Lima

Debue's Book Shop (NY81)   (716) 624-3730
7310 East Main Street 14485

Collection: General stock and ephemera.
# of Volumes: 10,000
Specialties: Children's
Hours: Mon & Wed-Sat 11-5.
Services: Search service, accepts want lists, mail order.
Travel: Located on Rtes. 20 & 5, near intersection of Rte. 15A. Map 16.
Credit Cards: No
Owner: William E. Buechel
Year Estab: 1991
Comments: From the little we could see looking through the window, the
                   shop appears to be a reasonably good source for used books.
                   Unfortunately, on the day we visited, the shop had closed 20 or
                   more minutes prior to its scheduled closing time making it
                   impossible for us to gain a better impression. If you're running a
                   tight schedule, we strongly suggest you call ahead to make
                   certain the shop will be open when you get there.

Maxwell's Treasures - Books & Ephemera (NY82)   (716) 624-4550
Route 5 & 20 at 15A 14485   (716) 359-3999

Collection:	General stock and ephemera.
# of Volumes:	5,000
Specialties:	New York State history; native Americans; black studies; women's studies.
Hours:	Sep-Jun: Wed, Sat & Sun 11-5. Jul & Aug: Wed, Thu, Sat & Sun 11-5. Other times by appointment.
Travel:	See above. Map 16.
Credit Cards:	No
Owner:	Ruth Kennedy
Comments:	Unfortunately, we find ourselves having to repeat here the comments we made above. (See Debue's Book Shop)

Livingston

Howard Frisch (NY83)   (518) 851-7493
Old Post Road
Mailing address: PO Box 75 Livingston 12541

Collection:	General stock.
# of Volumes:	10,000-20,000
Hours:	Apr-Nov: Fri-Sun 11-4. Other times by appointment.
Services:	Search service, catalog, accepts want lists.
Travel:	Just off Rte. 9. Follow signs into Livingston. Map 12.
Credit Cards:	No
Owner:	Howard Frisch & Fred Harris
Year Estab:	1954

Long Beach

Long Beach Books (NY84)   (516) 432-2265
17 East Park Avenue 11561

Collection:	General stock of new and used, paperback and hardcover.
Hours:	Daily 10-6 except Sun to 5.
Travel:	Meadowbrook Pkwy. to Loop Hwgy. Proceed on Lido Blvd. which becomes Park Ave. Shop is in Waldbaums Shopping Center on right. Map 13.
Credit Cards:	Yes
Owner:	Randy Bogash
Year Estab:	1950's
Comments:	Owner estimates stock is evenly divided between new and used books, the latter of which are primarily paperback.

Mabbettsville

Cooper Fox Farm Books (NY85)   (914) 677-3013
Route 44
Mailing address: PO Box 763 Millbrook 12545

Collection:	General stock.
# of Volumes:	50,000
Specialties:	Americana; military history; gardening; children's; horses; dogs; antiques.
Hours:	Jun-Aug: Tue-Sun 9-5. Sep-May: Sat & Sun 9-5 and other times by appointment.
Services:	Search service, accepts want lists, mail order.
Travel:	Rte. 44 exit off Taconic Pkwy. Proceed east for about 8-10 miles. Shop is on left, past the village of Millbrook. Map 12.
Credit Cards:	No
Owner:	George B. Davis
Year Estab:	1968
Comments:	It's always difficult to determine whether the conditions one views in a shop are temporary or part of the usual ambience. When we visited, this one story free standing building adjacent to the owner's home stocked at least twice as many books as could be displayed in a reasonable manner. The excess books were piled high in the aisles, making it extremely difficult to work one's way around them to examine the shelves that did display books. Many of the shelves had books lying on their sides rather than in the usual vertical position. The books we did manage to see represented various stages of condition, from very fine to barely acceptable, and included many titles not readily available in the typical used book shop. We note that our visit occurred immediately after two incidents that could have influenced the shop's appearance: a heavy rain and the owner's purchase of an extremely large collection.

Mechanicville

Uniquely Different (NY87)   (518) 664-6966
104 Park Avenue 12118

Collection:	General stock.
# of Volumes:	2,000
Hours:	Mon-Sat 10-5 but best to call ahead. Sun by chance.
Services:	Catalog planned, accepts want lists, mail order.
Travel:	Exit 9 off Rte. 87. Proceed east on Rte. 146 to Mechanicville. Right at second light on Park. Map 8.

Credit Cards:	No
Owner:	Kathy Buhl
Year Estab:	1988
Comments:	Shop also sells antiques and collectibles.

Melville

Arcadia Book Store (NY88)   (516) 351-3644
860 Route 110, Melville Mall 11747

Collection:	General stock of new, remainders and used books.
# of Volumes:	20,000
Specialties:	Technical.
Hours:	Mon-Sat 10-9. Sun 12-5.
Services:	Accepts want lists.
Travel:	Rte. 110 exit off I-495. Proceed north on Rte. 110 for 2-3 miles. The indoor mall is on right. Look for "Caldors" sign. Map 13.
Credit Cards:	Yes
Owner:	Pat Valluzzi
Year Estab:	1983

Millport

Lew Dabe Books at Serendipity II (NY89)   (607) 739-9413
4905 Watkins Road (Route 14)
Mailing address: RD 2, Box 388 Athens, PA 18810

Collection:	General stock and prints.
# of Volumes:	3,000-4,000
Specialties:	Art; architecture; photography; antiques.
Hours:	Daily 10-5.
Services:	Appraisals, accepts want lists, mail order.
Travel:	Rte. 14 north off Rte. 17. Located in a multi dealer antique shop. Map 10.
Credit Cards:	No
Owner:	Lew Dabe
Year Estab:	1962
Comments:	Although modest in size, the collection covers most subject areas and includes some odd and unusual titles. The books are in reasonably good condition. Very slightly overpriced.

Montgomery

Liberty Rock Books (NY90)   Shop: (914) 534-7522
At Antiques at Ward's Bridge, 87 Clinton Street   Dealer: (914) 457-9343
Mailing address: PO Box 680 Cornwall 12518-0680

Collection:	General stock.
# of Volumes:	45,000 (See Comments)
Hours:	Daily 11-5, except Wed & Thu. (See Comments)
Services:	Search service, accepts want lists, mail order.
Travel:	Middletown exit off Rte. 84. Right at exit and proceed on Rte. 211 into village. Left at Clinton St. The shop is one block before the intersection with Rte. 17K. Map 12.
Credit Cards:	Yes
Owner:	Thomas Liotta, James & Virgina Mahoney
Year Estab:	1975
Comments:	The owners note that their collection is divided between a "showroom" at the multi dealer antique shop listed above and their main office where the books can be viewed by appointment. Judging by the very modest number of volumes we saw when we visited the antique shop (considerably less than 1,500), unless you're in the Montgomery area, we suggest you call ahead for an appointment at the main office. The books we did see were mostly older, in mixed condition and reasonably priced.

Nedrow

Stonehouse Books (NY91)   (315) 469-6432
6612 South Salina Street 13120   Home: (315) 492-2713

Collection:	General stock of hardcover and paperback.
# of Volumes:	30,000
Specialties:	Children's; E.R. Burroughs.
Hours:	Mon 12-5:30. Tue-Fri 10-5:30. Sat 10-5. Other times by appointment.
Services:	Accepts want lists.
Travel:	Exit 16 off I-81. Proceed north on Rte. 11 (South Salina St.) for one mile. Shop is a corner store, on left. Map 10.
Credit Cards:	No
Owner:	Darrel & Lori Dillon
Year Estab:	1990
Comments:	While this bi-level shop's stock is predominately paper, there certainly is enough of a hardcover selection to provide some interesting titles. Prices are most reasonable (20%-30% less for many of the same items we saw elsewhere). The books are in mixed condition and represent mixed vintages.

Nelsonville
(See Cold Spring)

New Lebanon

G. J. Askins - Bookseller (NY93)   (518) 794-8833
2 West Street
Mailing address: PO Box 386   12125

Collection:	General stock and ephemera.
# of Volumes:	25,000
Specialties:	American communal societies; regional Americana; music; art; natural history; architecture. Books generally of an academic orientation.
Hours:	Apr-Nov: Fri-Mon 10-6. Dec-Mar: Sat & Sun 10-5.
Services:	Accepts want lists.
Travel:	Second building on West St. off the 1 mile strip where Rtes. 20 and 22 merge. Map 8.
Credit Cards:	No
Owner:	Grover J. Askins
Year Estab:	1982
Comments:	We concur with the owner's description of his collection (see above), with our added comment that most of the books we saw were in excellent condition. The ambience of the shop's several rooms is that of an academic or scholarly library.

New Paltz

Barner's (NY94)   (914) 255-2635
69 Main Street 12561   Fax: (914) 255-2636

Collection:	General stock.
# of Volumes:	20,000
Specialties:	Art; modern first editions; history; literature.
Hours:	Mon-Fri 10-6. Sat 10-7. Sun 12-6.
Services:	Search service, catalog in planning stage.
Travel:	Exit 18 off NY Twy. Left on Rte. 299. Shop is on the right past the fourth light. Map 12.
Credit Cards:	Yes
Owner:	James Barner
Year Estab:	1989
Comments:	This very neat and well organized shop, located on the main thoroughfare of a small college community, offers a modest collection of books, most in good or very good condition and quite reasonably priced. We saw few, if any, library or book club discards. The collection is mixed in terms of vintage and we spotted some prize items. Browsers will appreciate the ample supply of stools. Don't overlook the New Arrivals bookcase and the basket of free books at the shop's entrance.

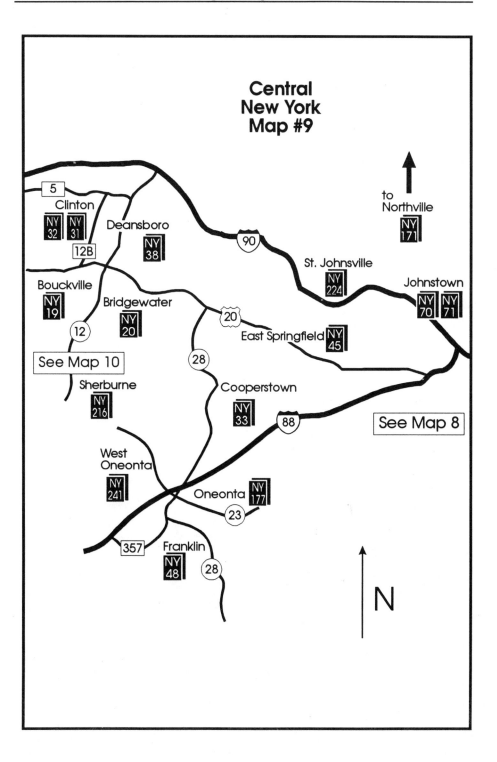

Central
New York
Map #9

to
Northville
NY
171

5

Clinton
NY   NY
32   31

Deansboro
NY
38

12B

90

St. Johnsville
NY
224

Johnstown
NY   NY
70   71

Bouckville
NY
19

Bridgewater
NY
20

20

East Springfield NY
45

12

See Map 10

28

Sherburne
NY
216

Cooperstown
NY
33

88

See Map 8

West
Oneonta
NY
241

Oneonta NY
177

23

357   Franklin
NY   28
48

N

New York City
(Brooklyn)

Avery Book Store   (718) 858-3606
308 Livingston Street 11217

Collection:	General stock of paperback and hardcover.
# of Volumes:	60,000
Hours:	Mon-Sat 10-6.
Services:	Accepts want lists.
Travel:	Downtown Brooklyn between Bond & Nevins Sts.
Credit Cards:	Yes
Year Estab:	1953
Comments:	Approximately 60% of the stock consists of paperbacks and we saw little that could be considered unusual in the hardcover volumes.

Bensonhurst Discount Book Store   (718) 232-7233
1908 86th 11214

Collection:	General stock of new and used hardcover and paperbacks.
Hours:	Mon, Tue, Thu, Fri 1-5. Wed & Sat 10-4.
Travel:	Between 19th & 20th Avenues.

J. Biegeleisen   (718) 436-1165
4409 16th Avenue 11204

Collection:	Specialty
Specialties:	Hebraica
Hours:	Mon-Thu & Sun 10:30-7. Fri 10:30-2:30.
Services:	Accepts want lists, catalog.
Credit Cards:	No
Owner:	J. Biegeleisen
Year Estab:	1930's

Binkins Book Center   (718) 855-7813
54 Willoughby Street 11201

Collection:	General stock.
Hours:	Mon-Fri 10:30-6. Sat 11-6.
Services:	Appraisals, accepts want lists.
Travel:	Downtown Brooklyn between Jay & Lawrence Sts.
Credit Cards:	No
Owner:	Robert Kanatous
Year Estab:	1935

Comments: Much as we would like to describe the books and the ambience of this shop, all we can honestly say is, "Don't arrive too early," as the posted opening hour of 10:30 cannot always be relied on. We were there at that hour and left 20 minutes later when the shop was still sealed tight. Perhaps if you call ahead you will be assured that someone will be there when you arrive and that you will have an opportunity to judge the shop's books for yourself.

New York City (Manhattan)

A & S Book Company   (212) 714-2712
304 West 40th Street 10018

Collection:	Specialty
Specialties:	Magazines
Hours:	Mon-Fri 10:30-6:30. Sat 11-5.
Services:	Appraisals, accepts want lists, mail order.
Travel:	Between 8th & 9th Avenues.
Credit Cards:	No
Owner:	Larry Kay
Year Estab:	1962

A Photographers Place   (212) 431-9358
133 Mercer Street 10012

Collection:	Specialty new and used books.
# of Volumes:	40,000 (combined)
Specialties:	Photography
Hours:	Mon-Sat 11-6. Sun 12-5.
Services:	Appraisals, catalog, mail order.
Travel:	Between Prince & Spring Streets.
Credit Cards:	Yes
Owner:	Harvey Zucker
Year Estab:	1980

Academy Book Store (NY101)   (212) 242-4848
10 West 18th Street 10011

Collection:	General stock, records and autographs.
# of Volumes:	15,000
Specialties:	Scholarly; art; photography.
Hours:	Mon-Sat 9:30-9. Sun 11-7.
Services:	Appraisals, accepts want lists, mail order.

Travel:	Between 5th & 6th Avenues. Map 14.
Credit Cards:	No
Owner:	Alan Weiner
Year Estab:	1977
Comments:	Although the store's name mentions only books, the shop has almost as many records and CDs as it has books. The books are in generally good condition and cover most categories.

Antiquarian Booksellers International, Inc. (NY102)   (212) 751-5450
125 East 57th Street, Gallery #48 10022   Fax: (212) 688-1139

Collection:	General stock and prints.
# of Volumes:	1,000-2,000
Specialties:	Antiquarian
Hours:	Mon-Sat 11-5:30
Services:	Mail order.
Travel:	Between Park & Lexington Avenues. Map 14.
Credit Cards:	Yes
Owner:	Raymond M. Wapner
Year Estab:	1988
Comments:	Located on the lower level of a building that houses a number of antique dealers, this group shop displays books of 30 dealers. Many of the books are kept behind locked glass bookcases. If you see something you would like to examine, the book will be shown to you. You will pay antiquarian prices for the books displayed here.

Appelfeld Gallery (NY103)   (212) 988-7835
1372 York Avenue 10021

Collection:	General stock.
# of Volumes:	5,000
Specialties:	Fine bindings; sets; first editions.
Hours:	Mon-Fri 10-5. Sat by appointment.
Services:	Appraisals, catalog, accepts want lists.
Travel:	Between 73rd & 74th Streets. Map 14.
Credit Cards:	No
Owner:	Louis Appelfeld
Year Estab:	1967

W. Graham Arader, III   (212) 628-3668
29 East 72nd Street 10021   Fax: (212) 879-8714

Collection:	Specialty books, prints and maps
Specialties:	Antiquarian (16th-19th centuries).
Hours:	Mon-Sat 10-6. Sun 11-5.

Services:	Appraisals, catalog, accepts want lists.
Travel:	Corner of Madison Avenue.
Credit Cards:	Yes
Owner:	W. Graham Arader, III
Year Estab:	1972
Comments:	While this shop is an "open shop" in the sense that it has regular hours, the nature of the collection is such that the owner prefers prospective buyers to call ahead for an appointment. The selection of volumes, carefully housed in two restricted rooms, are primarily for the connoisseur with a large bank account.

Archivia, The Decorative Arts Book Shop   (212) 439-9194
944 Madison Avenue 10021   Fax: (212) 744-1626

Collection:	Specialty new and used.
Specialties:	Decorative arts; gardening; architecture.
Hours:	Mon-Fri 10-6. Sat 11-5. Sun 12-4 (but best to call ahead).
Services:	Search service, catalog, accepts want lists.
Travel:	Between 74th & 75th Streets.
Credit Cards:	Yes
Owner:	Joan Gers & Cynthia Conigliaro
Year Estab:	1972
Comments:	If you're looking for an out of print or rare book dealing with art or the decorative arts, chances are, if it is a book respected in its field, you will find it here. If not, the owners promise a better than even chance of locating it for you. Prices for the older volumes are by no means inexpensive and some of the books could use some restoration.

Argosy (NY106)   (212) 753-4455
116 East 59th Street 10022   Fax: (212) 593-4784

Collection:	General stock, prints, autographs and maps.
# of Volumes:	300,000+
Specialties:	Americana; first editions; medicine; art; limited editions.
Hours:	Mon-Fri 9-5:30. Sat 10-4:30. Closed Sat May-Sep.
Services:	Appraisals, catalog.
Travel:	Between Park & Lexington Avenues. Map 14.
Credit Cards:	Yes
Owner:	Adina Cohen, Naomi Hample & Judith Lowry
Year Estab:	1927
Comments:	Book hunters will find this six story shop reminiscent of an earlier era when New York was a mecca for anyone interested in used books. The shop's ambience, especially its first floor, combines a bit of the old fashioned with the benefits of modern

technology. Indeed, all 300,000+ volumes in the shop's collection are on computer and book hunters interested in specific titles, can get an immediate response to their question: "Do you have..." From the basement to the 5th floor, bibliophiles will find books in every specialty imaginable, from the common to the rarest, from the popular to the antiquarian, from $1 to thousands of dollars. You name it, this shop has it. Considering its location and the excellent quality of the stock, we would certainly rate prices as being in the moderate category.

Richard B. Arkway, Inc.
538 Madison Avenue 10022

(212) 751-8135
Fax: (212) 832-5389

Collection:	Specialty books and maps.
Specialties:	Early travel; voyages; atlases, Jesuit relations; early science and technology; Americana.
Hours:	Mon-Fri 9:30-5. Appointment preferred.
Services:	Appraisals, catalog.
Travel:	Between 54th & 55th Streets.
Credit Cards:	Yes
Owner:	Richard B. Arkway
Year Estab:	1972

Back Issue Magazine Center
1133 Broadway, Room 620 10010

(212) 929-5255

Collection:	Specialty
Specialties:	Magazines, including Vogue, Vanity Fair, Apparel Arts, Harpers Bazaar, Esquire (U.S. and foreign editions).
Hours:	Mon-Fri 11-7.
Services:	Search service, accepts want lists.
Travel:	At West 26th Street.
Credit Cards:	Yes
Owner:	Basil A. Koyun
Year Estab:	1975

The Ballet Shop
1887 Broadway 10023

(212) 581-7990

Collection:	Specialty new and used.
# of Volumes:	3,000
Specialties:	Dance; opera; theatre.
Hours:	Mon-Sat 11-7. Sun 12-5.
Services:	Appraisals, search service, accepts want lists, mail order.
Travel:	Between 62nd & 63rd Streets.
Credit Cards:	Yes

Owner:	Norman Crider
Year Estab:	1974

J.N. Bartfield Books, Inc.   (212) 245-8890
30 West 57th Street 10019

Collection:	Specialty
Specialties:	Sets; fine bindings; foredge paintings; color plates; Audubon.
Hours:	Mon-Fri 10-5. Sat 10-3. Other times by appointment.
Travel:	Between 5th & 6th Avenues.
Credit Cards:	No
Year Estab:	1937

Bauman Rare Books   (212) 759-8300
301 Park Avenue 10022

Collection:	Specialty
Specialties:	Antiquarian; rare.
Hours:	Mon-Sat 10-7.
Services:	Catalog
Travel:	Located in lobby of Waldorf Astoria Hotel.
Credit Cards:	Yes
Owner:	David L. Bauman

Book-Friends Cafe (NY112)   (212) 255-7407
16 West 18th Street 10011

Collection:	General stock.
# of Volumes:	10,000
Specialties:	Biography; art; fiction.
Hours:	Mon-Fri 11:30-8:30. Sat & Sun 12-7.
Services:	Search service, accepts want lists, mail order.
Travel:	Between 5th & 6th Avenues. Map 14.
Owner:	Isabel Cymerman
Comments:	As the name implies, book lovers can combine their browsing with a pleasant lunch, dinner or afternoon tea in this attractively decorated and inviting book shop/cafe. The shop also features special evening literary events.

Bookleaves (NY113)   (212) 924-5638
304 West 4th Street 10014

Collection:	General stock.
# of Volumes:	4,000
Specialties:	Literature (20th century); art.
Hours:	Tue-Sun 12-8.

Travel:	Just off Bank Street in Greenwich Village. Map 14.
Credit Cards:	No
Owner:	Arthur Farrier
Year Estab:	1992
Comments:	Despite this shop's relatively small size and limited stock, the quality of the books, as well as their condition, suggests that you may be able to find an item or two of interest. If you're in the area, we recommend a visit.

Books and Binding (NY114)   (212) 229-0004
33 West 17th Street 10011

Collection:	General stock of used and new books and records.
# of Volumes:	50,000+ (See Comments)
Specialties:	Art; photography; science; poetry; children's; scholarly.
Hours:	Mon-Fri 9-8. Sat 10-7. Sun 11-6.
Services:	Appraisals, search service, catalog accepts want lists, book binding (on site).
Travel:	Between 5th & 6th Avenues. Map 14.
Credit Cards:	Yes
Owner:	Joseph Landau
Year Estab:	1993
Comments:	This extremely spacious and attractively decorated bi-level shop offers a combination of used, new and remainder books. Open for business only a short time prior to the authors' visit, the shelves were still being stocked with what the owner estimates will be a collection of about 100,000 volumes, approximately 50% of which will be used. Comfortable chairs and ladders abound for leisurely browsing.

Books of Wonder   (212) 989-3270
132 Seventh Avenue 10011   Fax: (212) 989-1203

Collection:	Specialty new and used books and collectibles.
# of Volumes:	2,000 (used)
Specialties:	Children's, including first editions, illustrated and Oz.
Hours:	Mon-Sat 11-7. Sun 12-6.
Services:	Catalog, accepts want lists.
Travel:	Corner of West 18th Street.
Credit Cards:	Yes
Owner:	Peter Glassman
Comments:	A spacious and attractively decorated combination new and used specialty shop. The books are in very good condition and are easy to locate on the shop's well organized shelves.

Bryn Mawr Book Shop (NY116)   (212) 744-7682
502 East 79th Street 10021

Collection:	General stock.
Hours:	Wed, Fri, Sat 10:30-4:30. Thu 12-7. Sun 12-4:30.
Travel:	Corner of York Ave. Map 14.
Comments:	Operated by volunteers for benefit of college scholarship fund. All books are donated.

Burlington Book Shop (NY117)   (212) 288-7420
1082 Madison Avenue 10028   Fax: (212) 249-3502

Collection:	General stock of new and used.
# of Volumes:	30,000 (combined)
Hours:	Mon-Fri 9:30-6. Sat 10-6. Sun 12-5.
Services:	Search service, accepts want lists, mail order.
Travel:	Between 81st & 82nd Streets. Map 14.
Credit Cards:	Yes
Owner:	Jane Trichter
Year Estab:	1962
Comments:	This very busy shop carries a mix of new and used books with the emphasis on new. The owner, a most charming and gregarious lady, knows her business and if she doesn't stock the book you're looking for, she will certainly try her best to locate it for you.

CFM Gallery   (212) 966-3864
112 Greene Street 10012   Fax: (212) 226-1041

Collection:	Specialty
# of Volumes:	1,000
Specialties:	Books by and about Leonor Fini; art (symbolists and figurative artists).
Hours:	Daily 12-6.
Credit Cards:	Yes
Owner:	Neil Zuckerman
Year Estab:	1982

Chartwell Booksellers   (212) 308-0643
55 East 52nd Street 10055

Collection:	Specialty (See Comments)
# of Volumes:	500 (used)
Specialties:	Modern first editions; Winston Churchill; jazz; angling; baseball.
Hours:	Mon-Fri 9:30-6:30. Third Sat of the month 12-6.
Services:	Appraisals, search service, catalog (Churchill only), accepts want

lists in specialty areas only, mail order.

Travel:	Between Park & Madison, in Park Avenue Plaza building.
Credit Cards:	Yes
Owner:	Barry Singer
Year Estab:	1983
Comments:	A general "new" book store, the used books are displayed in locked cabinets.

Chelsea Books and Records (NY120)   (212) 645-4340
111 West 17th Street 10011

Collection:	General stock and records.
# of Volume:	20,000-25,000
Hours:	Tue-Sun 11-7.
Travel:	Between 6th & 7th Avenues. Map 14.
Owner:	Isaac Kosman
Year Estab:	1993
Comments:	We discovered this shop just as it was getting ready to open and while the owner was still in the process of unpacking his stock. We look forward to a return visit when we hope to enjoy browsing the collection.

Complete Traveler   (212) 685-9007
199 Madison Avenue 10016   Fax: (212) 982-7628

Collection:	Specialty
Specialties:	Travel
Hours:	Mon-Fri 9-6:30. Sat 10-6. Sun 12-5.
Travel:	At 35th Street.
Owner:	Harriet Greenberg
Comments:	The Complete Traveler lives up to its name. It is, in effect, two stores in one. You enter what appears to be a new book store with traditional maps and travel publications for today's use. An adjoining room is devoted entirely to antiquarian and rare travel books and guides. Behind glass enclosures is a complete set of WPA guides to the various states. Other shelves have back issues of Baedekers and Cooke's guides that take you around the world in late 19th century and early 20th century editions. These older volumes are not inexpensive but where else could the armchair traveler or perhaps one who wants to do research on traveling conditions of yesteryear find better resources. All of the books we saw were in very good condition and attractively displayed.

The Compulsive Collector   (212) 879-7443
1082 Madison Avenue 10028

Collection:	Specialty
# of Volumes:	7,000
Specialties:	Children's; illustrated; first editions; art; Judaica (scholarly).
Hours:	Wed-Sat 2-6. Sun by chance.
Services:	Appraisals, lists, accepts want lists, mail order.
Travel:	Between 81st & 82nd Streets.
Credit Cards:	Yes
Owner:	Ami Megiddo
Year Estab:	1983
Comments:	Located on the mezzanine of a primarily new book store, the owner of this shop has room to display only a relatively small portion of his genuinely antiquarian and rare stock. It is no mean feat to climb the narrow stairs leading up to the mezzanine or to maneuver the single narrow aisle in order to view the books. Turn around space is at a premium. Given the logistical problems associated with viewing the collection, a phone call to the owner about a particular volume you are looking for might not be a bad idea.

James Cummins   (212) 688-6441
699 Madison Avenue 10021   Fax: (212) 688-6192

Collection:	Specialty
# of Volumes:	1,500
Specialties:	American literature; English literature; sets; Americana; travel; exploration; sporting.
Hours:	Mon-Fri 10-6. Sat 10-5.
Services:	Catalog, accepts want lists.
Travel:	Between 62nd & 63rd Streets.
Credit Cards:	Yes
Owner:	James Cummins
Year Estab:	1977
Comments:	This shop offers truly rare books, most in immaculate condition. You don't have to be a book connoisseur to fall in love with some of the bindings or to be impressed by the rare nature of the titles. There are sets galore by historical figures in addition to illustrated books that are worth their weight in more than paper. If you intend to buy, bring lots of money.

Bob Fein Books   (212) 807-0489
150 Fifth Avenue 10011

Collection:	Specialty

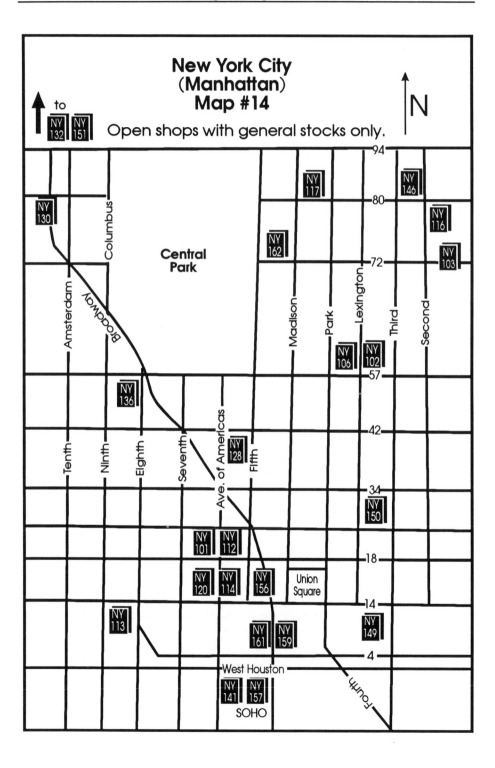

New York City
(Manhattan)
Map #14

N

to

Open shops with general stocks only.

# of Volumes:	4,000
Specialties:	Native Americans; North & South America; pre-Columbian art.
Hours:	Mon-Fri 12-5.
Services:	Appraisals, search service, catalog, accepts want lists.
Credit Cards:	Yes
Owner:	Bob Fein
Year Estab:	1988

Foul Play   (212) 675-5115
13 Eighth Avenue 10014 (See Comments)

Collection:	Specialty new and used.
Specialties:	Mystery
Hours:	Daily 11-9:45, except Sun till 7.
Travel:	Corner West 12th Street.
Owner:	John Douglas
Comments:	An uptown branch is located at 1465 Second Ave. at 76th St. (212) 517-3222. Hours: Mon-Sat 12-10. Sun 11:30-6:30.

Leonard Fox, Ltd.   (212) 879-7077
790 Madison Avenue 10021   Fax: (212) 772-9692

Collection:	Specialty
# of Volumes:	400
Specialties:	Illustrated (20th century); art deco; fashion; livres d'artiste.
Hours:	Mon-Fri 9-5 and by appointment.
Services:	Appraisals, occasional catalog, accepts want lists.
Travel:	Between 66th & 67th Streets.
Credit Cards:	Yes
Owner:	Leonard Fox
Year Estab:	1972

Fred Wilson-Chess Books   (212) 533-6381
80 East 11th Street, Ste. 334 10003

Collection:	Specialty new and used books and magazines
# of Volumes:	2,000
Specialties:	Chess
Hours:	Mon-Sat 12-7. (Often closed between 4 & 5 PM)
Services:	Appraisals, search service, catalog, accepts want lists.
Credit Cards:	No
Year Estab:	1972

Gallery 292   (212) 431-0292
120 Wooster Street 10012   Fax: (212) 941-7479

Collection:	Specialty

# of Volumes:	150
Specialties:	Photography
Hours:	Tue-Sat 11-6.
Travel:	In Soho, between Prince & Spring Streets.
Credit Cards:	Yes
Owner:	Vincent Cianni, Manager
Year Estab:	1992

Gotham Book Mart (NY128)   (212) 719-4448
41 West 47th Street 10036

Collection:	General stock and periodicals.
# of Volumes:	250,000 (combined)
Specialties:	Literature; literary criticism; theater; film; art; philosophy; current and back issues of literary periodicals.
Hours:	Mon-Fri 9:30-6:30. Sat 9:30-6.
Services:	Appraisals, search service, occasional catalog, accepts want lists, mail order.
Travel:	Between 5th & 6th Avenues. Map 14.
Credit Cards:	Yes ($20 minimum)
Owner:	Andreas Brown
Year Estab:	1920
Comments:	One of Manhattan's older and more established used book shops, this bi-level shop displays books wherever you look. Most categories are represented in depth and it is clear that the owner goes out of his way to stock sought after out of print titles. The second floor is devoted primarily to books dealing with art and a rare book room which may be visited upon request. If you're in Manhattan, this shop is a must.

Gryphon Bookshop (NY130)   (212) 362-0706
2246 Broadway 10024

Collection:	General stock.
# of Volumes:	20,000
Specialties:	Children's; first editions; art; New York City; music; dance.
Hours:	Daily 10-midnight.
Services:	Appraisals, search service, accepts want lists, mail order.
Travel:	Between 80th & 81st Streets. Map 14.
Credit Cards:	Yes
Owner:	Marc Lewis
Year Estab:	1974
Comments:	This bi-level shop offers an interesting assortment of some older, some rare and some unusual titles. Unfortunately, some of the shop's physical characteristics, at least when we visited, were not

conducive to leisurely browsing. The shop's narrow aisles were cluttered with shopping bags filed with new acquisitions waiting to be shelved. Also, the height of the first floor ceiling made browsing the top shelves somewhat difficult (we spotted only one ladder). A steep staircase provides access to the mezzanine.

Hacker Art Books   (212) 688-7600
45 West 57th Street 10036

Collection:	Specialty
Specialties:	Art; architecture; decorative arts.
Hours:	Mon-Sat 9:30-6.
Services:	Catalog
Travel:	Between 5th & 6th Avenues.
Credit Cards:	Yes
Owner:	Seymour Hacker
Year Estab:	1940's

Ideal Book Store (NY132)   (212) 662-1909
1125 Amsterdam Avenue 10025   Fax: (212) 662-1640

Collection:	General stock.
# of Volumes:	40,000
Specialties:	Judaica; classics; philosophy.
Hours:	Mon-Fri 10-6.
Services:	Appraisals, catalog.
Travel:	At 115th Street, opposite Columbia University. Map 14.
Credit Cards:	Yes
Owner:	Aron Lutwak
Year Estab:	1931

Imperial Fine Books, Inc.   (212) 861-6620
790 Madison Avenue, Room 200 10021   Fax: (212) 249-0333

Collection:	Specialty
# of Volumes:	3,000
Specialties:	Sets; fine bindings; children's; illustrated; first editions.
Hours:	Mon-Fri 10-5:30. Sat 10-5. Other times by appointment.
Services:	Appraisals, search service, catalog, accepts want lists, bookbinding; restoration, collection development.
Travel:	Between 66th & 67th Streets.
Credit Cards:	Yes
Owner:	Bibi T. Mohamed
Year Estab:	1989
Comments:	This small shop, located in an office building, features mostly sets representing the collected writings of well known 17th to

19th century writers and political figures. The sets are primarily leather bound and in pristine condition. Prices reflect the rarity of the items, e.g., a complete set of novels by Georges Sand was priced at $1800.

Jerry Ohlinger's Movie Material Store Inc.   (212) 989-0869
242 West 14th Street 10011   Fax: (212) 989-1660

Collection:	Specialty magazines and ephemera.
Specialties:	Film
Hours:	Daily 1-7:45.
Services:	Catalog
Travel:	Between 7th & 8th Avenues.
Owner:	Jerry Ohlinger
Year Estab:	1976

Harmer Johnson Books, Ltd.   (212) 535-9118
21 East 65th Street 10021   Fax: (212) 861-9893

Collection:	Specialty
# of Volumes:	10,000
Specialties:	Ancient and tribal art and archaeology.
Hours:	Mon-Fri 10-5:30. Sat by appointment.
Services:	Appraisals, search service, catalog, accepts want lists.
Credit Cards:	No
Owner:	Harmer Johnson & Peter Sharrer
Year Estab:	1975

Jonah's Whale-Zenith Books (NY136)   (212) 581-8181
935 Eighth Avenue 10019

Collection:	General stock.
# of Volumes:	50,000
Specialties:	Fine bindings; first editions.
Hours:	Sun-Thu 11-6:30.
Services:	Appraisals, search service, accepts want lists.
Travel:	Between 55th & 56th Streets. Map 14.
Credit Cards:	No
Owner:	Ann Abrams
Year Estab:	1962
Comments:	This crowded shop stocks a little of everything, from books to collectible bric a brac. Browsing the shop's narrow aisles can be a problem, though, especially if two people try to pass each other in the same aisle. The books we saw when we visited were in mixed condition and of mixed vintage.

Kolwyck-Jones Books on Art
588 Broadway, Ste. 905 10012

(212) 966-8698
Fax: (212) 966-0413

Collection:	Specialty
# of Volumes:	10,000
Specialties:	Fine art; architecture; design.
Hours:	Tue-Fri 11-6. Sat & Mon 11-5.
Services:	Search service, catalog, accepts want lists.
Travel:	In Soho, between Houston & Prince Streets.
Credit Cards:	Yes
Owner:	David Kolwyck
Year Estab:	1988

The Lawbook Exchange, Ltd.
135 West 29th Street 10001

(212) 594-4341 (800) 422-6686
Fax: (212) 465-8178

Collection:	Specialty
# of Volumes:	5,000
Specialties:	Law, including Anglo-American, Roman and Canon law, biographies, bibliographies, manuscripts, prints and reference works.
Hours:	Mon-Fri 9-5.
Services:	Appraisals, catalog, accepts want lists.
Credit Cards:	Yes
Owner:	Roland C. Hill & Gregory F. Talbot
Year Estab:	1982

James Lowe Autographs, Ltd.
30 East 60th Street, Ste. 907 10022

(212) 759-0775

Collection:	Specialty
Specialties:	Signed limited editions; 19th century photographs; autographs.
Hours:	Mon-Fri 9:30-5. Sat by appointment.
Services:	Catalog, accepts want lists.
Travel:	Between Madison & Park Avenues.
Credit Cards:	No
Owner:	James Lowe
Year Estab:	1968

Martayan Lan, Inc.
48 East 57th Street 10022

(212) 308-0018
Fax: (212) 308-0074

Collection:	Specialty books and maps.
# of Volumes:	1,000 (books only)
Specialties:	Early printings; history of science; history of medicine; architecture; early illustrated; technology; natural history; atlases; voyages.

Hours:	Mon-Fri 9:30-5:30. Sat and late evenings by appointment.
Services:	Appraisals, search service, catalog, accepts want lists.
Travel:	Between Fifth & Park Avenues.
Owner:	Seyla Martayan & Richard Lan
Year Estab:	1974

Mercer Street Books & Records (NY141)   (212) 505-8615
206 Mercer Street 10013

Collection:	General stock and records.
# of Volumes:	27,000
Specialties:	Fiction; poetry; film; art.
Hours:	Mon-Thu 10-10. Fri & Sat 12-midnight. Sun 11-10.
Services:	Accepts want lists.
Travel:	In Soho, between Bleecker & Houston Streets. Map 14.
Credit Cards:	Yes
Owner:	Wayne Conti, Brian Futterman & Sarah Gerhart
Year Estab:	1989
Comments:	Weary browsers are likely to appreciate the comfortable chairs in this well organized and pleasant shop. Most of the books are of post World War II vintage, in generally good condition and reasonably priced.

The Military Bookman Ltd.   (212) 348-1280
29 East 93rd Street 10128

Collection:	Specialty books and related prints and art.
# of Volumes:	10,000
Specialties:	Military; naval, military aviation; espionage.
Hours:	Tue-Sat 10:30-5:30.
Services:	Catalog, accepts want lists.
Travel:	Between Madison & Fifth Avenues.
Credit Cards:	Yes
Owner:	Harris & Margaretta Colt
Year Estab:	1976
Comments:	This very attractive book shop, easy to miss because it is located on an otherwise residential block, has the ultimate collection of books dealing with warfare. The shop is extremely well organized with shelves clearly delineating categories focusing on every aspect of military history. While the shop is relatively modest in size, it is spaciously laid out and easy to browse. The books are in generally good condition and are reasonably priced.

Arthur H. Minters, Inc., Booksellers　　　　　　(212) 587-4014
96 Fulton Street, 2nd Floor 10038　　　　　　Fax: (212) 406-0867

Collection:	Specialty
# of Volumes:	3,750
Specialties:	Art; architecture; modern literature; modern illustrated; photography; archaeology.
Hours:	Mon-Fri 10-6. Sat by appointment.
Services:	Appraisals, search service, catalog, accepts want lists, auction agents.
Credit Cards:	Yes
Owner:	Arthur H. Minters
Year Estab:	1957

Murder Ink　　　　　　　　　　　　　　　(800) 488-8123
2486 Broadway 10025

Collection:	Specialty new and used.
# of Volumes:	5,000 (used)
Specialties:	Mystery
Hours:	Daily 11-7. Closed Christmas, Thanksgiving and New Year's.
Services:	Appraisals, catalog, accepts want lists.
Travel:	Between 92nd & 93rd Streets.

Mysterious Bookshop　　　　　　　　　　　(212) 765-0900
129 West 56th Street 10019

Collection:	Speciality new and used.
Specialty:	Mystery
Hours:	Mon-Sat 11-7.
Owner:	Otto Penzler
Travel:	Between Sixth & Seventh Avenues.
Comments:	This bi-level shop offers primarily new books on the first floor and used and often rare titles on the second level. The owner also publishes the well known detective journal, *The Armchair Detective*.

Louis Nathanson Books (NY146)　　　　　　(212) 249-3235
219 East 85th Street 10028

Collection:	General stock.
# of Volumes:	10,000
Specialties:	Art; biography.
Hours:	Mon-Fri 11-7. Sat 10-5:30. Sun by appointment.
Services:	Mail order.
Travel:	Between Second & Third Avenues. Map 14.

Credit Cards: Yes
Owner: Louis J. Nathanson
Year Estab: 1951
Comments: This shop carries books. It also, as the sign over the door clearly reads, carries "junk." One man's junk is another man's treasures, but when we visited, we didn't find many treasures. Nor do we believe the books displayed merit a special visit.

New York Bound Bookshop   (212) 245-8503
50 Rockefeller Plaza 10020

Collection: Specialty
# of Volumes: 3,000
Specialties: New York State only, including history, literature, photography, immigration, transportation and architecture.
Hours: Mon-Fri 10-5:30. Sat 12-4 (except May-Sep).
Services: Appraisals, search service, catalog, accepts want lists.
Travel: Fifth Avenue & 51st Street.
Credit Cards: Yes
Owner: Barbara Cohen & Judith Stonehill
Year Estab: 1975

OAN/Oceanie-Afrique Noire   (212) 840-8844
15 East 39th Street, 2nd Fl. 10018-3806   Fax: (212) 840-3304

Collection: Specialty
# of Volumes: 10,000+
Specialties: Art of Africa, Oceania, North America, South America, Southeast Asia; cultural textiles; anthropology; ethnology.
Hours: Mon-Thu 11-5 and by appointment.
Services: Catalog, accepts want lists.
Credit Cards: Yes
Owner: Gail Feher
Year Estab: 1978

Pageant Book & Print Shop (NY149)   (212) 674-5296
109 East 9th Street 10003

Collection: General stock, prints and ephemera.
# of Volumes: 50,000+
Specialties: Americana; art; literature; maps.
Hours: Mon-Thu 10-7. Fri 10-8. Sat 11-7:30.
Travel: Between Third & Fourth Avenues. Map 14.
Credit Cards: Yes
Owner: Shirley Solomon
Year Estab: 1945

Comments:　　One of the very few remaining veterans of New York City's once thriving Fourth Avenue Book Mart, this bi-level shop still retains much of the aura of yesteryear. This is a used book store in the classic sense and the mix of titles from recently used to truly antiquarian makes for a perfect marriage. We found the second generation owner most hospitable and the ample supply of chairs and ladders most welcome.

Pak Books (NY150)　　　　　　　　　　　　　　(212) 213-2177
137 East 27th Street 10016

Collection:	General stock of hardcover and paperback.
# of Volumes:	5,000+
Specialties:	Middle East; Islam
Hours:	Mon-Sat 11-6:30.
Travel:	Between Lexington & Third Avenues. Map 14.
Credit Cards:	Yes
Comments:	A small shop featuring new and used books in English and foreign languages.

Pomander Bookshop (NY151)　　　　　　　　　(212) 866-1777
955 West End Avenue 10025

Collection:	General stock.
Hours:	Sun-Fri 12-8. Sat 11-11.
Services:	Search service, catalog.
Travel:	At 107th Street. Map 14.
Credit Cards:	Yes
Owner:	Suzanne Zavrian
Year Estab:	1976
Comments:	A small but spacious shop that is comfortable to browse. The books are of mixed vintage and in generally good condition. Few bargains. The entrance is down a few steps.

Kenneth W. Rendell Gallery, Inc.　　　　　　(212) 717-1776
989 Madison Avenue 10021　　　　　　　　Fax: (212) 717-1492

Collection:	Specialty books and autographs.
Specialties:	Signed books in fall back boxes.
Hours:	Mon-Sat 10-6. Other times by appointment.
Services:	Catalog, accepts want lists.
Travel:	At 76th Street.
Credit Cards:	Yes
Owner:	Kenneth Rendell

Comments: If you're looking for the autograph of a world renowned writer, musician and/or anyone who has been in the public eye, it's more than likely that if the Kenneth Rendell Gallery doesn't have it in its vast stock, a copy can be located for you. While the signed books make up only a very small portion of the stock, the manner in which they are displayed, will awe the typical book lover.

Mary S. Rosenberg, Inc.   (212) 307-7733
1841 Broadway, 11th Floor 10023

Collection:	Specialty new and used.
Specialties:	German books only in a variety of subject categories; Judaica.
Hours:	Mon-Fri 9-5:30. Sat 9-3:30.
Services:	Appraisals, accepts want lists, mail order.
Travel:	At corner of 60th Street.
Credit Cards:	Yes
Owner:	Thomas Tyrrell
Year Estab:	1940
Comments:	Approximately one third of the collection is used.

Science Fiction, Mysteries & More   (212) 385-8798
140 Chambers Street 10007

Collection:	Specialty
# of Volumes:	3,000
Specialties:	Science fiction; mystery.
Hours:	Mon-Fri 11-7. Sat & Sun 2:30-6:30.
Services:	Accepts want lists
Travel:	5 blocks north of the World Trade Center.
Credit Cards:	Yes
Owner:	Alan Zimmerman
Year Estab:	1992

The Science Fiction Shop   (212) 473-3010
163 Bleecker Street 10014   Fax: (212) 475-9727

Collection:	Specialty new and used.
# of Volumes:	300-400 (used, mostly paperback).
Specialties:	Science fiction; horror; fantasy.
Hours:	Mon-Sat 11-7. Sun 12-6.
Services:	Catalog
Travel:	Between Sullivan and Thompson.
Credit Cards:	Yes

Owner:	Joseph Lihach
Year Estab:	1972

Skyline Books & Records, Inc. (NY156)   (212) 759-5463
13 West 18 Street 10011

Collection:	General stock and records.
# of Volumes:	75,000
Specialties:	Modern first editions; photography; art history; vintage paper-backs; jazz.
Hours:	Mon-Sat 9:30-8. Sun 11-7.
Services:	Appraisals, search service, catalog, accepts want lists.
Travel:	Between Fifth & Sixth Avenues. Map 14.
Credit Cards:	Yes
Owner:	Rob Warren
Year Estab:	1991
Comments:	Despite its urban location, this well stocked shop has the ambience of a tightly packed but inviting rural used book shop. The store is divided into a series of alcoves, nooks and crannies with stools scattered about for the comfort of browsers. The rear portion of the store is two steps up. The collection offers an excellent selection of titles in all categories.

Soho Books (NY157)   (212) 226-3395
351 West Broadway 10013

Collection:	General stock.
# of Volumes:	40,000-50,000.
Hours:	Mon-Fri 10:30-10. Sat 12-midnight. Sun 12-10.
Travel:	In Soho, between Broome and Grand Streets. Map 14.
Comments:	A well organized, well labeled collection of books in generally good condition. The shop offers a good selection of mixed vintage books in most categories with an emphasis on post World War II titles and some more recent volumes. Moderately priced. Worth a visit, especially if you're planning additional stops in Soho. The entrance is up a few steps.

Richard Stoddard - Performing Arts Books   (212) 645-9576
18 East 16th Street, #305 10003

Collection:	Specialty books and ephemera.
# of Volumes:	8,000
Specialties:	Performing arts (theater, film, dance, music, popular entertainments); costume design; scenic design.
Hours:	Daily except Wed and Sun 11-6.
Services:	Appraisals, search service, catalog, accepts want lists.

Travel:	Between Fifth Avenue & Union Square.
Credit Cards:	No
Owner:	Richard Stoddard
Year Estab:	1975

Strand Book Store (NY159)   (212) 473-1452
828 Broadway 10003   Fax: (212) 473-2591

Collection:	General stock.
# of Volumes:	2,000,000+
Specialties:	Scholarly; first editions; art; photography; books about books; Americana; performing arts; children's; children's illustrated; travel; fine bindings; fiction reference, sets; science; natural history.
Hours:	Main store: Mon-Sat 9:30-9:30. Sun 11-9:30. Rare Book Department: Mon-Sat 9:30-6:30. Sun 11-6:30. South Street Seaport shop: Mon-Sat 10-9. Sun 10-8.
Services:	Appraisals, catalog, accepts want lists, collection development; rentals.
Travel:	Corner of East 12th Street. Map 14.
Credit Cards:	Yes
Owner:	Fred Bass
Year Estab:	1927
Comments:	The description of this shop as containing eight miles of shelves is no exaggeration. If you love books, come early and plan to stay late. The shelves are well organized and the subjects are clearly marked. A store directory, including a map of the shop, is available at the entrance. The stock contains a heavy emphasis on inexpensive copies (often remainders) of newer books as well as review copies which can be purchased at half price although we had no trouble spotting plenty of older volumes as we browsed the shelves. Prices are clearly marked and fall within the expected range of what a book buyer should expect to pay. Don't miss the large selection of books available in the basement. For book hunters interested in rare or signed books, there's a separate rare book department located on the third floor of the adjacent office building.

No true book lover making a one time visit to New York City should miss the opportunity to visit this landmark establishment. Although the authors have not checked with the *Guinness Book of Records*, the store may very well qualify as the largest antiquarian book store in the English speaking world. In addition to the main store, there is a branch shop at 159 John St. at the South Street Seaport, and between April and October, kiosks at 59th St. & Second Ave. and 59th St. & Fifth Ave.

Stubbs Books & Prints   (212) 772-3120
153 East 70th Street 10021   Fax: (212) 794-9071

Collection:	Specialty books and prints.
# of Volumes:	3,000
Specialties:	Landscape architecture; decorative arts; social history; cookbooks; biography; fashion.
Hours:	Mon-Sat 10-6.
Travel:	Between Lexington & Third Avenues.
Credit Cards:	Yes
Owner:	John & Jane Stubbs
Year Estab:	1982
Comments:	An attractively decorated bi-level specialty shop. In addition to a small entry level room, a winding staircase leads to a second floor with additional books and prints. The books are generally well cared for and are not unreasonably priced.

University Place Book Shop (NY161)   (212) 254-5998
821 Broadway, 9th Floor 10003

Collection:	General stock and ephemera.
# of Volumes:	60,000
Specialties:	Africa; African-American; French Revolution pamphlets.
Hours:	Mon-Fri 10-5. Sat by chance.
Services:	Appraisals, search service, catalog, accepts want lists.
Travel:	Corner East 12th St. Entrance is on East 12th St. Map 14.
Credit Cards:	No
Owner:	William French
Year Estab:	1932
Comments:	This shop is distinguished by its narrow, cluttered and poorly lit aisles. The organization of the collection varies depending on the room and the ephemera is not well displayed. For book hunters who don't mind dust and some disarray, the collection is a good source for antiquarian searches and offers a good academically oriented general stock. Not all the books are in good condition.

Ursus Books And Prints, Ltd. (NY162)   (212) 772-8787
981 Madison Avenue 10021   Fax: (212) 737-9306

Collection:	General stock and prints. (See Comments)
# of Volumes:	10,000
Specialties:	Art reference; antiquarian.
Hours:	Mon-Fri 10-6. Sat 11-5. (See Comments)
Services:	Appraisals, search service (art only), accepts want lists, catalog.
Travel:	Between 76th & 77th Streets. Map 14.

Credit Cards:	Yes
Owner:	T. Peter Kraus
Year Estab:	1972
Comments:	Located on the 2nd floor of the Hotel Carlyle, this shop concentrates primarily on art but also has a small selection of modern first editions as well as a rare book room carrying a more traditional antiquarian stock. If books on art are your thing, this is a place you would not want to miss.

The owner operates a second shop in Soho, at 375 West Broadway, specializing in 19th & 20th century art books and exhibition catalogs only. The shop is open Mon-Fri 10-6 and Sat 11-5. (212) 226-7858.

Michael R. Weintraub Book Annex   (212) 924-8088
135 West 26th Street (5th Floor) 10001   Fax: (212) 874-2481

Collection:	Specialty
# of Volumes:	2,500
Specialties:	Modern illustrated; decorative arts; fine arts; performing arts; architecture; photography; children's illustrated.
Hours:	Tue & Wed 10-6. Other times by appointment.
Services:	Accepts want lists, mail order.
Travel:	Between Sixth & Seventh Avenues. Ring buzzer #13 for entry.
Credit Cards:	No
Owner:	Michael R. Weintraub
Year Estab:	1980
Comments:	See additional listing in By Appointment section.

Samuel Weiser, Inc.   (212) 777-6363
132 East 24th Street 10010

Collection:	Specialty
# of Volumes:	3,000-5,000
Specialties:	Occult; metaphysical; eastern philosophy; new age, spiritual.
Hours:	Mon-Wed 9-6. Thu & Fri 10-7. Sat 9:30-5:30. Sun 12-5.
Services:	Catalog, accepts want lists.
Travel:	Between Lexington & Park Avenues.
Credit Cards:	Yes
Owner:	Donald Weiser
Year Estab:	1926
Comments:	For serious students of the occult or the mysterious East, or for book hunters with a religious bent, this shop offers an outstanding collection of both recent and crumbling volumes of every possible sub topic dealing with the specialties listed above. Some of the books are displayed on open shelves while other rare

volumes can be found behind glass enclosed bookcases or behind counters. In addition to the books, the shop sells miscellaneous related items. Prices vary depending on rarity and condition. The entrance to the shop is a few steps down.

Weitz, Weitz & Coleman   (212) 831-2213
1377 Lexington Avenue 10128   Fax: (212) 427-5718

Collection:	Specialty
# of Volumes:	6,000
Specialties:	Illustrated; sets; fine bindings; art.
Hours:	Mon-Thu 9-7. Fri 9-5. Sat 12-5. Sun by appointment.
Services:	Custom bookbinding; boxes; restoration.
Travel:	Between 90th and 91st Streets.
Credit Cards:	No
Owner:	Elspeth Coleman & Herbert Weitz
Year Estab:	1909
Comments:	If you have a favorite book that you want to preserve in an artistic and creative manner, this shop can do wonders for you. The shop displays some attractive books with covers done by the craftsmen who work there. It also has a small stock of other used books, not necessarily distinctive. We give an A+ to the shop's book covers and a more average grade to its other collection. The shop offers classes in restoration and the owners are proud to show visitors their collection of hand bookbinding decorating tools.

Ximenes Rare Books   (212) 744-0226
19 East 69th Street 10021   Fax: (212) 472-8075

Collection:	Specialty
# of Volumes:	5,000
Specialties:	Rare books (English and American) in all subjects, 1500-1900.
Hours:	Mon-Fri 9:30-5:30.
Services:	Catalog
Credit Cards:	No
Owner:	Stephen Weissman
Year Estab:	1965

New York City
(Queens)

Jackson Heights Discount Bookstore   (718) 426-0202
77-15 37th Avenue 11372   Fax: (718) 426-0202

Collection:	General stock of used and some new paperback and hardcover.

# of Volumes:	1,000,000
Hours:	Mon-Sat 9-9. Sun 11:30-6:30.
Services:	Accepts want lists.
Travel:	Northern Blvd. East exit off Grand Central Pkwy. Proceed on Northern Blvd. to 78th St. Left on 78th St. and proceed 3 blocks to 37th Ave. right on 37th Ave.
Credit Cards:	Yes
Owner:	Ava & Elliott Grubman
Year Estab:	1976
Comments:	The owner estimates that the used stock is about 60% paperback.

Austin Book Shop   (718) 441-1199
104-29 Jamaica Avenue   (800) 676-4556
Mailing address: Box 36 Kew Gardens 11415

Collection:	General stock.
# of Volumes:	75,000
Specialties:	Baseball; law; women's studies; American history; immigration; ethnic studies.
Hours:	Fri & Sat 12-6. Other times by appointment.
Services:	Catalog, accepts want lists. Computer printouts by subject.
Travel:	Jamaica Ave. exit off Van Wyck Expy. Proceed east for about 1 mile.
Credit Cards:	Yes
Owner:	Titowsky Family
Year Estab:	1954
Comments:	If you're searching for books in the specialties noted above, there is an excellent chance you'll find what you're looking for here although you're likely to pay premium prices for the items. The bi-level shop is packed tightly with books, sometimes multiple copies of the same title. You'll also find several new copies of out of print volumes, suggesting that the late owner had been buying as an investment in the books' future desirability. The basement stock is not as well organized as the first floor and some subject categories are located on both levels. In addition to the specialties noted above, the shop has a collection of the "Year's Best Short Stories" and the "Year's Best Plays" that go back many many years.

Book hunters should note that the shop's founder, Bernard Titowsky, a well known and well respected book dealer passed away shortly before this book went to press and that the family has put the shop up for sale.

Newburgh

Clough's Bookshop (NY170)   (914) 561-5522
159 Liberty Street 12550

Collection:	General stock.
# of Volumes:	30,000+
Specialties:	Natural history; New York State.
Hours:	Tue-Sat 10-5.
Services:	Accepts want lists, mail order.
Travel:	Downtown Newburgh, 2 miles east of the NY Twy. and 1 mile from I-84. Follow signs to downtown. From Broadway (the main thoroughfare), proceed east toward the river. Map 12.
Credit Cards:	No
Owner:	Franzen Clough
Year Estab:	1985
Comments:	Browsing the collection in this storefront shop can be somewhat difficult due to narrow aisles made even narrower by piles of books stacked in the aisles. Despite this logistical drawback, the shop does have many older volumes, including several titles in the "hard to find" category. If you're patient and adventurous, you may pick up some items you've been searching for. The books are most reasonably priced.

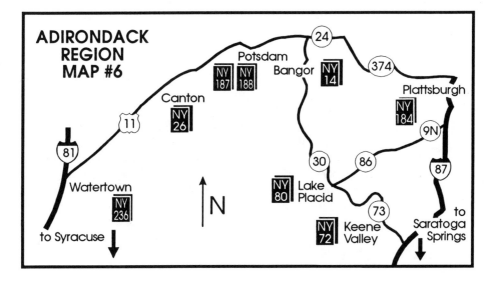

Northville

Carriage House Book Store (NY171)   (518) 863-8533
102 Prospect Street 12134

Collection:	General stock.
# of Volumes:	40,000
Hours:	1st week of May-Labor Day: Thu-Sun 11-5.
Travel:	Fultonville exit off NY Twy. Proceed north on Rte. 30A to Northville. Shop is in heart of village. Map 9.
Credit Cards:	No
Owner:	Robert Komornik
Year Estab:	1989

Nyack

Ben Franklin Bookshop (NY172)   (914) 358-0440
18 North Broadway 10960

Collection:	General stock.
# of Volumes:	35,000
Specialties:	New York State (regional).
Hours:	Mon-Fri 11-5:30. Sat & Sun 11-6:30.
Services:	Occasional catalog, accepts want lists.
Travel:	Nyack exit off NY Twy. Right at light at end of exit ramp. Left at next light on Main. Left at Broadway (3rd light). Map 11.
Credit Cards:	No
Owner:	Michael Houghton
Year Estab:	1979
Comments:	Upon entering this long established shop, one is immediately taken by the 20 foot ceilings and the rolling library ladders that provide access to the shop's two story high bookcases. Despite the handles on both sides of the ladders though, one does have to be quite agile to search the upper shelves. The majority of the books are in good to excellent condition and quite reasonably priced. Most subjects are well represented with literature and literary criticism collections particularly strong. Some rare items can be found in a glass bookcase. Book hunters may also want to check out the New Arrivals section in the front room.

Pickwick Book Shop (NY173)   (914) 358-9126
8 South Broadway 10960

Collection:	General stock used and new.
# of Volumes:	50,000 (used)
Specialties:	Hudson River; American history; biography.

Hours:	Mon-Sat. Open at 9AM. Closing time varies. Sun 11-5:30.
Services:	Appraisals, search service, accepts want lists, mail order.
Travel:	See above. Map 11.
Credit Cards:	Yes
Owner:	John Dunnigan
Year Estab:	1946
Comments:	This combination new/used book shop overflows with titles with most of the used books (about 50% of the stock) located toward the middle and rear of the shop. Portions of the used book collection, which consists primarily of more recent titles, can be difficult to browse for all but the most dedicated book hunter because of the shop's high shelves and the paucity of ladders; we saw only one during our visit.

Oceanside

Stan's Book Bin (NY174)   (516) 766-4949
234 Merrick Road 11572

Collection:	General stock.
# of Volumes:	50,000-60,000
Hours:	Mon-Fri 12-6. Sat 9-6. Sun 11-5.
Services:	Accepts want lists, mail order.
Travel:	Exit 20 off Southern State Pkwy. Right at exit on Grand Ave. Proceed for 3 miles. Right on Merrick Rd. Proceed for 1 mile. Shop is on left. Map 13.
Credit Cards:	No
Owner:	Stan Simon
Year Estab:	1983
Comments:	Book lovers who are also inveterate browsers may end up spending far more time in this shop than they may have originally planned. In addition to a crowded and well stocked main level, the shop has a basement level that, standing alone, would make many book dealers envious. The only problem we experienced in the basement was that in order to display all of the stock, the shelves were arranged in a series of extremely tight alcoves. Non weight watchers beware, or you may have a bit of trouble fitting into some of the alcoves. The area was consistently well lit and most of the shelves were double stacked.

Olean

Knieser's Used & Rare Books (NY175)   (716) 372-0915
309½ North Union Street 14760

Collection:	General stock, magazines and ephemera.

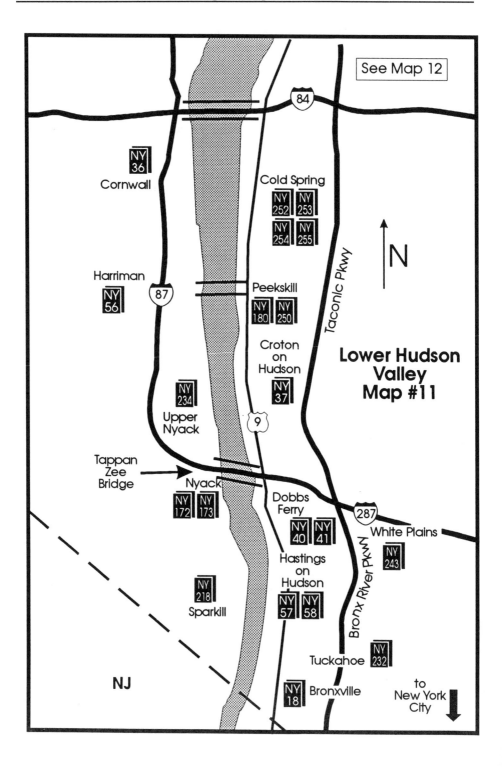

See Map 12

NY 36
Cornwall

Cold Spring
NY 252 NY 253
NY 254 NY 255

84

N

Harriman
NY 56

87

Peekskill
NY 180 NY 250

Taconic Pkwy

Croton on Hudson
NY 37

Lower Hudson Valley Map #11

NY 234
Upper Nyack

9

Tappan Zee Bridge

Nyack
NY 172 NY 173

Dobbs Ferry
NY 40 NY 41

287
White Plains
NY 243

Hastings on Hudson
NY 57 NY 58

Bronx River Pkwy

NY 218
Sparkill

Tuckahoe
NY 232

NJ

NY 18 Bronxville

to New York City

# of Volumes:	15,000-20,000
Specialties:	History; American history.
Hours:	Mon-Sat 10-5, except Fri till 8.
Services:	Appraisals, search service, accepts want lists, mail order.
Travel:	Rte. 17 to Rte. 16. Proceed south on Rte. 16 into Olean. Rte. 16 becomes North Union St. Shop is one block after Olean Center Mall, above a men's clothing shop. The entrance to the book shop is through the clothing shop. Map 10.
Credit Cards:	Yes
Owner:	Paul & Sarah Knieser
Comments:	This shop offers several rooms of mostly older books, including some collectible items. A discriminating book person may find some titles of interest here. Moderately priced.

Darlene Morgan (NY176)   (716) 372-8171
At Olean Antique Center,   269 North Union Street 14760

Collection:	General stock.
Hours:	Mon-Sat 10-6. Sun 1-5.
Travel:	See above. Map 10.
Credit Cards:	Yes
Owner:	Darlene Morgan
Comments:	A modest display in a multi dealer antique mall. See also By Appointment section.

Oneonta

Susquehanna Valley Book Mart (NY177)   (607) 433-1034
RD 2, Box 2024, Route 23 13820

Collection:	General stock.
# of Volumes:	20,000+
Hours:	Daily 10:30-5:30. The shop usually closes for vacation, so a call ahead is advised if you're coming from a distance.
Services:	Accepts want lists, mail order.
Travel:	Exit 15 off I-88. Proceed on Rte. 23 East for approximately 2 miles. Shop is just east of Holiday Inn in yellow one story stand alone building. Map 9.
Credit Cards:	Yes
Owner:	Joe Campbell
Year Estab:	1982
Comments:	An inauspicious entrance sign reads "New books and comics." However, the shop, which is larger than it initially appears, does have several rooms containing older hardcover books and a separate room devoted entirely to paperbacks. We noted lots of

interesting titles but we did feel that the prices being asked were a bit steep. Unfortunately, many of the shelves were unmarked.

Owego

Riverow Bookshop (NY178)   (607) 687-4094
187 Front Street 13827   (607) 687-1248

Collection:	General stock, ephemera and prints.
# of Volumes:	20,000
Specialties:	New York State; architecture; trade catalogs.
Hours:	Mon-Sat 9:30-5:30, except Thu until 8. Also 1st & 3rd Sun of month 10-5.
Services:	Appraisals
Travel:	In heart of downtown. Map 10.
Credit Cards:	Yes
Owner:	John D. Spencer
Year Estab:	1976
Comments:	This multi level shop may be what some would call a sleeper. The first floor displays new books in addition to used hardcover titles, including some very old (19th century) items, for the most part in reasonably good condition. The second floor houses the shop's better, rare and more unusual titles, while the basement level contains a mix of bargain books, sets, and historical items. The books were not inexpensive. However, if your wants are not easily available elsewhere, this shop, in our judgment, is worth making the extra effort to reach.

Patchogue

Side Street Books (NY179)   (516) 475-2617
76 North Ocean Avenue 11772

Collection:	General stock of new and used paperback and hardcover.
Hours:	Mon-Fri 10-6. Sat 10-5. Sun 11-3.
Travel:	Exit 52A (North Ocean Ave.) off Sunrise Hwgy. Proceed south. Shop is 1½ blocks north of Main St. Map 13.
Owner:	Linda M. Sella & Jacqueline Roberts
Comments:	Primarily paperback.

Peekskill

Field Library Annex (NY250)   (914) 528-4488
Westchester Mall, Rte. 6 10566

Collection:	General stock.

Hours:	Mon-Sat 10-5. Sun 1-5.
Travel:	Rte. 6 exit off Taconic Pkwy. Proceed west on Rte. 6 for about 2 miles to mall. Map 11.
Manager:	Hortense Saperstein
Comments:	Operated by and for benefit of Peekskill Public Library. All books are donated.

Wishing Well Books (NY180)   (914) 739-4813
101 South Division Street 10566

Collection:	General stock of new and used books, prints and maps.
# of Volumes:	8,000 (used)
Specialties:	Americana; metaphysics; occult; regional.
Hours:	Mon-Sat 10-6. Thu & Fri till 8. Mid Oct-Apr only: Sun 12:30-5.
Services:	Accepts want lists, mail order.
Travel:	South St. exit off Rte. 9. Take South St. to end. Map 11.
Credit Cards:	Yes
Owner:	Robert Downing & Carol Staudohar
Year Estab:	1989
Comments:	The authors were pleased to find a "real" used book store fairly close to their backyard. This modest sized storefront shop carries new books, cards, gemstones and an assortment of jewelry in a front room while a second room is devoted exclusively to used and even a few antiquarian books. The books are moderately priced and generally in good condition and well organized.

Penn Yan

Belknap Hill Books (NY181)   (315) 536-1186
106 Main Street 14527   Fax: (315) 536-1186

Collection:	General stock, prints, maps and original art.
# of Volumes:	30,000
Specialties:	Military; children's; cookbooks; religion; philosophy; Americana.
Hours:	Mon-Fri 10-6. Sat 10-3. Sun 10-2.
Services:	Appraisals, search service, accepts want lists, mail order.
Travel:	From Geneva, proceed south on Rte. 14, then follow signs for Rte. 54 to Penn Yan. Map 10.
Credit Cards:	No
Owner:	Eileen O'Reilly
Year Estab:	1985
Comments:	A lovely shop with a little bit of everything, including some interesting older titles. The collection is well organized and moderately priced and the owner most helpful.

Pittsford

Strawberry Hill Books (NY182)   (716) 586-8707
Northfield Common, 50 State Street 14534

Collection:	General stock.
# of Volumes:	7,000-10,000
Hours:	Mon-Sat 10-5, except Thu till 8.
Services:	Search service, accepts want lists, mail order.
Travel:	Rte. 31 (Monroe Ave.) becomes State St. in Pittsford. Shop is in an outdoor shopping center across the bridge. Map 16.
Owner:	Mary Lou Gastin

Plainview

Bonmark Books, Inc. (NY183)   (516) 938-9000
998 Old Country Road 11803

Collection:	General stock of used and new.
# of Volumes:	30,000
Hours:	Mon-Fri 10-8:30. Sat 10-6. Sun 11-5.
Services:	Search service, mail order, accepts want lists.
Travel:	Northern State Pkwy. to Seaford Expy. Proceed south on Seaford Expy. for 2 exits. Left on Old Country Rd. and proceed east for 3 lights. The shop is in the shopping center on the left, next to a movie theater. Map 13.
Credit Cards:	Yes
Owner:	Mark & Rita Blinderman
Comments:	What a pleasant surprise to discover an old fashioned and rather large used book store in the middle of a suburban shopping center. While the front of the store offers new titles, magazines, paperbacks and comics, the center and rear of the shop is devoted to row after row after row of used, out of print and occasionally rare titles. Most of the books are in good condition, and as far as we could tell, priced quite reasonably.

Plattsburgh

The Corner-Stone Bookshop (NY184)   (518) 561-0520
110 Margaret Street 12901

Collection:	General stock and records.
# of Volumes:	50,000
Hours:	Mon-Sat 10-9. Sun 12-6.
Services:	Search service, mail order.

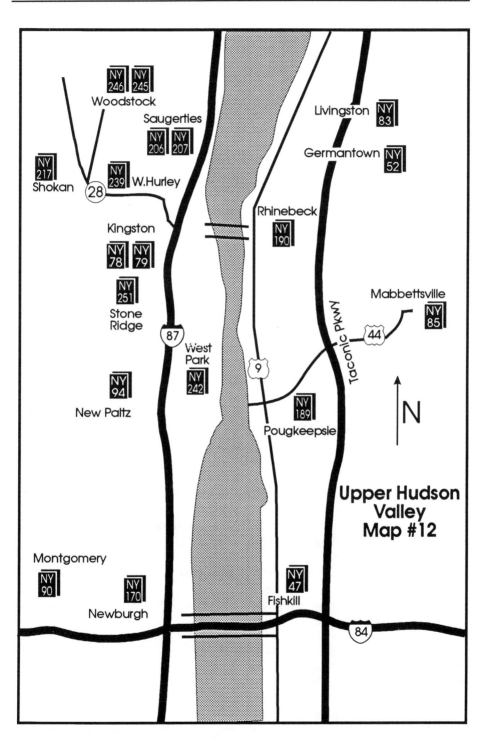

NY 246 NY 245
Woodstock

Saugerties
NY 206 NY 207

Livingston NY 83

Germantown NY 52

NY 217
Shokan

NY 239 W.Hurley

(28)

Rhinebeck
NY 190

Kingston
NY 78 NY 79

NY 251

Stone
Ridge

Mabbettsville
NY 85

Taconic Pkwy

(44)

(87)

West
Park
NY 242

NY 94

New Paltz

(9)

NY 189

Pougkeepsie

N

**Upper Hudson
Valley
Map #12**

Montgomery

NY 90

NY 170

NY 47

Fishkill

Newburgh

(84)

Travel:	From Rte. 87, take exit to Rte. 3 in Plattsburgh. Proceed east on Rte. 3 to downtown. Shop is at corner of Margaret and Court Sts. Map 6.
Credit Cards:	Yes
Owner:	Nancy Duniho
Year Estab:	1975
Comments:	If you're looking for older books, you're likely to find many bargains in this bi-level shop. However, you'll require much patience if you want to see everything the shop has to offer as many of the shelves were somewhat in disarray due to over-stocked conditions.

Port Jefferson

The Good Times Bookshop (NY185)   (516) 928-2664
150 East Main Street 11777

Collection:	General stock, ephemera and sheet music.
# of Volumes:	20,000
Specialties:	Humanities; Long Island history.
Hours:	Tue-Sat 11-6. Sun 1-5 but best to call ahead.
Services:	Appraisals, lists, accepts want lists, mail order.
Travel:	Exit 64 off I-495. Proceed north on Rte. 112 (Main St.) to harbor. Right on East Broadway, then right on East Main. Shop is 1 block ahead on right. Shop is 1 block from the Port Jefferson/Bridgeport ferry. Map 13.
Credit Cards:	Yes
Owner:	Michael & Mary Mart
Year Estab:	1972
Comments:	This immaculately kept bi-level shop offers a nice collection of well organized, reasonably priced books in good condition. According to the owner, the shop is Long Island's oldest antiquarian book shop.

Port Washington

Collectors Antiques, Inc. (NY186)   (516) 883-2098
286 Main Street 11050

Collection:	General stock, antiques and art.
# of Volumes:	A few hundred.
Specialties:	Children's; art; history.
Hours:	Tue-Sun 9-5, except Fri 9-1.
Services:	Appraisals
Travel:	Searington Rd. North exit off I-495. Continue on Searington

which becomes Port Washington Blvd. Continue to Main St. Left on Main. Map 13.

Credit Cards:	No
Owner:	Jean Feigenbaum
Year Estab:	1965

Potsdam

BirchBark Bookshop (NY187)   (315) 265-3875
Route 4, Aston Road 13676

Collection:	General stock.
# of Volumes:	15,000
Specialties:	Adirondacks; New York State.
Hours:	Thu-Sun 1-6 or by chance or appointment.
Travel:	From Rte. 56 south in Potsdam, proceed on Rte. 72 for 6 miles to Parishville Center. Right on Ashton Rd. and follow book signs. Shop is 1 mile ahead on left. Map 6.
Credit Cards:	No
Owner:	Tim Strong
Year Estab:	1989
Comments:	If you're willing to drive several miles off the beaten track to find a book shop that is likely to have unusual titles that have not been "picked over" by other avid collectors, you'll find a visit to this bi-level barn most rewarding. The books are generally in good condition, prices are extremely reasonable and the owner knowledgeable, helpful and pleasant. A well stocked children's corner on the second floor should occupy the younger set while their parents are browsing.

Cabin in the Pines Bookshop (NY188)   (315) 265-9036
Route 5, Box 409 13676

Collection:	General stock.
# of Volumes:	4,000
Hours:	Mon-Fri 9-5.
Services:	Appraisals, search service, accepts want lists.
Travel:	From Rte. 11 proceeding north to Potsdam, left on County Rte. 35 and proceed to third major intersection (West Potsdam.) Left on Bucks Bridge Rd. and proceed for about 1/2 mile. Shop is a log cabin on right but park in driveway of house immediately after cabin. Map 6.
Credit Cards:	No
Owner:	Charles Penrose
Year Estab:	1978

Comments: When we visited this shop, there were few books on the shelves and no one was on hand to answer any questions about the stock. A sign on the desk advised visitors to leave their money in the drawer if they saw a book or two they wanted.

Poughkeepsie

The Three Arts (NY189)   (914) 471-3640
3 Collegeview Avenue 12603

Collection:	Specialty
# of Volumes:	300 (used)
Specialties:	Local history; Hudson Valley.
Hours:	Mon-Sat 9:30-5:30.
Services:	Search service, mail order.
Travel:	Rte. 44/55 exit from Taconic Pkwy. Proceed on Rtes. 44/55 to downtown. Left on Rte. 376 South (Raymond Ave). Collegeview is the third light. The shop is on the corner of Collegeview and Raymond. Map 12.
Credit Cards:	Yes
Owner:	Walter Effron
Year Estab:	1946
Comments:	Primarily a new book shop with a limited selection of used books in the specialty areas noted above.

Rhinebeck

Recyled Reading (NY190)   (914) 876-7849
Route 9, Astor Square Plaza 12574

Collection:	General stock of paperback and hardcover.
# of Volumes:	400,000+
Hours:	Mon-Wed 10:30-5. Thu & Fri 10:30-7. Sat 10-5. Sun 12-4.
Services:	Search service, mail order.
Travel:	One mile north of Rhinebeck, on the left. Map 12.
Credit Cards:	Yes
Owner:	Jayne Brooks
Year Estab:	1980
Comments:	While this shop is certainly not for the used book "purist" in that the collection is primarily paperback, almost every category also includes hardcover titles in addition to paperbacks. Sadly, most, but certainly not all, of the hardcover volumes are book club editions. If the reader is searching for a popular best seller, particularly in the areas of science fiction, mystery or romance, this shop is bound to have a copy. Perhaps caught up

in the snobbery of some of our peers, we expected less and found a great deal more.

Rochester

ABACUS Bookshop (NY191)   (716) 325-7950
350 East Avenue 14604

Collection:	General stock, prints, maps and autographs.
# of Volumes:	15,000
Specialties:	Art; architecture; photography; literature; scholarly.
Hours:	Mon-Sat 12-6, except Thu till 8. Other times by appointment.
Services:	Appraisals, catalog, accepts want lists.
Travel:	Goodman St. exit off Rte. 490. Proceed north on Goodman to East Ave. (4th light). Left on East and proceed to next light. The shop is a few doors past the light on the right at Alexander St. Map 15.
Credit Cards:	Yes
Owner:	John Tribone
Year Estab:	1987

Armchair Books   (716) 338-3240
545 Titus Avenue 14617

Collection:	General stock of new and used hardcover and paperback.
# of Volumes:	15,000+
Specialties:	Science fiction; fantasy; horror; mystery.
Hours:	Tue-Fri 11-7. Sat 10-6. Open daily during Christmas season.
Services:	Accepts want lists, mail order.
Travel:	From Rte. 104, take Hudson Ave. exit north till it ends at Titus Ave. Left on Titus and immediate left into mall lot.
Credit Cards:	Yes
Owner:	Gary Reilly
Year Estab:	1990
Comments:	Most of the titles we saw here were standard for combination new/used mall book shops. It's not likely, in our judgment, that even the mystery or horror fan will find anything unusual here. While some books were priced at substantial discounts, others were advertised as being half the new price, not necessarily a bargain in our view.

The Backward Glance (NY193)   (716) 442-8450
1796 East Avenue 14610   (716) 442-8387

Collection:	General stock.
# of Volumes:	2,000+

Hours:	Wed-Sat 1-5. Spring only: Also Mon by chance or appointment.
Services:	Accepts want lists, mail order.
Travel:	From I-490 westbound, University Ave. exit. Left on Winton, then right on East Ave. From I-490 eastbound, take Winton Rd. exit, then left on Winton and left on East. Map 15.
Credit Cards:	Yes
Owner:	Diane Chichelli
Year Estab:	1992
Comments:	Shop also sells antiques, decorative art, oriental rugs and pottery.

The Bookshelf (NY194)   (716) 247-7670
1994 Chili Avenue 14624

Collection:	General stock of paperback and hardcover.
# of Volumes:	15,000-20,000
Hours:	Mon-Fri 10-8. Sat 10-5.
Services:	Accepts want lists, mail order.
Travel:	At intersection of Howard, Brooks and Chili Rds. Map 15.
Credit Cards:	Yes
Owner:	Barbara D. Flannery
Year Estab:	1975
Comments:	Primarily paperbacks.

Brown Bag Bookshop (NY195)   (716) 271-3494
678 Monroe Avenue 14607

Collection:	General stock of used and new hardcover and paperback.
# of Volumes:	8,000
Hours:	Mon-Sat 11-6, except Thu till 8:30. Sun 12-5.
Services:	Accepts want lists, occasional catalog.
Travel:	Rte. 490 from NY Twy. Exit at Monroe Ave. and proceed north toward city. Shop is 4 blocks ahead. The entrance is from a side yard between two shops. Map 15.
Credit Cards:	Yes
Owner:	James Gould
Year Estab:	1982
Comments:	Most of the used books we saw were in such excellent condition that it was not always easy to distinguish the used books from the new ones. The shop has a warm, browser friendly ambience.

Bryn Mawr Bookshop (NY196)   (716) 454-2910
147 State Street 14614

Collection:	General Stock.
# of Volumes:	3,000

Hours:	Mon-Fri 10-3. Sat 9:30-12:30. Jul & Aug: Mon-Fri 11-3.
Travel:	See map. Map 15.
Credit Cards:	No
Comments:	Operated by volunteers for benefit of college scholarship fund. Books are donated.

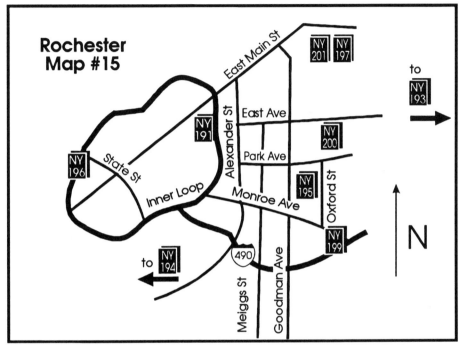

Rochester Map #15

DeSimone and Yount Booksellers (NY197)   (716) 242-9349
274 North Goodman Street, Box K-6 14607

Collection:	General stock.
# of Volumes:	10,000
Specialties:	Americana; Civil War, military.
Hours:	Daily 11-6, except Thu and Fri till 8PM. Call ahead for summer hours.
Services:	Appraisals, search service, catalog, accepts want lists.
Travel:	Goodman St. exit off Rte. 490. Proceed north to Village Gate Square, a renovated 2 story red brick building. Map 15.
Credit Cards:	Yes
Owner:	Jerold DeSimone & Terrance & Eugene Yount
Year Estab:	1992
Comments:	Located on the first level of a former factory turned indoor shopping mall, this modest sized shop carries a mix of recent and vintage book and some very old volumes.

The Earl of Clarendon

(716) 458-3990
(716) 482-4590

At Lee-Way Antique Co-Op, 1221 Lee Road 14606

Collection:	General stock and ephemera.
# of Volumes:	1,000
Hours:	Mon-Sat 11-5. Sun 12-5.
Services:	Accepts want lists, mail order.
Travel:	Rte. 390 North to Ridgeway Ave. Right on Ridgeway. Right on Lee.
Credit Cards:	Yes
Owner:	Jason Karp
Year Estab:	1981
Comments:	Multi dealer antique mall.

Gutenberg Books (NY199)

(716) 442-4620

675 Monroe Avenue 14607

Collection:	General stock.
# of Volumes:	8,000
Specialties:	Gardening; literature; history.
Hours:	Daily 11-6, except Thu till 8:30. Sun 12-5.
Services:	Appraisals, search service, catalog, accepts want lists.
Travel:	See Brown Bag Bookshop above. Map 15.
Credit Cards:	Yes
Owner:	Martha Kelly
Year Estab:	1982
Comments:	A class act shop with a not overly large but quality collection. Reasonably priced.

Park Avenue Book Store (NY200)

(716) 271-6120

370 Park Avenue 14607

Collection:	General stock of new and used.
# of Volumes:	3,000 (used)
Specialties:	History; biography.
Hours:	Mon, Wed, Fri 10-6. Tue & Thu 12-9. Sat 10-5. Sun 1-5.
Services:	Appraisals, catalog.
Travel:	Monroe or Culver St. exits off Rte. 490. Map 15.
Credit Cards:	Yes
Owner:	Herb Leventer
Year Estab:	1976
Comments:	Primarily a new book store, this shop offers a modest sized collection of used books of mixed vintage. Most of the books have been selected with care and are in reasonably good condition.

Yankee Peddler Book Shop (NY201)   (716) 271-5080
274 North Goodman Street
Mailing address: P.O. Box 118 Pultneyville 14538

Collection:	General stock, ephemera and prints.
# of Volumes:	20,000
Specialties:	Aeronautics, Americana; Arabia; autographs; black studies; children's; first editions; illustrated; music; Roycroft Press; women's studies; Great Lakes Maritime.
Hours:	Mon-Sat 11-6. Sun 12-5.
Services:	Appraisals, search service.
Travel:	See DeSimone and Yount Booksellers above. Shop is on second level. Map 15.
Credit Cards:	Yes
Owner:	Jane S. & John Westerberg
Year Estab:	1970
Comments:	A large selection of well displayed books with some interesting titles. While we believe the shop is worth a visit, we don't believe that the "down under" flavor associated with the shop's name is reflected in the prices of its books.

Roslyn Heights

Bookmarx (NY202)   (516) 621-0095
28 Lincoln Ave. 11577

Collection:	General stock.
# of Volumes:	8,000
Hours:	Mon-Fri 10:30-6, except Thu till 7. Sat 1:30-5.
Travel:	Exit 37 off I-495. Proceed east on service road to Roslyn Rd. Left on Roslyn. Proceed for 2 lights. Left on Lincoln. Map 13.
Credit Cards:	Yes
Owner:	Evan Marx
Year Estab:	1980
Comments:	The adage regarding not being able to tell a book by its cover is most appropriate for this shop. The first image of this storefront shop is that it caters to baseball card collectors. Once you pass through the front of the store though and enter the back room, you'll find a solid collection of older books and the atmosphere of a "real" used book shop. The collection is modest in size and appropriately organized and labeled. We noted many interesting titles and were pleased to find a vintage item that had long been on our own want list, always a bright sign for us. Moderately priced. When we visited, we saw fewer books displayed than noted above.

Sag Harbor

Canio's Books (NY203)   (516) 725-4926
Upper Main Street
Mailing address: PO Box 1962   11963

Collection:	General stock of new and used.
# of Volumes:	5,000 (used)
Specialties:	Poetry; literature.
Hours:	March-December: Daily 12-6. January & February: Sat & Sun only 12-6.
Services:	Appraisals, search service, accepts want lists, mail order.
Travel:	Exit 70 off I-495. Proceed south to Rte. 27 (Sunrise Hgwy), then east on Rte. 27 to Bridgehampton. Left at Sag Harbor Tpk. and proceed north for about 3 miles. The shop is on the left. Map 13.
Credit Cards:	Yes
Owner:	Canio Pavone

Saratoga Springs

Lyrical Ballad Bookstore (NY204)   (518) 584-8779
7 Phila Street 12866

Collection:	General stock, framed and unframed prints, magazines.
# of Volumes:	75,000+
Specialties:	Art; music; dance; children's; illustrated; literature; horse racing.
Hours:	Mon-Sat 10-6. Sun (except Jan-Mar) 12-4.
Services:	Appraisals, search service, accepts want lists, mail order.
Travel:	Just off Broadway (Rte. 9) in downtown. Map 8.
Credit Cards:	Yes
Owner:	John & Janice DeMarco
Year Estab:	1971
Comments:	If you love books, you'll fall in love with this shop which consists of a labyrinth of rooms, filled floor to ceiling, with fiction and non fiction titles from every period and representing the most esoteric of tastes. If one makes allowances for books over 150 years old, the books are in generally good to excellent condition. Needless to say, this shop is a winner and a "must see."

Saratoga Science Fiction & Mystery Bookshop (NY205)
454 Broadway 12866   (518) 583-3743

Collection:	Specialty used and new.
# of Volumes:	20,000+

Specialties:	Science fiction; mystery; horror.
Hours:	Mon-Sat 10-6. Sun 12-5.
Services:	Catalogs, accepts want lists.
Travel:	See above. Shop is located on 1st floor rear of an indoor mall. Map 8.
Credit Cards:	Yes
Owner:	Mary Southworth & Karl Olsen
Year Estab:	1989
Comments:	If you're a mystery or science fiction buff looking for titles reprinted in paperback, this shop is worth a visit. The hardcover collection is sparse and mostly of a more recent vintage. The shop also carries pulps, comics and some related ephemera.

Saugerties

Booktrader (NY206)   (914) 246-3522
252 Main Street 12477

Collection:	General stock of used hardcover and paperback.
# of Volumes:	25,000
Specialties:	Regional history; science fiction; mystery; children's.
Hours:	Mon-Sat 10-6. Sun 12-4. Closed for major holidays.
Travel:	Exit 20 off NY Twy. Proceed east on Ulster Ave. for about 1 mile. Right on Market St. Proceed for 2 blocks to light. Left on Main. Shop is on the right. Map 12.
Credit Cards:	Yes
Owner:	Lou Saylor
Year Estab:	1986
Comments:	This stock in this storefront shop is about evenly divided between hardcover and paperback titles. The books are generally well organized, reasonably priced, and represent older, previously owned volumes.

Hope Farm Press & Bookshop (NY207)   (914) 679-6809
1708 Route 212 12477

Collection:	Specialty
# of Volumes:	2,000
Specialties:	New York State; Hudson Valley; Catskill Mountains.
Hours:	Thu-Sat 1-6 and other times by appointment or chance.
Services:	Search service, catalog, research library. Also publishes new books and reprints dealing with regional history.
Travel:	Exit 20 off NY Twy. Proceed west on Rte. 212 for about 6 miles until you see the South Peak Veterinary Hospital. Map 12.
Credit Cards:	Yes

Owner: Richard Frisbie
Year Estab: 1959

Sayville

Words and Music (NY208)   (516) 563-1665
273 Railroad Avenue 11782

Collection: General stock of paperback and hardcover and records.
# of Volumes: 15,000
Hours: Mon-Sat 11-6.
Services: Accepts want lists.
Travel: Exit 44 East off Sunrise Hgwy. Right on Lakeland Ave. Proceed
                  for 1.5 miles. After the railroad tracks, the street becomes Rail-
                  road Ave. The shop is just after the tracks on left. Map 13.
Credit Cards: No
Owner: Dave & Joan Eimer
Year Estab: 1983
Comments: This small storefront shop consists of two rooms with the rear
                  room devoted mostly to records. The used book collection in the
                  front room consists primarily of paperbacks with a sprinkling of
                  hardcovers and very few titles that were unusual. If you're
                  looking for recycled paperbacks, this shop has an adequate
                  supply. Otherwise, unless you're passing through the neighbor-
                  hood, the shop is not worth going out of the way for.

Schenectady

Bibliomania (NY209)   (518) 393-8069
129 Jay Street 12305

Collection: General stock.
# of Volumes: 15,000
Specialties: Americana; literature; mystery; fishing; New York State.
Hours: Mon-Sat 10-5, except Thu till 9. Closed Mon Jun-Sep.
Services: Catalog, accepts want lists, mail order.
Travel: In downtown Schenectady, 1/2 block off US Rte. 5 and directly
                  opposite Proctor's Theatre. From exit 25 of NY Twy, proceed on
                  Rte. 890 to exit 3 (Broadway) exit. Follow signs for the "down-
                  town parking loop." Shop is in pedestrian mall. Map 8.
Credit Cards: No
Owner: Bill Healy
Year Estab: 1981
Comments: While this shop may not offer a selection of antiquarian titles, it
                  is certainly worth a browse if you're in the area. The books have

been selected with good taste, are in generally good condition and are well organized.

Collins Books (NY210)   (518) 372-1495
160 Jay Street   12305

Collection:	General stock of paperback and hardcover.
# of Volumes:	15,000
Hours:	Mon-Fri 11-6, except Thu till 8:30. Sat 10-5:30.
Services:	Search service, accepts want lists, mail order.
Travel:	See above. Map 8.
Credit Cards:	Yes
Owner:	Thomas Collins
Year Estab:	1990
Comments:	Most of the books we saw when we visited were fairly common and not always in the best condition.

W. Somers, Bookseller (NY211)   (518) 393-5266
841 Union Street   12308

Collection:	General stock.
# of Volumes:	10,000
Hours:	Mon-Fri 1-5. Sat 10-5.
Services:	Catalog (under business name of Hammer Mountain Book Halls).
Travel:	Michigan Ave. exit off Rte. 890. Turn north. Michigan becomes Brandywine. Proceed on Brandywine to Union. Left on Union. Shop is on right about 11 blocks ahead. Map 8.
Credit Cards:	No
Owner:	Wayne Somers
Year Estab:	1971
Comments:	Located in a quiet residential neighborhood, this pleasant shop carries books of mixed vintage that are in generally good condition and reasonably priced.

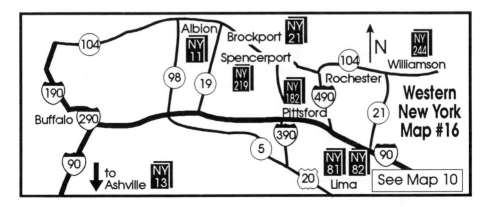

Sea Cliff

Book Emporium (NY212)   (516) 671-6524
235 Glen Cove Avenue 11579

Collection:	General stock.
# of Volumes:	80,000
Specialties:	Philosophy; history.
Hours:	Tue-Sat 12-5:30. Sun 12-5.
Travel:	Exit 39N off I-495. Proceed north on Glen Cove Rd. Cross Northern Blvd. Left after 3rd light and bear right at fork. Proceed 3 miles. Shop will be on left. Map 13.
Credit Cards:	Yes
Owner:	Robert J. Pucciariello
Year Estab:	1983
Comments:	This shop does offer book hunters as many books as it claims, although we did see many duplicates. The majority of the books are of more recent vintage with some older volumes and a small section of leather bindings, most of which looked new. Popular and some serious paperbacks are shelved separately. This is not a shop for collectors looking for truly unusual items. Mystery books are shelved with general fiction. Prospective visitors should note that at press time, the shop was for sale.

Sea Cliff Books (NY213)   (516) 676-6088
327 Sea Cliff Avenue 11579

Collection:	General stock and prints.
# of Volumes:	30,000
Hours:	Wed-Sun 12 to 6.
Services:	Appraisals, search service.
Travel:	See above. Left on Sea Cliff Ave. which is past The Book Emporium. Map 13.
Credit Cards:	No
Owner:	Charles Oppizi
Year Estab:	1950
Comments:	This shop offers a good supply of older books with many unusual titles. We were impressed by the section of first editions, many signed. The back room, which contained mostly fiction and mysteries should not be missed. In our view, the shop is worth extra browsing time.

Seneca Falls

Tallcot Bookshop Volume II (NY214)
31 State Street 13148

Collection:	General stock.
Hours:	Call (See Comments)
Services:	Search service, accepts want lists, mail order.
Travel:	Just off Rte. 20, around the corner from Gould Hotel. Map 10.
Credit Cards:	Yes
Owner:	Connie Tallcot
Year Estab:	1993
Comments:	Scheduled to open in the summer of 1993, this shop will also feature a tea room. The owner operates a second shop in nearby Union Springs.

Shelter Island Heights

Books & Video (NY215)   (516) 749-8925
17 Grand Avenue, Box 636 11965

Collection:	General stock of new and used books and ephemera.
Specialties:	Military; regional; nautical.
Hours:	Daily 10-8.
Services:	Accepts want lists, mail order.
Travel:	I-495 to end. Follow Rte. 25 to Greenport and take ferry to Shelter Island. Map 13.
Credit Cards:	Yes
Owner:	Paul Olinkiewicz
Year Estab:	1980

Sherburne

Curioddity Shop (NY216)   (607) 674-2375
14 West State Street
Mailing address: PO Box 627 13460

Collection:	General stock.
# of Volumes:	30,000
Specialties:	Hunting; fishing.
Hours:	Daily 10-4:30, but best to call ahead on Sat & Sun.
Services:	Mail order.
Travel:	300 yards west of intersection of Rtes. 12 & 80, across the street from fire department. Look for a five story weathered warehouse like building set back from the road. Map 9.
Credit Cards:	No
Owner:	Tracy Law
Year Estab:	1972
Comments:	The owner is in the process of cleaning out an accumulation of clutter in order to display his collection of used books (currently

in storage) and collectibles. When we visited, we were able to view only a few book shelves containing older volumes, many of an interesting and unusual nature. With any luck, and lots of hard work, thousands of additional volumes may be available for browsing in the future. When this occurs, we suspect a patient book hunter may find several treasures here because of the age of the collection and the relative isolation of the shop.

Shokan

Editions (NY217)   (914) 657-7000
153 Route 28 12481

Collection:	General stock and records.
# of Volumes:	40,000
Hours:	Daily 10-5.
Travel:	Exit 19 off NY Twy. Proceed on Rte. 28 west for about 9 miles. Shop is on right after the Kingdom Hall Church. Look for a one story building with blue and yellow sign. Map 12.
Credit Cards:	Yes
Owner:	Norman & Joan Levine
Year Estab:	1948
Comments:	This quite large shop has expanded considerably (and is still expanding) since our last visit. You name the subject and there should be a good selection in the category of your choice. The shop is divided into a series of rooms, some small (but not cramped), some large. Each room is well organized and carefully numbered and labeled for the convenience of the browser. An easy to read directory at the shop's entrance lists the contents of each room. The books are in generally good condition and are carefully, but not inexpensively priced. The shop is a pleasure to browse and book hunters should plan to spend lots and lots of time here.

Sparkill

The Dragon & The Unicorn (NY218)   (914) 353-0313
722 Main Street 10976

Collection:	Specialty paperback and hardcover (all used).
# of Volumes:	5,000
Specialties:	Science fiction; fantasy; horror; mystery.
Hours:	Tue-Sun 11-8. Summer only till 9.
Services:	Search service, catalog, accepts want lists.

Travel:	From Nyack exit off NY Twy, proceed south on Rte. 9W for 3 lights. At 3rd light, turn right and proceed down hill. At light, jog to the left and cross the intersection. The shop is on the right in the middle of the block. Map 11.
Credit Cards:	No
Owner:	George W. Hiller
Year Estab:	1992
Comments:	This relatively new shop currently occupies a space that can best be described as the size of a newspaper kiosk stand. The stock is 95% paperback with a few hardcover items interspersed. The owner is hoping to expand into slightly larger quarters which would give him a chance to display his stock more attractively. If you are deeply into science fiction and interested in older paperbacks, we recommend a call ahead to see if the titles you want are available.

Spencerport

Book Centre (NY219)   (716) 352-1890
Village Plaza 14559

Collection:	General stock of used and remainders.
# of Volumes:	30,000+
Hours:	Mon-Wed 9:30-6. Thu & Fri 9:30-8. Sat 9-5.
Services:	Accepts want lists.
Travel:	Rte. 259 (Union St.) exit off I-490 (west of Rochester). Proceed north on Rte. 259 into Spencerport. Shop is in a shopping plaza in heart of village. Map 16.
Credit Cards:	No
Owner:	Michael Palozzi
Year Estab:	1981
Comments:	The overwhelming majority of the used stock (about 80% of the total stock) consists of paperbacks.

St. James

Antique Bookworm (NY220)   (516) 862-6572
541 Lake Avenue 11780

Collection:	General stock and ephemera.
# of Volumes:	30,000+
Specialties:	Transvestite/transsexual; Long Island; automotive brochures.
Hours:	Mon-Sat 10-6.
Services:	Search service, accepts want lists.

Travel:	Northern State Pkwy. to the end. Continue on Rte. 347 to Moriches Rd. Proceed on Moriches to North Country Rd. Right on North Country, then first right on Lake (at fire house). Shop is a few blocks ahead on left. Map 13.
Credit Cards:	Yes
Owner:	Paul Hirschhorn
Year Estab:	1972
Comments:	The ambience of this storefront shop is very typical of the "traditional used book shop" in the sense that it is crowded, there are piles of books in the narrow aisles and the books are in mixed condition (and not always where you might expect to find them). Most subjects are represented. This is a shop where book hunters should have more than an even chance of finding some unusual or rare titles. We found the owner to be most friendly.

The Book Gallery (NY221)   (516) 862-7982
532 North Country Road 11780

Collection:	General stock of new and used.
Specialties:	Science fiction; horror.
Hours:	Tue-Sat 10:30-5. Sun 12-4.
Services:	Appraisals, search service, accepts want lists.
Travel:	See above. Shop is at intersection of North Country and Moriches Rds. Map 13.
Credit Cards:	Yes
Owner:	Genevieve Mancini
Year Estab:	1983
Comments:	A small, compact shop in which the owner says she shelves the used books with new titles by category. If we had trouble spotting the used books, it could have been because they were either so new looking or there weren't too many; we're not sure which. The rear room is devoted almost exclusively to horror and science fiction. If you're visiting the other used book shops in St. James just a few blocks away, or if you collect science fiction or horror, you may wish to stop by.

Science Fiction Store (NY222)   (516) 584-6858
21 Hobson Avenue 11780

Collection:	Specialty used and new.
# of Volumes:	15,000 (used)
Specialties:	Science fiction; horror; fantasy.
Hours:	Sat 10-6. Sun 12-5. Other times by appointment.
Services:	Appraisals, search service, accepts want lists.

Travel:	See above. Three blocks from Lake Ave. Map 13.
Credit Cards:	Yes
Owner:	Jean Gonzalez
Year Estab:	1978
Comments:	Approximately 75% of the stock is used and all the used books are hardcover.

St. Johnville

The Book Case (NY224)   (518) 568-2774
13 West Main Street 13452

Collection:	General stock and prints.
# of Volumes:	50,000+
Hours:	Mon-Fri 10-5. Sat 10-3:30.
Services:	Search service, accepts want lists, mail order.
Travel:	Little Falls exit off I-90. Proceed on Rte. 5 for 5 miles into St. Johnsville. Map 9.
Credit Cards:	No
Owner:	Vivian Walsh
Year Estab:	1987
Comments:	If you have a lot of patience and arrive early in the day, you would certainly have an opportunity to examine thousands of older volumes and possibly (but not likely) discover a rare item upon a shelf. While this storefront shop lives up to its claim of having 50,000 or more books on hand, organization is lacking and few if any of the shelves are labeled. Fiction and non fiction titles are frequently shelved side by side and books are not always alphabetically shelved by author or subject matter. The books are not all in the best condition.

Stephentown

Down In Denver Books (NY225)   (518) 733-6856
HCR 19 12168

Collection:	General stock and ephemera.
# of Volumes:	10,000
Hours:	Fri-Mon 10-6. Other days by chance.
Services:	Appraisals, search service, mail order.
Travel:	Rte. 22 to Stephentown. At light, turn west on Rte. 43 and proceed for 2½ miles. Shop is on right in a 140 year old farmhouse. Map 8.
Credit Cards:	No
Owner:	Daniel Lorber

Year Estab: 1989
Comments: This bi-level shop offers a relatively modest collection with a
                 focus on the beat generation. When we visited, the size of the
                 collection seemed smaller than the number indicated above.

Stone Ridge

H.A.S. Beane Books (NY251)   (914) 687-7091
Route 209
Mailing address: PO Box 244 12484

Collection: General stock.
# of Volumes: 5,000
Specialties: Modern first editions; children's.
Hours: Sat 10-6. Sun 12-6. Best to call ahead. Other times by appoint-
                  ment.
Services: Search service, accepts want lists, mail order.
Travel: Kingston exit off NY Twy. Proceed south on Rte. 209 for about
                  10 miles to Stone Ridge. Shop is in heart of village, across from
                  gas station, in owner's house. Map 12.
Credit Cards: No
Owner: Karen Cinquemani
Year Estab: 1986

Syracuse

Book Warehouse (NY226)   (315) 471-3803
212 Bear Street 13208

Collection: General stock of remainders and used.
# of Volumes: 75,000
Hours: Daily 8:30-6:30.
Services: Search service.
Travel: Southbound on Rte. 81: Hiawatha Bear St. exit. Follow Bear St.
                  signs and make left at light at end of ramp. Proceed one block.
                  Shop is ahead on right in a two story red brick building. North-
                  bound on Rte. 81: Court St. exit. Proceed one block to Bear.
                  Right on Bear. Map 10.
Credit Cards: No
Year Estab: 1950's
Comments: If you're patient enough to carefully go through shelf after shelf
                  of fairly recent titles at marked down prices, you'll find some
                  older (sometimes quite a bit older) books at bargain prices in
                  this large warehouse like shop. Even if you don't walk away
                  with a purchase, this is an interesting place to visit.

Books & Memories (NY227)   (315) 434-9268
2600 James Street 13206   Fax: (315) 434-9269

Collection:	General stock, records, posters and comics.
# of Volumes:	40,000
Specialties:	Film; literary criticism; books about books; games; magazines.
Hours:	Mon-Sat 12-6.
Services:	Appraisals, catalog, accepts want lists. The owner also sells BookMaster III software for used book dealers.
Travel:	Midler Ave. exit off I-690. Proceed north to James St. Left on James and go 4 blocks to Woodbine. Shop is at corner of Woodbine and James. Map 10.
Credit Cards:	Yes
Owner:	Sam Melfi
Year Estab:	1984
Comments:	This bi-level shop is like two stores in one. While one room concentrates on collectible items, including old games, records and posters, a second room stocks used books, with a good sized section devoted to entertainment, especially film. The basement is filled with thousands of old magazines. The owner's claim to offering bargain prices was upheld by the three items we purchased. When we visited, the size of the collection seemed smaller than the number indicated above.

Books End (NY228)   (315) 437-2312
2443 James Street 13206

Collection:	General stock of new and used paperback and hardcover and ephemera.
# of Volumes:	25,000
Specialties:	Modern first editions; New York State; science fiction; film; literature; performing arts; military; mystery.
Hours:	Mon-Fri 10-6. Sat 10-5. Sun 12-5.
Services:	Appraisals, search service, accepts want lists.
Travel:	Exit 14 off Rte. 690. Proceed north on Teall, then right on James. Shop is about 1/4 mile ahead on left across from a movie theater. Map 10.
Credit Cards:	Yes
Owner:	James Roberts
Year Estab:	1985
Comments:	The shop carries a mix of new and used books of a fairly common variety.

The Juke Box Shop (NY229)
2612 James Street 13206

Collection:	General stock, ephemera and magazines.
# of Volumes:	A few hundred
Services:	Accepts want lists.
Travel:	See above. Map 10.
Credit Cards:	No
Owner:	Tom Egleston
Year Estab:	1993
Comments:	A general nostalgia stop with a limited collection of used books. Worth a quick browse if you're visiting the two other nearby shops.

Tales Twice Told (NY230)   (315) 475-5925
546 Westcott Street 13210

Collection:	General stock of paperback and hardcover.
# of Volumes:	19,000
Specialties:	Children's illustrated; first editions (science fiction only); art; illustrated.
Hours:	Mon, Tue, Wed & Sat 10-8. Thu & Fri 12-8. Sun 12-5. Other times by appointment.
Services:	Appraisals, search service, catalog (science fiction only), accepts want lists.
Travel:	Rte. 81 to Rte. 690. Take Teall St. exit. (Note: Teall becomes Columbus). From east, turn left on Teall. From west, turn right. Cross over Erie Blvd. and left on East Genesse. Right on Westcott and proceed 1/4 mile. Shop is on right. Map 10.
Credit Cards:	Yes
Owner:	John O'Shea
Year:	Estab: 1987
Comments:	While this storefront shop does carry a general stock, its special interests, as noted above, take up much of the space. The remaining general stock is limited with little depth. Approximately 25% of the stock is hardcover.

Troy

Book Outlet (NY231)   (518) 272-0010
403 Fulton Street 12180

Collection:	General stock of new and used, hardcover and paperback.
# of Volumes:	20,000 (combined)
Hours:	Mon-Sat 10-5:30, except Thu & Fri till 9.

Services:	Accepts want lists.
Travel:	Green Island Bridge exit off Rte. 787. Right at light at foot of ramp. Proceed 1/4 mile to next light. Turn right and proceed over bridge. Right at end of bridge. Proceed to second light and make left on Fulton. Shop is 1 block ahead on far right corner of 4th & Fulton. Map 8.
Credit Cards:	No
Year Estab:	1980
Comments:	This shop stocks mainly new paperbacks, remainders and used paperbacks with very few used hardcover titles. Unless you're driving right by the shop, we really don't believe additional travel is in order.

Tuckahoe

Willowpond Antiques (NY232)   (914) 961-7973
36 Oak Avenue 10707

Collection:	General stock.
# of Volumes:	2,000
Specialties:	Americana; children's.
Hours:	Tue-Sat 11-4 and by appointment.
Services:	Accepts want lists.
Travel:	Tuckahoe exit from Bronx River Pkwy. Proceed to Oak Ave. Shop is adjacent to train depot. Map 11.
Credit Cards:	No
Owner:	Madeline Buckley & Mike Romano
Year Estab:	1992

Union Springs

Tallcot Bookshop (NY233)   (315) 889-5836
28 South Cayuga Street (Route 90) 13160

Collection:	General stock.
# of Volumes:	20,000
Specialties:	Local history; New York State; Civil War, nature; children's; Tasha Tudor; cookbooks.
Hours:	Mon-Sat 10-6. Sun by chance or appointment. Closed Feb.
Services:	Search service, accepts want lists, mail order.
Travel:	Weedsport exit off NY Twy. Take Rte. 34 south to Auburn. Turn right and proceed west on Rte. 5 in front of Holiday Inn for about 5 miles. Left at Free Bridge and proceed south on Rte. 90. Proceed for about 8½ miles on Rte. 90. The shop is in the center of the village. Map 10.

Credit Cards:	Yes
Owner:	Connie Tallcot
Year Estab:	1987
Comments:	A real find and most certainly worth a visit. While the collection is not tremendous in size, the books have been carefully selected and are most reasonably priced; the prices of the children's series books we saw were a fraction of the price of similar books offered in some specialty shops. The owner operates a second shop in nearby Seneca Falls.

Upper Nyack

The Book-Nook (NY234)   (914)358-1114
366 Route 9W North 10960

Collection:	General stock, magazines and ephemera.
# of Volumes:	10,000
Specialties:	Autobiography; biography; film; children's; poetry.
Hours:	Mon, Wed-Fri 12-4. Sat and Sun 12-5:30. Tue by chance or appointment.
Services:	Accepts want lists, mail order.
Travel:	Exit 11 off NY Twy. Proceed north on Rte. 9W. Shop is on the left, about 3/4 of a mile after Main St. and just past the hospital. Map 11.
Owner:	Mildred Markowitz
Comments:	This stand alone shop, located next to an antique shop, offers a wide variety of books in mixed condition, plus a good stock of ephemera, including magazines, sheet music and pamphlets. The shelves are well marked. While it is possible to find many fascinating items here, don't look for bargains.

Warrensburg

Antiques & Decorative Arts (NY235)   (518) 623-3426
84 Main Street 12885

Collection:	General stock.
# of Volumes:	6,000
Hours:	Thu-Sat 10-5. Sun 12-5.
Services:	Accepts want lists, mail order.
Travel:	Map 8.
Credit Cards:	No
Owner:	Brother Calvin
Year Estab:	1985

Watertown

Barracks Books (NY236)   (315) 782-9471
302 Court Street (Globe Mall) 13601

Collection:	General stock.
# of Volumes:	2,000
Specialties:	Military; hunting; fishing; children's.
Hours:	Tue-Fri 10:30-5:30. Sat 10:30-5.
Services:	Accepts want lists, mail order.
Travel:	Exit 46 off I-81. Proceed east on Coffeen St. for about 2 miles until street comes to an end at a blinking red light. Proceed straight through light into parking lot for Globe Mall. Shop is on main level. Map 6.
Credit Cards:	No
Owner:	Frederick S. Lockwood, IV
Year Estab:	1987

Watervliet

The Book Barn (NY237)   (518) 786-1368
184 Troy-Schenectady Road 12189

Collection:	General stock of remainders, paperback and hardcover.
# of Volumes:	45,000
Hours:	Mon-Sat 10-8. Sun 12-5.
Services:	Accepts want lists.
Travel:	Latham exit off Rte. 87. Proceed east on Rte. 2 (Troy-Schenectady Rd) for about 3 miles. Left at light into Colonnade Shopping Center. Map 8.
Credit Cards:	Yes
Owner:	Daniel Driggs
Year Estab:	1991
Comments:	This shop stocks remainders, used paperbacks and a modest number of recent vintage and older hardcover fiction titles. We saw few items that stirred our imagination and don't recommend going out of your way to visit.

West Hempstead

Mystery Bookstore (Oceanside Books) (NY238)   (516) 565-4710
173-A Woodfield Road 11552

Collection:	Specialty books and ephemera.
# of Volumes:	8,000

Specialties:	Mystery; detective.
Hours:	Thu-Sat 12-6.
Services:	Appraisals, search service, catalog, accepts want lists, collection development (for clients only).
Travel:	Exit 18 (Eagle Ave) off Southern State Pkwy. Left and proceed on Eagle for 3 blocks to light. Right on Woodfield. The shop is 3/4 mile ahead on right in a building that looks like the garage for the adjoining single family house. Map 13.
Credit Cards:	Yes
Owner:	Adrienne & Jeffrey Williams
Year Estab:	1973
Comments:	If you're one of the legion of mystery book buyers, you should fall in love with this small, compact shop. Unlike so many other mystery specialty shops that concentrate heavily in current and more recent fiction, this shop, in addition to having a healthy supply of modern mysteries, is also quite strong in the golden age of mystery and detective fiction. The owner travels far and wide to assure her customers pristine copies of desirable titles. Approximately 85% of the collection consists of used titles.

West Hurley

Many Feathers Books (NY239)   (914) 679-6305
Routes 28 & 375
Mailing address: PO Box 117 Lake Hill 12448

Collection:	General stock.
# of Volumes:	10,000
Specialties:	Literature.
Hours:	Daily except Wed 10-5.
Services:	Appraisals, search service, accepts want lists, mail order.
Travel:	On Rte. 28 at intersection with Rte. 375. Map 12.
Credit Cards:	No
Owner:	Anthony Sackett
Year Estab:	1980

West Oneonta

Popek's Pages Past (NY241)   (607) 432-8036
Route 23 West 13861
Mailing address: RD #3, Box 44C Oneonta 13820

Collection:	General stock and ephemera.
# of Volumes:	20,000
Specialties:	Children's literary sets; literature.

Hours:	Sat & Sun 10-5, or by appointment.
Services:	Accepts want lists, mail order.
Travel:	Exit 13 off I-88. Proceed on Rte. 205 North to Rte. 23 West. Look for a green barn with a 16' knight outside. The barn is set back from the road behind a yellow two story house about six houses past the post office. Map 9.
Credit Cards:	No
Owner:	Pete & Connie Popek
Year Estab:	1983
Comments:	Most of the books in this bi-level barn are located on the second floor. The books, many of an older vintage, are reasonably priced. Although the stock displayed appears to be less than what is indicated above, it is quite possible that you might find some long lost item you've been searching for.

West Park

Gordon & Gordon Booksellers (NY242)   (914) 384-6361
Route 9W   Fax: (914) 384-6800
Mailing address: PO Box 128   12493

Collection:	General stock.
# of Volumes:	10,000+
Specialties:	Children's; modern first editions; local history; radical.
Hours:	Wed-Sat 10-5. Closed in Feb.
Services:	Appraisals, catalog, accepts want lists.
Travel:	Exit 18 off NY Twy. Proceed on Rte. 299 east for 6 miles, then 4 miles north on Rte. 9W. The shop is on the right in a slate colored stand alone building. Map 12.
Credit Cards:	No
Owner:	Anne & Louis Gordon
Year Estab:	1986
Comments:	This small and attractively decorated shop, located adjacent to the owner's home, is absolutely worth visiting for anyone interested in quality books. The subject matter of many of the books is unusual and prices, considering the rare nature of many of the titles, are moderate. Where else would you find an entire shelf devoted to the works of William Morris? Needless to say, we were most impressed by this modest sized but hardly modest collection.

White Plains

Bryn Mawr Book Shop (NY243)   (914) 946-5356
170 Grand Street 10601

Collection:	General stock.
Hours:	Mon-Sat 10-4.
Travel:	Between Post Rd. and Quarapos in downtown. Map 11.
Comments:	Operated by volunteers for the benefit of college scholarship fund. Books are donated.

Williamson

Yankee Peddler Book Shop (NY244)   (315) 589-2063
3895 Route 104
Mailing address: P.O. Box 118 Pultneyville 14538

Collection:	General stock, ephemera and prints.
# of Volumes:	20,000
Specialties:	Aeronautics; Americana; Arabia; autographs; black studies; children's first editions; illustrated; music; Roycroft Press; women's studies; Great Lake Maritime.
Hours:	Mon-Wed 10-5. Thu-Sun 1-5.
Services:	Appraisals, search service.
Travel:	Manchester exit off NY Twy. Proceed north on Rte. 21 to Rte. 104. West on Rte. 104. Shop is 1/2 mile ahead. Map 16.
Credit Cards:	Yes
Owner:	Jane S. & John Westerberg
Year Estab:	1970
Comments:	Like its sister shop in Rochester, this roadside establishment has a large collection of mixed vintage titles with a good portion of older items. Our prejudice is that since we found an item to purchase, we believe there is a good chance that the average browser may experience the same good luck.

Woodstock

Blue Mountain Books & Manuscripts, Ltd. (NY245)   (914) 679-5991
9 Rock City Road
Mailing address: PO Box 363 Catskill 12444

Collection:	General stock and ephemera.
# of Volumes:	10,000
Specialties:	Literature; scholarly books; children's; illustrated; Americana; travel; history; Judaica; science; occult; history of ideas; art; decorative art; architecture; signed books; autographs.
Hours:	Fri & Sat 11-6. Sun 11-5.
Services:	Appraisals, catalog.
Travel:	Exit 22 off NY Twy. Proceed on Rte. 212 west for about 9 miles

to downtown. Right at village square on Rock City Rd. The shop is down the first driveway on left. Map 12.

Credit Cards:	Yes
Owner:	Ric Zank
Year Estab:	1990
Comments:	Seasoned book hunters learn quickly that the size of a shop does not always denote the quality of the books inside, nor the likelihood of finding something one is looking for. We think this modest sized bi-level shop is definitely worth visiting and we believe you will indeed see many titles worth perusing. The abundance of chairs and a comfortable sofa are a clear indication that the owner hopes his visitors will enjoy browsing his collection and will spend time in his shop. Prices are quite reasonable.

Reader's Quarry (NY246)   (914) 679-9572
70 Tinker Street 12498

Collection:	General stock.
# of Volumes:	5,000
Hours:	May-Nov: Daily except Tue 12:30-5. Dec-Apr: Thu-Sat 12:30-5.
Services:	Appraisals, accepts want lists.
Travel:	See above. Rte. 212 becomes Tinker St. in village. Shop is about 3 blocks past village square on right. Map 12.
Credit Cards:	No
Owner:	Margaret Lauchner
Comments:	Although relatively modest in terms of square footage, this small shop packs in a lot of books for its size. The books are in varied condition with some unusual titles mixed in with more common stock. We managed to purchase three books of 1930's and 1940's vintage we had not previously seen. The shop's entrance is up a few steps.

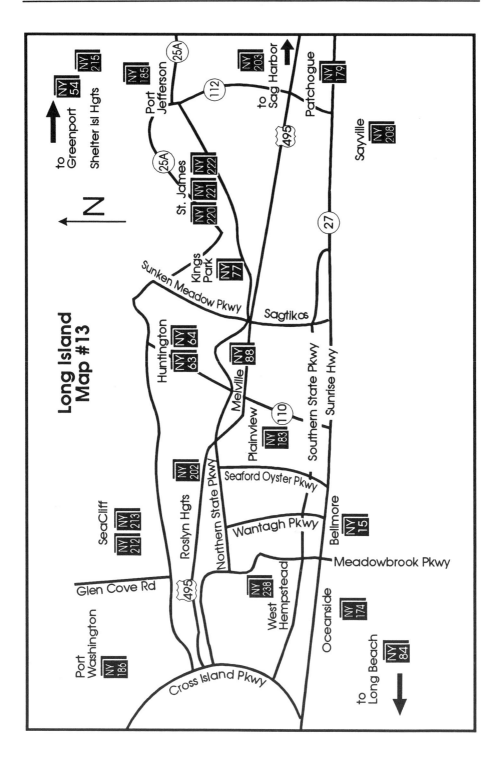

Long Island
Map #13

Albany

AMP Books   (518) 438-2156
8 Ableman Avenue 12203

Collection:	General stock.
# of Volumes:	7,000
Hours:	Best to call between 8-10 AM or 11 PM-midnight.
Services:	Appraisals, accepts want lists.
Credit Cards:	No
Owner:	Arnold M. Patashnick
Year Estab:	1978

Michael R. Linehan, Bookseller   (518) 436-4669
275 North Pearl Street 12207

Collection:	General stock.
# of Volumes:	5,000+
Specialties:	Rare (all subjects, except modern fiction).
Services:	Appraisals, catalog.
Credit Cards:	No
Year Estab:	1975

Amherst

Kevin T. Ransom - Bookseller   (716) 839-1510
116 Audubon Drive
Mailing address: PO Box 176 14226

Collection:	Specialty and limited general stock.
# of Volumes:	8,000
Specialties:	Modern first editions; children's illustrated; fine bindings; detective; science fiction.
Services:	Appraisals, accepts want lists, occasional catalog.
Credit Cards:	No
Year Estab:	1977

Arkville

Heritage Publications   (914) 586-3810
Box 335, Church Street, A21 12406   Fax: (914) 586-2797

Collection:	Specialty
# of Volumes:	3,000
Specialties:	Cookbooks
Services:	Appraisals, catalog, accepts want lists.
Credit Cards:	No
Owner:	Mary Barile
Year Estab:	1986

Aurora

Talbothays Books   (315) 364-7550
Box 118, Black Rock Road 13026

Collection: General stock
# of Volumes: 6,000-8,000
Services: Search service, catalog, accepts want lists.
Credit Cards: No
Owner: Paul C. Mitchell
Year Estab: 1974

Bakers Mills

Heyday Antiques & Books   (518) 251-2217
Box 111, Bartman Road 12811

Collection: Specialty
# of Volumes: 300-400
Specialties: Adirondacks; sports.
Services: Appraisals, accepts want lists.
Credit Cards: No
Owner: Tom Akstens
Year Estab: 1986

Bayport

Maestro Books   (516) 472-1222
PO Box 848 11705

Collection: General stock.
# of Volumes: 5,000+
Specialties: Children's
Services: Accepts want lists, mail order.
Credit Cards: No
Owner: Michael Signorelli

Bedford

Judith Bowman - Books   (914) 234-7543
Pound Ridge Road 10506   Fax: (914) 234-0122

Collection: Specialty
# of Volumes: 25,000
Specialties: Hunting; fishing; allied outdoor sports and natural history.
Services: Appraisals, search service, catalog, accepts want lists.
Credit Cards: No
Year Estab: 1980

Big Flats

Best Cellar Books   (607) 562-3781
2700 County Line Drive 14814

Collection:	General stock and ephemera.
# of Volumes:	15,000
Hours:	July and August only.
Services:	Search service, accepts want lists.
Credit Cards:	No
Owner:	Nancy Doutt
Year Estab:	1984

Brewster

Olana Gallery   (914) 279-8077
2 Carillon Road 10509   Fax: (914) 279-8079

Collection:	Specialty
# of Volumes:	8,000
Specialties:	Art (American paintings and sculpture).
Services:	Appraisals, search service, accepts want lists, mail order.
Credit Cards:	No
Owner:	Bernard Rosenberg
Year Estab:	1971

Buffalo

Frontier Antiques   (716) 823-9415
308 Choate Avenue 14220

Collection:	General stock of hardcover and paperbacks.
# of Volumes:	7,000
Services:	Catalog
Credit Cards:	No
Owner:	Janice Clifford
Year Estab:	1987
Comments:	The shop also sells collectibles.

Canaan

Sydney R. Smith Sporting Books   (518) 794-8998
PO Box 81 12029

Collection:	Specialty
Specialties:	Horses; dogs; fishing; shooting.
Services:	Appraisals, search service, occasional catalog, accepts want lists, mail order.
Credit Cards:	No
Owner:	Camilla P. Smith

Catskill

McDonald's Book Ends   (518) 943-3520
125 Water Street 12414

Collection:	General stock.
# of Volumes:	100,000
Specialties:	Local history; Hudson River; New York State.
Services:	Appraisals, accepts want lists, mail order.
Credit Cards:	No
Owner:	Francis McDonald
Year Estab:	1959

Cattaraugus

Rockland Bookman   (716) 257-5121
102 Washington Street 14719   Fax: (716) 257-9116

Collection:	General stock.
# of Volumes:	5,000
Specialties:	Fine printing; fine bindings; rare; color plate; Americana; manuscripts, autographs.
Services:	Appraisals, catalog, accepts want lists.
Credit Cards:	No
Owner:	Thomas Cullen
Year Estab:	1968

Clarence

Vi & Si's Antiques   (716) 634-4488
8970 Main Street 14031

Collection:	Specialty
# of Volumes:	400
Specialties:	Music (automatic and mechanical); catalogs, advertising books.
Services:	Appraisals, catalog, accepts want lists.
Credit Cards:	Yes
Year Estab:	1950

Clarence Center

Deirdre's Books   (716) 741-9236
8110 Northfield Road 14032

Collection:	General stock.
# of Volumes:	3,000
Specialties:	Children's; illustrated; cookbooks.
Services:	Appraisals, search service, accepts want lists, mail order.
Credit Cards:	No
Year Estab:	1984

Cold Spring Harbor

Well Read Books   (516) 692-8257
2 Folly Field Court 11724   (516) 261-7373

Collection:	General stock and ephemera.

# of Volumes:	10,000
Specialties:	Children's; children's series; illustrated; New York.
Services:	Accepts want lists.
Credit Cards:	No
Owner:	Bea Coryell & Penelope Daly
Year Estab:	1989

Cooperstown

Classical Forms Bookstore   (607) 547-6135
PO Box 668 13326

Collection:	Specialty
# of Volumes:	1,000+
Specialties:	Ancient civilizations of Greece, Rome, Egypt and Middle East.
Services:	Search service, catalog, accepts want lists.
Credit Cards:	No
Owner:	Linda M. Medwid
Year Estab:	1991

Omnibus Books   (607) 547-2763
County Route 28
Mailing Address: RR 1, Box 21 13326

Collection:	Specialty
# of Volumes:	7,000
Specialties:	Natural history; birds; insects; reptiles; natural history writers; travel.
Credit Cards:	No
Owner:	George & Jane Hymas
Year Estab:	1986

Corning

Michael Gilmartin, Bookseller   (607) 936-3237
288 East 3rd Street 14830

Collection:	General stock.
# of Volumes:	2,000
Specialties:	Baseball; military (20th century).
Services:	Search service, catalog, accepts want lists.
Credit Cards:	No
Year Estab:	1978

Cragsmoor

Cragsmoor Books   (914) 647-5588
Clark Road, PO Box 66 12420

Collection:	General stock.
# of Volumes:	8,000

Services: Search service, accepts want lists, mail order.
Credit Cards: No
Owner: L. Kroul
Year Estab: 1970

Deansboro

Stuffinder   (315) 841-4444
PO Box 222 13328

Collection: Specialty books and ephemera
# of Volumes: 3,000
Specialties: Aviation; transportation.
Services: Accepts want lists, mail order, appraisals (specialty areas only).
Credit Cards: No
Owner: Tom Heitzman
Year Estab: 1986

Delanson

Speleobooks   (518) 295-7978
RD 1, Box 349, Sheldon Road   Fax: (518) 295-7981
Mailing address: PO Box 10 Schoharie 12157

Collection: Specialty used and new books and related items.
# of Volumes: 1,500
Specialties: Caves; bats.
Services: Appraisals, search service, catalog, accepts want lists.
Credit Cards: Yes
Owner: Emily Davis Mobley
Year Estab: 1977

Dobbs Ferry

N. & N. Pavlov   (914) 693-1776
37 Oakdale Drive 10522

Collection: Specialty
# of Volumes: 500
Specialties: Early printed books; books about early printed books; illuminated manuscripts.
Services: Mail order.
Credit Cards: No
Owner: Nicolai & Nina Pavlov
Year Estab: 1976

Roy Young   (914) 693-6116
145 Palisade Street 10522   Fax: (914) 693-6275

Collection: General stock.
# of Volumes: 20,000

Specialties:	Architecture; art; private presses, books on books; scholarly.
Hours:	Mon-Fri 9-5.
Services:	Appraisals, catalog, accepts want lists.
Credit Cards:	Yes
Owner:	Roy Young
Year Estab:	1980

Dolgeville

Watkins Natural History Books   (518) 568-2280
7036 State Highway 29 13329

Collection:	Specialty
# of Volumes:	8,500
Specialties:	Mammalogy; ornithology; herpetology; ichtyology.
Services:	Appraisals, search service, catalog.
Credit Cards:	Yes
Owner:	Larry C. Watkins
Year Estab:	1971

East Northport

M & M Books   (516) 368-4858
21 Perth Place 11731

Collection:	Specialty
# of Volumes:	9,000
Specialties:	Americana; American history; books on books; Judaica; regional history; American literature; English literature.
Services:	Search service, catalog, accepts want lists.
Credit Cards:	No
Owner:	Marvin & Miriam Feinstein
Year Estab:	1987

Merlin   (516) 368-7371
28 Orton Drive 11731

Collection:	Specialty books and ephemera.
# of Volumes:	4,000
Specialties:	Military; history; first signed editions.
Services:	Appraisals and search service (specialty areas only); occasional catalog.
Credit Cards:	No
Owner:	Edward & Lilian Oresky
Year Estab:	1968

Edmeston

Ingeborg Quitzau, Antiquarian Books   (607) 965-8605
PO Box 5160, Route 80 13335

Collection:	General stock.

# of Volumes:	3,000-5,000
Specialties:	Modern literature; children's illustrated; books about books; private presses; beat literature; miniature books; German books (especially literary first editions).
Services:	Search service; catalog; accepts want lists.
Credit Cards:	No
Year Estab:	1971

Fayetteville

Ronald W. Becker   (315) 637-3273
197 Brookside Lane 13066

Collection:	General stock.
# of Volumes:	8,000
Specialties:	Local history.
Services:	Accepts want lists, mail order.
Credit Cards:	No
Year Estab:	1990

Jim Hodgson Books   (315) 637-6264
908 South Manlius Street 13066

Collection:	General stock.
# of Volumes:	10,000
Specialties:	Americana; travel; voyages; fishing; hunting; New York State.
Services:	Accepts want lists, mail order.
Credit Cards:	No
Year Estab:	1980

Freedom

D'Shams-Horse Books & Treasures   (716) 676-3036
10317 Sandbank Road 14065

Collection:	Specialty
# of Volumes:	500
Specialties:	Horses, with sub specialty in Arabian horses.
Services:	Search service, catalog.
Credit Cards:	Yes
Owner:	Marion V. Roth
Year Estab:	1984

Garrison

Antipodean Books, Maps & Prints   (914) 424-3867
4 Depot Square 10524   Fax: (914) 424-3617
Mailing Address: PO Box 189 Cold Spring 10516

Collection:	Specialty books, maps and prints.
# of Volumes:	3,000

Specialties:	Hudson River; Antarctica; Australia.
Services:	Accepts want lists, appraisals, catalog, search service, international auction bidding.
Credit Cards:	No
Owner:	David Lilburne
Year Estab:	1976
Comments:	Closed October-December. See also Cold Spring in Open Shop section.

Getzville

Roy W. Clare - Antiquarian and Uncommon Books   (716) 688-8723
47 Woodshire South
Mailing address: PO Box 136 14068-0136

Collection:	Specialty
# of Volumes:	200
Specialties:	Early printing; witchcraft (to 1750); early original bindings (15th-17th centuries); early illustrated (15th-17th centuries).
Services:	Appraisals, catalog.
Credit Cards:	No
Owner:	Roy W. Clare
Year Estab:	1969

Glen Head

Xerxes Fine and Rare Books and Documents   (516) 671-6235
818 Glen Cove Avenue   Fax: (516) 676-0243
Mailing address: PO Box 428 Glen Cove 11545

Collection:	General stock.
# of Volumes:	50,000+
Specialties:	Americana; medicine; science; Latin America; travel, China; psychology; scholarly; unusual non-fiction.
Services:	Mail order.
Credit Cards:	No
Owner:	Carol & Dennis Travis
Year Estab:	1980

Great Neck

Estates Of Mind   (516) 487-5160
85 Bayview Avenue 11021   Fax: (516) 487-5160

Collection:	Specialty
Specialties:	Rare literature; philosophy; science; alchemy; occult; fine printing; illustrated.
Services:	Catalog
Owner:	David Waxman

Greenwich

Country Books   (518) 692-2585
RD 1, Box 200 12834

Collection: General stock.
Specialties: Adirondacks; children's; illustrated.
Services: Accepts want lists.
Credit Cards: No
Owner: Barbara Wells
Year Estab: 1974

Hastings-on-Hudson

Christopher P. Stephens   (914) 478-2522
7 Terrace Drive 10706

Collection: Specialty
# of Volumes: 50,000
Specialties: Modern first editions; science fiction; fiction in translation; letters and manuscripts; proof copies; signed; sets.
Services: Appraisals, search service, catalog, accepts want lists.
Credit Cards: Yes
Year Estab: 1970

Hempstead

Stanson's Books   (516) 565-0761
6 Sealey Avenue, #3L 11550

Collection: General stock.
# of Volumes: 8,000
Specialties: Art; military; entertainment.
Services: Appraisals, accepts want lists, mail order.

High Falls

Ridge Books   (914) 687-9774
150 Mohonk Road
Mailing address: PO Box 58 Stone Ridge 12484

Collection: Specialty
# of Volumes: 1,000
Specialties: American literature (20th century).
Services: Catalog, accepts want lists.
Owner: Peter E. Scott

Ithaca

D. C. Kellogg   (607) 273-0709
10 Hawthorne Circle 14850

Collection:	General stock.
# of Volumes:	20,000
Specialties:	Modern first editions; literary criticism.
Services:	Search service, accepts want lists, catalog.
Credit Cards:	No
Owner:	D.C. Kellogg
Year Estab:	1982

Jericho

Gaslight   (516) 938-9510
9 Lewis Avenue 11753   Fax: (516) 433-9363

Collection:	Specialty
Specialties:	Magazines; ephemera.
Services:	Accepts want lists, search service, mail order.
Credit Cards:	No
Owner:	Ruth Kravette
Year Estab:	1968

Johnstown

Bob's Book Business   (518) 762-8919
3 Spring Street 12095

Collection:	General stock.
# of Volumes:	10,000
Specialties:	Science fiction; mystery; occult.
Services:	Accepts want lists.
Credit Cards:	No
Owner:	Robert Komornik
Year Estab:	1988

Katonah

Katonah Book Scout   (914) 232-5768
75 Meadow Lane 10536

Collection:	General stock and ephemera.
# of Volumes:	5,000-6,000
Specialties:	Black studies; children's; regional American history; performing arts; literary first editions.
Services:	Appraisals, catalog and accepts want lists in black studies only.
Credit Cards:	No
Owner:	Anne M. Lange
Year Estab:	1980
Comments:	A free bonus book is offered with each purchase.

Kinderhook

L.E. Gobrecht - Books   (518) 758-7341
Mile Hill Road 12106

Collection: Specialty
Specialties: American culture; architecture; decorative arts.
Services: Accepts want lists, mail order.
Owner: L.E. Gobrecht
Year Estab: 1969

Larchmont

Dog Ink   (914) 834-9029
46 Cooper Lane 10538   Fax: (914) 834-9029

Collection: Specialty books and art.
Specialties: Dogs
Services: Appraisals, catalog (by breed), accepts want lists.
Credit Cards: Yes
Owner: Kathy Darling
Year Estab: 1974

F. A. Bernett Inc.   (914) 834-3026
2001 Palmer Avenue 10538   Fax: (914) 834-0084

Collection: Specialty books and ephemera.
# of Volumes: 15,000
Specialties: Art; architecture; archaeology; theater; dance.
Services: Appraisals, catalog, accepts want lists.
Credit Cards: Yes
Owner: Peter Bernett & Lawrence Malam
Year Estab: 1942

Leicester

Warbirds & Warriors   (716) 382-3234
PO Box 266 14481

Collection: Specialty new and out of print.
# of Volumes: 1,200
Specialties: World War II aircraft and armor.
Services: Catalog, accepts want lists.
Credit Cards: No
Owner: Tom Roffe
Year Estab: 1987

Liverpool

Edward J. Monarski, Books & Military Souvenirs   (315) 652-0267
119 Woodside Lane 13090-2258

Collection:	Specialty books and souvenirs.
# of Volumes:	3,000+
Specialties:	Military (Civil War to present).
Services:	Appraisals, search service, catalog, accepts want lists.
Year Estab:	1960's

Mamaroneck

Jens J. Christoffersen, Rare Books   (914) 698-3495
221 S. Barry Avenue 10543

Collection:	Specialty
# of Volumes:	1,000
Specialties:	Illustrated; Greek and Latin classics; press books; books about books.
Services:	Appraisals, catalog.
Credit Cards:	No
Year Estab:	1930's

Elaine S. Feiden   (914) 698-6504
525 Lawn Terrace 10543

Collection:	Specialty
Specialties:	First editions; literature; architecture; private presses, illustrated; art.
Credit Cards:	No
Year Estab:	1976

George Lewis/Golfiana   (914) 698-4579
PO Box 291 10543

Collection:	Specialty books, magazines and ephemera.
# of Volumes:	1,500
Specialties:	Golf
Services:	Appraisals, search service, catalog, accepts want lists.
Credit Cards:	Yes
Year Estab:	1980

Manhasset

Margaret Zervas, Rare Books   (516) 767-0907
PO Box 562 11030

Collection:	Specialty
# of Volumes:	5,000
Specialties:	Literature; printing.
Services:	Mail order.

Mattituck

Herb Jacobs, Rare Books   (516) 298-4135
PO Box 1286 11952   Fax: (516) 298-4181

Collection:	Specialty
# of Volumes:	3,500
Specialties:	Magic; aviation.
Services:	Appraisals (specialty areas only); occasional catalog, mail order.
Credit Cards:	No
Year Estab:	1978

Middletown

T. Emmett Henderson   (914) 343-1038
130 West Main Street 10940   Fax: (914) 343-1038

Collection:	General stock.
# of Volumes:	13,000
Specialties:	American Indian; Americana.
Services:	Appraisals, accepts want lists, catalog.
Credit Cards:	No
Year Estab:	1948

Monsey

Judaix Art   (914) 352-0359
PO Box 248 10952

Collection:	Specialty books, prints and ephemera.
Specialties:	Judaica
Services:	Accepts want lists.
Credit Cards:	No
Year Estab:	1980

Montrose

Gary White - Bookseller   (914) 739-3460
17 Kings Ferry Road   10548

Collection:	General stock.
# of Volumes:	4,000
Specialties:	New York; regional Americana; Western Americana; sports; boxing; modern first editions; Civil War; true crime; John Steinbeck.
Services:	Accepts want lists, mail order.
Credit Cards:	No
Year Estab:	1988

New City

Larry McGill - Books   (914) 634-0729
41 Third Street 10956

Collection:	Specialty
# of Volumes:	3,000-4,000
Specialties:	Americana; arts; classics; theater; travel; biography; literature;

history; military; religion; poetry; selected fiction.
Credit Cards: No
Year Estab: 1978

New York City
(Bronx)

Denbry Books   (718) 881-7459
3555 Rochambeau Avenue 10467

Collection: General stock.
# of Volumes: 5,000-10,000
Services: Appraisals, mail order, accepts want lists.
Credit Cards: No
Owner: Ray Denbry
Year Estab: 1950's

New York City
(Brooklyn)

The American Experience   (718) 522-2665
254 4th Avenue 11215

Collection: Specialty books, art and ephemera.
# of Volumes: 900
Specialties: Western Americana, including military, Indians, gold rush, territorial imprints, overland journals, cattle trade, cowboys, outlaws, fur trade.
Services: Accepts want lists, mail order.
Credit Cards: No
Owner: Gordon C. Turner
Year Estab: 1966

De Simone Company, Booksellers   (718) 965-1392
184 Eighth Avenue 11215

Collection: Specialty
# of Volumes: 600
Specialties: Rare books.
Services: Appraisals, catalog, accepts want lists.
Credit Cards: No
Owner: Daniel De Simone
Year Estab: 1978

Enchanted Books   (718) 891-5241
2435 Ocean Avenue, 6J 11229

Collection: General stock.
Specialties: Illustrated; children's; illustrated Judaica; literature..
Services: Search service, catalog, accepts want lists.
Credit Cards: No

Owner:	Susan Weiser Liebegott
Year Estab:	1985

Lawrence Feinberg Rare Books   (718) 235-7106
68 Ashford Street 11207

Collection:	Specialty
Specialties:	Rare books.
Services:	Appraisals, accepts want lists, catalog.
Credit Cards:	No
Year Estab:	1977

Yosef Goldman Rare Books & Manuscripts   (718) 434-4088
750 East 18th Street 11230   Fax: (718) 421-4887

Collection:	Specialty books and manuscripts
Specialties:	Judaica; Hebraica.
Services:	Appraisals, accepts want lists, catalog.
Credit Cards:	No
Year Estab:	1973

Stephen Lupack   (718) 834-0310
247 President Street 11231

Collection:	Specialty
# of Volumes:	2,000-3,000
Specialties:	Literary first editions (19th and 20th centuries).
Services:	Lists, accepts want lists, mail order.
Credit Cards:	No

Rona Schneider Fine Prints & Rare Books   (718) 858-9297
12 Monroe Place 11201   Fax: (718) 875-5121

Collection:	Specialty
# of Volumes:	250
Specialties:	American art (1850-1920); art reference; graphic art.
Services:	Accepts want lists, mail order.
Credit Cards	No
Year Estab:	1978

Select Books-Richard L. Hoffman   (718) 965-8442
420 12th Street, #F-3R 11215

Collection:	Specialty
# of Volumes:	5,000
Specialties:	Signed books; manuscripts; autographs; black studies; modern literature; sports; film; theater.
Services:	Appraisals, catalog, accepts want lists.
Credit Cards:	No
Year Estab:	1987

New York City
(Manhattan)

Arcade Books   (212) 724-5371
PO Box 5176, FDR Station 10150-5176

Collection:	Specialty
# of Volumes:	7,000
Specialties:	Architecture; design; city planning; New York City; printmaking; art.
Services:	Search service, catalog, accepts want lists.
Credit Cards:	No
Owner:	Michael T. Sillerman
Year Estab:	1980

Asian Rare Books   (212) 316-5334
175 West 93rd Street, Ste. 16D 10025   Fax: (212) 316-5334

Collection:	Specialty
# of Volumes:	3,000
Specialties:	Asia; Orient; Middle East.
Services:	Mail order, lists.
Credit Cards:	No
Owner:	Stephen Feldman
Year Estab:	1974

Aurora Fine Books   (212) 947-0422
547 West 27th Street, Ste.570 10001   Fax: (212) 947-0422

Collection:	Specialty
# of Volumes:	12,000
Specialties:	Judaica; art (American, European, Islamic, Jewish); classical studies (Greek and Roman culture); German (all aspects).
Services:	Catalog
Credit Cards:	No
Owner:	Dr. Y. Mashiah
Year Estab:	1989

Rick Barandes - Periodicals   (212) 941-0826
41 North Moore Street, #6 10013   Fax: (212) 941-0826

Collection:	Magazines
# of Volumes:	40,000
Specialties:	American and foreign periodicals from 1800's-1970's.
Services:	Search service, collection development.
Credit Cards:	No
Year Estab:	1984

C. Richard Becker, Bookseller   (212) 243-3789
PO Box 20261, London Terrace Station 10011

Collection:	Specialty

# of Volumes:	3,000
Specialties:	Fine art; decorative art; antique reference.
Services:	Appraisals, catalog, accepts want lists.
Credit Cards:	No
Year Estab:	1977

Biography House   (212) 714-2004
547 West 27th Street, 6th Fl. 10001

Collection:	Specialty
# of Volumes:	36,000
Specialties:	Biography; autobiography; diaries; memoirs.
Services:	Accepts want lists, mail order.
Credit Cards:	No
Owner:	Ned Pollsky
Year Estab:	1986

Black Sun Books   (212) 688-6622
157 East 57th Street 10022   Fax: (212) 751-6529

Collection:	Specialty
# of Volumes:	2,000
Specialties:	French illustrated; rare literature.
Services:	Catalog, appraisals.
Credit Cards:	Yes
Owner:	Harvey Tucker
Year Estab:	1968

The Bohemian Bookworm   (212) 678-6011
215 West 95th Street 10025   Fax: (212) 678-6011

Collection:	Specialty
# of Volumes:	4,000
Specialties:	Travel; adventure; cookbooks; natural history; domestic arts; European history.
Services:	Appraisals, search service, accepts want lists, mail order.
Credit Cards:	Yes
Owner:	Myrna Adolph & Ronald Morris
Year Estab:	1989

The Book Chest   (212) 246-8955
322 West 57th Street, 34S 10019

Collection:	Specialty
# of Volumes:	5,000
Specialties:	Humor
Services:	Mail order, search service, accepts want lists.
Credit Cards:	No
Owner:	Estelle Chessid
Year Estab:	1972

Book Ranger   (212) 924-4957
105 Charles Street 10014

Collection:	General stock.
# of Volumes:	3,000
Specialties:	Americana; travel.
Services:	Search service, mail order.
Credit Cards:	No
Owner:	Shepard Rikfin
Year Estab:	1974

William G. Boyer   (212) 724-9402
Box 763, Planetarium Station 10024

Collection:	Specialty
# of Volumes:	3,000
Specialties:	Americana; architecture; art; illustrated; children's; music; travel, plate books (on occasion).
Services:	Search service, accepts want lists, mail order.
Credit Cards:	No
Year Estab:	1970

Brazen Head Books   (212) 879-9830
235 East 84th Street 10028

Collection:	General stock.
# of Volumes:	10,000
Specialties:	Modern first editions.
Services:	Search service, catalog in planning stage, accepts want lists, mail order.
Credit Cards:	No
Owner:	Michael Seidenberg
Year Estab:	1978

James F. Carr   (212) 535-8110
227 East 81st Street 10028

Collection:	General stock.
# of Volumes:	20,000
Specialties:	Christmas keepsake; Mari Sandoz; American art and artists; exhibition catalogs; pamphlets.
Credit Cards:	No
Year Estab:	1959

Howard D. Daitz-Photographica   (212) 929-8987
PO Box 530 10011

Collection:	Specialty books, images and autographs.
# of Volumes:	3,000
Specialties:	Photography
Credit Cards:	No
Year Estab:	1970

Dramatis Personae - Booksellers
71 Lexington Avenue 10010

(212) 679-3705
Fax: (212) 679-3705

Collection:	Specialty books, prints and ephemera.
# of Volumes:	700
Specialties:	Theatre; magic; puppetry; pyrotechnics; circus.
Services:	Catalog, accepts want lists..
Credit Cards:	No
Owner:	Jonathan & Lisa Reynolds
Year Estab:	1986

El Cascajero-The Old Spanish Book Mine
506 West Broadway 10012

(212) 254-0905

Collection:	Specialty
# of Volumes:	5,000-10,000
Specialties:	Hispanica
Services:	Appraisals, search service, catalog, accepts want lists.
Credit Cards:	No
Owner:	Anthony Gran
Year Estab:	1956

Ex Libris
160A East 70th Street 10021

(212) 249-2618
Fax: (212) 249-1465

Collection:	Specialty
# of Volumes:	20,000
Specialties:	20th century European artists.
Services:	Occasional catalog, accepts want lists, mail order.
Credit Cards:	No
Owner:	Elaine Cohen
Year Estab:	1975

Richard C. Faber, Jr.
230 East 15th Street 10003

(212) 228-7353
Fax: (212) 533-9124

Collection:	Specialty books and ephemera.
Specialties:	Ocean liners.
Services:	Appraisals, catalog, accepts want lists.
Credit Cards:	Yes
Year Estab:	1980

VF Germack Professional Photography Collectors
1199 Park Avenue 10028

(212) 289-8411

Collection:	Specialty
# of Volumes:	2,000-3,000
Specialties:	Photography
Services:	Appraisals, mail order.
Credit Cards:	No
Owner:	V.F. Germack
Year Estab:	1978

Bruce Gimelson
305 East 24th Street 10010

(212) 889-4273
Fax: (212) 683-8305

Collection:	Specialty
Specialties:	Autographs; manuscripts; books from presidential libraries.
Services:	Appraisals, mail order.
Credit Cards:	No
Year Estab:	1964

Elliot Gordon/Books
150 East 69th Street 10021

(212) 861-2892
Fax: (212) 838-0380

Collection:	Specialty
# of Volumes:	2,000
Specialties:	Art
Services:	Search service, accepts want lists, mail order.
Credit Cards:	No
Year Estab:	1980

Gunson & Turner Books
166 East 63rd Street 10021

(212) 826-9381
Fax: (212) 980-5736

Collection:	Specialty
# of Volumes:	7,000-10,000
Specialties:	Fashion; photography; social history; first editions.
Services:	Appraisals, mail order.
Credit Cards:	No
Owner:	Shaun Gunson
Year Estab:	1988

Harvard Gallery
315 East 86th Street 10028

(212) 427-9191
Fax: (212) 427-5879

Collection:	Specialty books and related art.
# of Volumes:	300-500
Specialties:	Natural history; sports.
Services:	Accepts want lists, occasional catalog, mail order.
Credit Cards:	No
Owner:	Elliot Rayfield
Year Estab:	1988

J. N. Herlin, Inc.
40 Harrison Street, Apt. 25D 10013

(212) 732-1086

Collection:	Specialty
# of Volumes:	5,000
Specialties:	Art (from 1950).
Services:	Appraisals, catalog, accepts want lists.
Credit Cards:	No
Owner:	J.N. Herlin
Year Estab:	1971

Jonathan A. Hill, Bookseller, Inc.
470 West End Avenue 10024-4933

(212) 496-7856
Fax: (212) 496-9182

Collection:	Specialty
# of Volumes:	2,000-3,000
Specialties:	Science; medicine; natural history; bibliography.
Services:	Catalog
Credit Cards:	No
Year Estab:	1979

David Johnson
360 East 65th Street, #4G 10021

(212) 879-1853

Collection:	Specialty books, manuscripts and autographs.
# of Volumes:	1,000+
Specialties:	English & American literature (first editions); books about books; bibliography; fine printings; early printed books; proof copies.
Services:	Appraisals, catalog planned, accepts want lists, mail order.
Credit Cards:	No
Year Estab:	1969

Arnold B. Joseph
1140 Broadway, Rm 701 10001

(212) 532-0019

Collection:	Specialty books and ephemera.
# of Volumes:	7,000
Specialties:	Railroads; transportation.
Hours:	By chance Mon-Sat 11-7, but subject to change.
Services:	Search service, accepts want lists, mail order, lists.
Credit Cards:	No
Year Estab:	1970

Thomas Keith
237 Eldridge Street, #13 10002

(212) 533-8842

Collection:	Specialty
# of Volumes:	200
Specialties:	Robert Burns; Tennessee Williams.
Services:	Appraisals, mail order.
Credit Cards:	No
Year Estab:	1989

Judith & Peter Klemperer
400 Second Avenue 10010

(212) 684-5970

Collection:	General stock, ephemera and magazines.
# of Volumes:	5,000
Specialties:	New York City; New York State.
Services:	Catalog (New York City and State).
Credit Cards:	No
Year Estab:	1972

Kendra Krienke   (212) 580-6516
230 Central Park West 10024

Collection:	Specialty art only.
Specialties:	Original illustrations created for children's books.
Services:	Appraisals, catalog, accepts want lists.
Credit Cards:	No

Larry Lawrence Rare Sports   (212) 255-9230
150 Fifth Avenue, Room 842 10011

Collection:	Specialty
# of Volumes:	1,000-1,500
Specialties:	Sports
Services:	Appraisals, accepts want lists, catalog.
Credit Cards:	No
Year Estab:	1978

Janet Lehr Inc.   (212) 288-1802
PO Box 617 10028   Fax: (212) 288-6234

Collection:	Specialty
# of Volumes:	4,000
Specialties:	Photography
Services:	Appraisals, search service, accepts want lists, occasional catalog.
Credit Cards:	Yes
Year Estab:	1972

Andrew Makowsky Fine Books   (212) 675-7789
63 Downing Street 10014

Collection:	Specialty
# of Volumes:	4,000
Specialties:	Photography
Services:	Search service, catalog, accepts want lists.
Credit Cards:	No
Year Estab:	1989

David Malamud, Books   (212) 866-8478
382 Central Park West 10025

Collection:	General stock.
# of Volumes:	1,000+
Specialties:	First editions; history; politics (especially F.D. Roosevelt, A.E. Stevenson & J.F. Kennedy); city planning; New York City; fine art; music.
Credit Cards:	No
Year Estab:	1989

Issac Mendoza Book Company   (212) 362-1129
77 West 85th Street, 6F 10024

Collection:	Specialty
# of Volumes:	20,000
Specialties:	Science fiction; horror; mystery; fantasy; first editions.
Services:	Appraisals, accepts want lists.
Credit Cards:	No
Owner:	Walter Caron
Year Estab:	1972

Jeryl Metz, Books
697 West End Avenue, #13A 10025

(212) 864-3055
Fax: (212) 222-8048

Collection:	General stock.
# of Volumes:	1,000
Specialties:	Children's
Services:	Search service, catalog, accepts want lists.
Credit Cards:	No
Year Estab:	1989

MJS Books and Graphics
9 East 82nd Street 10028

(212) 517-8565
Fax: (212)650-9561

Collection:	Specialty
Specialties:	Early 20th century Dutch, Russian and German avant-garde; contemporary fine printing; illustrated.
Services:	Catalog, accepts want lists.
Credit Cards:	No
Owner:	Monica J. Strauss
Year Estab:	1987

Naturalist's Bookshelf
540 West 114th Street 10025

(212) 865-6202
Fax: (212) 865-2718

Collection:	Specialty
# of Volumes:	20,000-25,000
Specialties:	Natural history, including natural history art and biographies; exploration.
Services:	Appraisals, accepts want lists, catalog.
Credit Cards:	No
Owner:	Herman Kitchen
Year Estab:	1980

Irving Oaklander Books
547 West 27th Street 10001

(212) 954-4210

Collection:	Specialty
# of Volumes:	5,000
Specialties:	Books about books; graphic design; art (modern); typography.
Services:	Catalog in planning stage, accepts want lists, mail order.
Credit Cards:	No
Year Estab:	1988

Fred & Elizabeth Pajerski
250 West 24th Street, Apt 4GE 10011

(212) 255-6501
Fax: (212) 255-6501

Collection:	Specialty
# of Volumes:	2,500
Specialties:	Photography
Services:	Appraisals, catalog, accepts want lists.
Credit Cards:	No
Year Estab:	1985

R.M. Smythe & Co., Inc.
26 Broadway 10004

(212) 943-1880

Collection:	Specialty
Specialties:	Signed books; historic autographs.
Hours:	Mon-Fri 9-5.
Services:	Appraisals, auctions.
Credit Cards:	Yes
Owner:	Diana Herzog
Year Estab:	1890

Bruce J. Ramer
401 East 80th Street, Ste. 24-J 10021

(212) 772-6211
Fax: (212) 650-9032

Collection:	Specialty with limited general stock.
# of Volumes:	3,500
Specialties:	Science; medicine; natural history; technology; early illustrated; occult; 16th and 17th century books.
Services:	Appraisals, catalog, accepts want lists.
Credit Cards:	No
Year Estab:	1980

Richard C. Ramer, Old & Rare Books
225 East 70th Street 10021

(212) 737-0222
Fax: (212) 288-4169

Collection:	Specialty
# of Volumes:	10,000
Specialties:	Spain; Portugal (including former overseas possessions).
Services:	Appraisals, search service, catalog, accepts want lists.
Credit Cards:	No
Year Estab:	1969

Paulette Rose Fine & Rare Books
360 East 72nd Street 10021

(212) 861-5607

Collection:	Specialty
# of Volumes:	1,000
Specialties:	Literary women; books by and about women.
	Appraisals (in specialty only); accepts want lists, catalog.
Credit Cards:	No
Year Estab:	1978

Rostenberg & Stern
40 East 88th Street 10128

(212) 831-6628
Fax: (212) 831-1961

Collection:	Specialty books and ephemera.
# of Volumes:	3,000
Specialties:	Early printed books; books about books; literature; political theory.
Services:	Catalog
Credit Cards:	No
Owner:	Leona Rostenberg & Madeleine Stern
Year Estab:	1944
Comments:	The partners have also co-authored several books about the book business.

Justin G. Schiller, Ltd.
125 East 57th Street, Gallery 48 10150

(212) 832-8231
Fax: (212) 688-1139

Collection:	Specialty
# of Volumes:	5,000
Specialties:	Children's
Services:	Appraisals, catalog, accepts want lists.
Credit Cards:	Yes
Owner:	Justin G. Schiller & Raymond Wapner
Year Estab:	1968

David Schulson Autographs
11 East 68th Street 10021

(212) 517-8300

Collection:	Specialty
Specialties:	Historic manuscripts, letters and documents; signed books.
Services:	Appraisals (autographs only), accepts want lists, catalog.
Credit Cards:	Yes
Year Estab:	1973

Theatron
250 Fort Washington Avenue #2H 10032

(212) 923-5814

Collection:	Specialty
# of Volumes:	6,000
Specialties:	Theater; film.
Credit Cards:	No
Owner:	Max Gulack

Tollett and Harman
175 West 76 Street 10023

(212) 877-1566

Collection:	Specialty
# of Volumes:	200-300 (books)
Specialties:	Signed books; manuscripts, autographs.
Services:	Catalog, accepts want lists.

Credit Cards:	No
Owner:	Robert Tollett
Year Estab:	1984

Vieux Livres d'Europe
16 East 65th Street 10021

(212) 861-5694
Fax: (212) 861-1434

Collection:	Specialty
Specialties:	French illustrated (17th & 18th centuries).
Services:	Appraisals, catalog.
Credit Cards:	No
Owner:	Ketty Maisonrouge
Year Estab:	1987

Andrew D. Washton Books on the Fine Arts
411 East 83rd Street 10028
Mailing Address: 88 Lexington Avenue, Ste. 10G 10028

(212) 481-0479
Fax: (212) 861-0588

Collection:	Specialty
# of Volumes:	2,000
Specialties:	Art history; West European art and architecture. Scholarly (not "coffee table" books).
Services:	Appraisals, catalog, accepts want lists..
Credit Cards:	No
Year Estab:	1982

Michael R. Weintraub, Inc.
263 West 90th Street, #3 10024

(212) 769-1178
Fax: (212) 874-2481

Collection:	Specialty
# of Volumes:	6,000
Specialties:	Modern illustrated; decorative arts; applied art; performing arts; livres d'artistes; children's; photography; art and design; architecture.
Services:	Accepts want lists, mail order.
Credit Cards:	No
Year Estab:	1980
Comments:	See additional listing in Open Shop section.

Lorraine Wilber Gramercy Book Shop
22 East 17th Street 10003

(212) 255-5568

Collection:	Specialty
# of Volumes:	8,000
Specialties:	English literature; American literature; STC and Wing books; Wright books; modern first editions.
Services:	Accepts want lists.
Credit Cards:	No
Year Estab:	1941.

Randolph Williams, Bookman   (212) 759-5816
122 East 61st Street 10021   Fax: (212) 759-5816

Collection:	General stock.
# of Volumes:	6,000
Specialties:	American literature (18th & 19th C.); English literature (18th & 19th C); fine bindings; modern first editions; classics; foreign greats in translation; Anthony Trollope.
Services:	Appraisals, search service, catalog, accepts want lists.
Credit Cards:	No
Year Estab:	1987

Wurlitzer-Bruck   (212) 787-6431
60 Riverside Drive 10024

Collection:	Specialty books, ephemera and autographs.
# of Volumes:	1,000
Specialties:	Music
Services:	Appraisals, accepts want lists, mail order.
Credit Cards:	No
Owner:	Marianne Wurlitzer & Gene Bruck
Year Estab:	1976

Irving Zucker Art Books, Inc.   (212) 679-6332
303 Fifth Avenue, Ste.1407 10016

Collection:	Specialty
# of Volumes:	250-300
Specialties:	Illustrated (16th-20th centuries); modern French illustrated.
Services:	Appraisals
Credit Cards:	No
Owner:	Irving Zucker
Year Estab:	1946

New York City
(Queens)

David Bergman   (718) 274-9036
28-44 35th Street Astoria 11103

Collection:	General stock.
# of Volumes:	10,000
Specialties:	Paleontology; jazz.
Credit Cards:	No
Year Estab:	1988

Henry Feldstein   (718) 544-3002
PO Box 398 Forest Hills 11375

Collection:	Specialty
# of Volumes:	2,000
Specialties:	Photography

Services:	Accepts want lists, catalog.
Credit Cards:	No
Year Estab:	1976

Nancy L. McGlashan, Inc.   (718) 849-0020
PO Box 303 Kew Gardens 11415

Collection:	Specialty
Specialties:	Autographs; manuscripts; signed photographs in all fields except sports, Nazis and Hollywood.
Services:	Appraisals, search service, catalog, accepts want lists, represents clients at auctions.
Credit Cards:	No
Year Estab:	1984

Safka & Bareis Autographs   (718) 263-2276
PO Box 886 Forest Hills 11375

Collection:	Specialty autographs and ephemera.
Specialties:	Music; film; performing arts.
Services:	Search service, catalog, accepts want lists.
Credit Cards:	No
Owner:	Bill Safka & Arbe Bareis
Year Estab:	1983

Leonard Toelk Bookseller   (718) 497-1573
464 Woodward Avenue Queens 11385

Collection:	Specialty
# of Volumes:	Several hundred.
Specialties:	Decorative arts.
Services:	Mail order.
Credit Cards:	No
Year Estab:	1988

New York City
(Staten Island)

Harlow McMillen   (718) 816-3063
PO Box 140-965 10314-0003
Mailing address: 131 Manor Road 10310

Collection:	General stock.
# of Volumes:	12,000+
Hours:	Collection can be viewed all year, but spring thru fall is preferred.
Services:	Search service, accepts want lists, mail order.
Credit Cards:	No

Great Expectations   (718) 351-5043
30 Barton Avenue 10306

Collection:	General stock.
# of Volumes:	4,000
Specialties:	Dickens & Dickensiana; literature; first editions; illustrated.
Services:	Catalog, accepts want lists.
Credit Cards:	No
Owner:	Richard Colletti
Year Estab:	1982

North Bellmore

Main Street Booksellers   (516) 221-6155
923 Old Britton Road 11710-1347

Collection:	General stock.
# of Volumes:	5,000
Specialties:	Chess; P.G. Wodehouse; first editions; antiquarian.
Credit Cards:	No
Owner:	Arnold Cohen
Year Estab:	1968

North Java

Bob Cook   (716) 861-4918
Box 129 14113

Collection:	General stock.
# of Volumes:	3,000-5,000
Credit Cards:	No
Year Estab:	1971

Nyack
(Grandview)

Fred Rosselot - Books   (914) 358-0254
586 Route 9W 10960

Collection:	General stock.
# of Volumes:	30,000-50,000
Specialties:	Free thought; geology.
Travel:	Nyack exit off NY Twy. Proceed south on Rte. 9W. Shop is in private house on right.
Credit Cards:	No
Year Estab:	1977
Comments:	If you're an ambitious book hunter and you're planning a visit to the Nyack area, we recommend a call ahead to this amicable dealer. The collection is housed in the home of a bachelor who makes no bones about his housekeeping skills. If you don't mind ducking and stooping, there's a good chance you'll be find some titles not readily available in a typical used book shop. Because of his contacts with local antique dealers, the owner often gets the "first crack" at newly discovered items.

Old Bethpage

G. Montlack   (516) 249-5632
12 Harrow Lane 11804

Collection:	Specialty
# of Volumes:	2,000
Specialties:	Decorative arts; applied arts; antiques; fashion; furniture; needlework; textiles; trade catalogs; ornament and design; ceramics; related subjects.
Services:	Search service, catalog, accepts want lists.
Owner:	Gloria Montlack
Year Estab:	1984

Old Chatham

Bookstar   (518) 794-8328
Route 13 12136

Collection:	General stock.
Specialties:	Science fiction.
Owner:	Alan Naftal
Year Estab:	1985

Old Field

JoAnn & Richard Casten, Ltd.   (516) 689-3018
4 Dodge Lane 11733   Fax: (516) 689-8909

Collection:	Specialty
Specialties:	Antique maps; atlases.
Services:	Appraisals, catalog, accepts want lists.
Credit Cards:	No
Year Estab:	1972

Olean

Dar's Book Menage   (716) 373-4141
127 North 2nd Street
Mailing address: PO Box 356 14760

Collection:	General stock.
# of Volumes:	15,000
Hours:	See Comments.
Services:	Appraisals, search service, accepts want lists, mail order.
Credit Cards:	Yes
Owner:	Darlene J. Morgan
Year Estab:	1980
Comments:	Owner also maintains a booth at a multi dealer antique shop. See Olean in Open Shop section.

Olivebridge

Rigaud Books & Arcana
PO Box 1369 12461

(914) 657-8231

Collection:	Specialty
# of Volumes:	Several hundred.
Specialties:	Medieval; Celtic.
Services:	Appraisals; search service, accepts want lists, catalog.
Credit Cards:	No
Owner:	Michael Rigaud
Year Estab:	1992

Wilsey Rare Books
23 Mill Road 12461

(914) 657-7057
Fax: (914) 657-2366

Collection:	Specialty
# of Volumes:	600-700
Specialties:	Fine bindings; color plate books; private presses; illustrated; calligraphy; typography; papermaking and book arts.
Services:	Appraisals, catalog, accepts want lists.
Credit Cards:	No
Owner:	Edward Ripley Duggan
Year Estab:	1972
Comments:	Appointments made with serious collectors or dealers interested in the "high end" of the price range.

Oneonta

Carney Books
44 Elm Street 13820

(607) 432-5360

Collection:	General stock.
# of Volumes:	25,000
Specialties:	Ireland; local history.
Services:	Appraisals, search service, catalog, accepts want lists.
Credit Cards:	No
Owner:	John & Margaret Carney
Year Estab:	1970's
Comments:	The owners advise potential visitors that the building is not usually heated and that during very cold weather, the lights do not come on.

Ossining

Bev Chaney Jr. Books
73 Croton Avenue 10562

(914) 941-1002

Collection:	Specialty
# of Volumes:	4,000
Specialties:	Modern American first editions; limited editions.

Credit Cards: No
Year Estab: 1985

JLM's Bookcase   (914) 923-4546
7 Cherry Hill Circle 10562

Collection: Specialty
Specialties: Business; science; technical; telecommunications standards, data
                   compression (JPGE).
Services: Catalog (in planning stage), accepts want lists, mail order.
Credit Cards: No
Owner: Joan L. Mitchell
Year Estab: 1990

Peekskill

Timothy Trace, Bookseller   (914) 528-4074
144 Red Mill Road 10566

Collection: Specialty
# of Volumes: 5,000
Specialties: Decorative arts; antiques; architecture; trade catalogs.
Services: Search service, occasional catalog, accepts want lists.
Credit Cards: No
Owner: Elizabeth Trace
Year Estab: 1950's

Plainview

Bengta Woo - Books   (516) 692-4426
One Sorgi Court 11803

Collection: Specialty hardcover and paperbacks.
# of Volumes: 20,000+
Specialties: Mystery; detective; science fiction; fantasy.
Services: Accepts want lists, mail order.
Credit Cards: No
Year Estab: 1970

Plandome

Lee And Mike Temares   (516) 627-8688
50 Heights Road 11030   Fax: (516) 627-7822

Collection: General stock.
# of Volumes: 35,000
Specialties: Children's series; books about books; Heritage Press; limited
                   editions club; art; illustrated; Judaica; modern first editions;
                   Modern Library.
Services: Appraisals, search service, accepts want lists, mail order, collec-
                   tion development.

Credit Cards: No
Year Estab: 1963

Port Washington

Andra Kustin   (516) 944-7035
127 Reid Avenue 11050   Fax: (516) 944-7035

Collection: Specialty, limited general stock, and prints.
# of Volumes: 5,000
Specialties: Science; technical; fashion; textiles; art; antiques; illustration art.
Services: Appraisals, search service, catalog, accepts want lists, collection development.
Credit Cards: No
Year Estab: 1980

Poughkeepsie

Americana Research   (914) 454-5158
19 North Randolph Avenue 12603

Collection: General stock.
# of Volumes: 10,000
Specialties: Americana; children's; art.
Services: Mail order.
Credit Cards: No
Owner: Martha Mercer
Year Estab: 1977

Rochester

Graham Holroyd   (716) 225-4879
19 Borrowdale Drive 14626

Collection: Specialty hardcover and vintage paperbacks.
# of Volumes: 100,000
Specialties: Science fiction; fantasy; horror; pulps.
Services: Catalog, accepts want lists.
Credit Cards: Yes
Year Estab: 1972

Rye

High Ridge Books, Inc.   (914) 967-3332
PO Box 286 10580

Collection: Specialty
# of Volumes: 2,000
Specialties: Americana; American maps and atlases (19th century).
Services: Accepts want lists, catalog.

Credit Cards:	Yes
Owner:	Frederick Baron
Year Estab:	1978

Scarsdale

Nancy Scheck Art Reference Books   (914) 723-6974
164 Boulevard 10583

Collection:	Specialty
# of Volumes:	3,000
Specialties:	Art reference; books on prints and drawing.
Services:	Appraisals, accepts want lists, catalog.
Credit Cards:	No
Year Estab:	1981

Schenectady

Aide deCamp Books   (518) 346-4966
PO Box 9250 12309

Collection:	Specialty
# of Volumes:	2,000
Specialties:	Military history.
Services:	Appraisals, catalog, accepts want lists.
Credit Cards:	No
Owner:	Art & Louise Fossa
Year Estab:	1987

Books Remembered   (518) 346-0269
Box 1157 12301

Collection:	General stock.
# of Volumes:	10,000
Services:	Search service, accepts want lists.
Credit Cards:	No
Owner:	Jill S. Titus
Year Estab:	1985

Schenevus

Atelier Books   (607) 638-9962
PO Box 314 12155

Collection:	General stock.
# of Volumes:	10,000
Specialties:	Architecture; design.
Services:	Catalog, accepts want lists.
Credit Cards:	No
Owner:	Ed Brodzinsky
Year Estab:	1986

Scotia

Bob Van Flue, Bookseller   (518) 887-2661
RD #4, Waters Road 12302

Collection:	Specialty books and ephemera.
# of Volumes:	1,000
Specialties:	New York State.
Services:	Catalog, accepts want lists.
Credit Cards:	No
Year Estab:	1991

Sea Cliff

Sefton Books   (516) 671-0465
41 Park Way 11579

Collection:	General stock.
# of Volumes:	4,000
Specialties:	Art; architecture; performing arts.
Services:	Search service, accepts want lists, mail order.
Credit Cards:	No
Owner:	Isabel & Robert Sefton
Year Estab:	1985

Spencertown

Berkshire Books   (518) 392-5701
PO Box 185 12165

Collection:	General stock.
# of Volumes:	5,000
Specialties:	Modern first editions.
Services:	Search service, accepts want lists, mail order.
Credit Cards:	No
Owner:	Kaarin & R.J. Lemstrom-Sheedy
Year Estab:	1991

Springfield Center

James Hurley, Books   (315) 858-2012
PO Box 334 13468

Collection:	Specialty
# of Volumes:	5,000
Specialties:	South and Central Asia; Middle East; Islam.
Services:	Accepts want lists, catalog.
Credit Cards:	No
Year Estab:	1991

Stillwater

Book-In-Hand   (518) 587-0040
103 Condon Road 12170   Fax: (518) 587-0040

Collection:	General stock and specialty.
# of Volumes:	20,000
Specialties:	Children's; American Revolution; Civil War; New York State.
Credit Cards:	No
Owner:	Helen & Bill Crawshaw
Year Estab:	1979

Syosset

Cornucopia/Carol A. Greenberg   (516) 921-4813
2108 Edge Road 11791   Fax: (516) 921-7339

Collection:	Specialty
# of Volumes:	2,000
Specialties:	Cookbooks; etiquette; domestic arts and history (primarily 19th century to 1940); needlework.
Services:	Appraisals, search service, accepts want lists, mail order.
Credit Cards:	No
Year Estab:	1986

Syracuse

The Angliphle Owl & The Yankee Frog   (315) 479-9032
506 Dewitt Street 13203

Collection:	General stock.
# of Volumes:	30,00-40,000
Specialties:	Canals
Services:	Mail order, accepts want lists.
Credit Cards:	No
Owner:	Todd & Connie Weseloh
Year Estab:	1985

Tivoli

Douglas S. Penn - Books   (914) 757-3961
29 Broadway, CR 78
Mailing address: PO Box 449   12583

Collection:	Specialty
Specialties:	Nautical; regional New York; New England.
Services:	Accepts want lists.
Credit Cards:	No
Year Estab:	1986

Valhalla

Educo Services International Ltd.   (914) 997-7044
75 North Kensico Avenue
Mailing address: PO Box 226 10595

Collection:	Specialty books and periodicals.
# of Volumes:	5,000 (combined)
Specialties:	Back issues of scholarly periodicals.
Hours:	Mon-Fri 9-5. Sat & Sun by appointment.
Services:	Catalog (periodicals only).
Credit Cards:	No
Owner:	Charles Cecere
Year Estab:	1978

Valley Cottage

Aleph-Bet Books   (914) 268-7410
218 Waters Edge 10989

Collection:	Specialty
# of Volumes:	4,000
Specialties:	Children's; illustrated.
Services:	Appraisals, accepts want lists; catalog.
Credit Cards:	Yes
Owner:	Helen Younger
Year Estab:	1978

Valley Stream

Thomas & Ahngana Suarez, Rare Maps   (516) 285-7419
1146 Irving Street 11580

Collection:	Specialty
Specialties:	Maps; atlases.
Services:	Appraisals, accepts want lists, catalog.
Credit Cards:	No
Year Estab:	1978

Victor

Joshua Heller Books, Photographica & Miscellany   (716) 924-1740
1184 Cunningham Drive 14564

Collection:	General stock and ephemera.
# of Volumes:	3,500
Specialties:	Photography; photographic periodicals; stereoviews; photographic images; art; regional Americana; literature; architecture; New York City; politics; "weird" science.
Services:	Appraisals, search service, catalog, accepts want lists.
Credit Cards:	No
Year Estab:	1980

West Hempstead

Gloves and Old Glory
184 Hempstead Avenue 11552

(516) 486-1400
Fax: (516) 486-1716

Collection:	Specialty
# of Volumes:	1,000
Specialties:	Boxing
Services:	Appraisals
Credit Cards:	No
Year Estab:	1986
Owner:	Stephen A. Tuchman

John Valle Books
Box 544 11552

(516) 887-3342

Collection:	Specialty
# of Volumes:	2,000
Specialties:	Hunting; fishing.
Services:	Appraisals, search service, catalog, accepts want lists.
Credit Cards:	Yes
Year Estab:	1984

Wynantskill

A Gatherin'
PO Box 175 12198

(518) 674-2979

Collection:	Specialty books and ephemera.
Specialties:	Transportation; communication; manuscripts.
Services:	Appraisals, catalog, accepts want lists.
Credit Cards:	No
Owner:	Robert Dalton Harris & Diane DeBlois
Year Estab:	1973

Yonkers

Crux Books
58 Ramsey Avenue 10701

(914) 969-1554

Collection:	Specialty books and ephemera.
# of Volumes:	1,500
Specialties:	Mountaineering; travel (Asia); exploration.
Services:	Catalog, accepts want lists.
Credit Cards:	No
Owner:	James Havranek
Year Estab:	1987

Abbot Books   (718) 671-9800
100-26 Benchley Place Bronx 10475

Collection:	General stock.
# of Volumes:	10,000
Specialties:	Children's; illustrated; business; finance.
Services:	Accepts want lists.
Credit Cards:	No
Owner:	B. Abbot
Year Estab:	1983

Felix Albert Books   (516) 922-2315
4 Bromley Lane Great Neck 11023

Collection:	General stock.
# of Volumes:	25,000
Specialties:	Art; music; literary first editions.
Services:	Occasional catalog, accepts want lists.
Credit Cards:	No
Year Estab:	1978

Jerry Alper, Inc.   (914) 793-2100
PO Box 218 Eastchester 10707   Fax: (914) 793-7811

Collection:	Specialty
Specialties:	Sells books in collection form, primarily to university libraries.
Services:	Appraisals, search service, catalog, accepts want lists.
Credit Cards:	No
Year Estab:	1980

American Crossword Federation   (516) 795-8823
PO Box 69 Massapequa Park 11762

Collection:	Specialty
# of Volumes:	1,000
Specialties:	Crosswords
Services:	Accepts want lists.
Credit Cards:	Yes
Owner:	Stanley Newman
Year Estab:	1983

The American Dust Company   (718) 442-8253
47 Park Court Staten Island 10301

Collection:	General stock and specialty.
# of Volumes:	10,000+
Specialties:	Rare paperbacks; modern first editions; signed books; African American literature; mystery; crime; poetry; antique games and amusements; theatrical posters.
Services:	Catalog, accepts want lists.
Credit Cards:	No
Owner:	Albert Newgarden

Ampersand Books   (212) 674-6795
PO Box 674 New York 10276

Collection:	Specialty
# of Volumes:	8,000
Specialties:	Modern first editions.
Services:	Appraisals, search service, catalog, accepts want lists.
Credit Cards:	No
Owner:	George Bixby
Year Estab:	1967

The Anglican Bibliopole   (518) 587-7470
858 Church Street Saratoga Springs 12866

Collection:	Specialty books and periodicals.
# of Volumes:	12,000
Specialties:	Anglican/Episcopal church, including liturgy, biography, history, music, and devotional.
Services:	Search service, catalog, accepts want lists, collection development.
Credit Cards:	Yes
Owner:	Robert D. Kearney & Paul Evans
Year Estab:	1979
Comments:	Collection may also be viewed by appointment.

Antheil Booksellers   (516) 826-2094
2177 Isabelle Court North Bellmore 11710

Collection:	Specialty new and used.
# of Volumes:	7,500
Specialties:	Maritime; military; aviation.
Services:	Appraisals, search service, catalog, accepts want lists.
Credit Cards:	No
Owner:	Sheila & Nate Rind
Year Estab:	1957

ArtBooks   (607) 547-9748
PO Box 665 Cooperstown 13326-0665

Collection:	Specialty
# of Volumes:	2,000
Specialties:	Fine art; decorative arts; interior design; art history. Out of print books, catalogs, monographs and scholarly works.
Services:	Catalog, accepts want lists.
Credit Cards:	No
Owner:	Doris Motta
Year Estab:	1983

B.K. Books   (914) 997-7184
PO Box 1681 White Plains 10606

Collection:	General stock.

# of Volumes:	15,000
Specialties:	Literature; history; performing arts; women's studies; black studies.
Services:	Search service, accepts want lists, collection development for libraries.
Credit Cards:	No
Owner:	Barbara & Kenneth Leish
Year Estab:	1980

Bay View Books   (516) 324-3145
595 Fireplace Road East Hampton 11937

Collection:	Specialty
# of Volumes:	3,000
Specialties:	Maritime; boat building; model building; whaling; exploration.
Services:	Catalog, accepts want lists.
Credit Cards:	No
Owner:	Burt Van Deusen
Year Estab:	1986

C. Wm. Beebe Books
24 South Catherine Street, #16 Plattsburgh 12901

Collection:	Specialty
# of Volumes:	400+
Specialties:	C. Wm. Beebe.
Credit Cards:	No
Owner:	Oliver A. Stromberg
Year Estab:	1991

T.D. Bell, Bookseller   (518) 885-5577
526 Leahy Lane Ballston Spa 12020

Collection:	Specialty paperbacks (new and used).
# of Volumes:	16,000
Specialties:	Science fiction; horror; mystery.
Services:	Catalog, accepts want lists.
Credit Cards:	No
Owner:	Timothy Bell
Year Estab:	1986

Carl Sandler Berkowitz   (914) 341-0255
7 Crane Road Middletown 10940

Collection:	Specialty
# of Volumes:	30,000
Specialties:	Ancient world; mediaeval and renaissance Europe; Middle East. (All subject matter.)
Services:	Catalog, accepts want lists.
Credit Cards:	No
Year Estab:	1979

Bernard Book Company
(516) 239-4095

Box 387 Long Beach 11561

Collection:	Specialty and limited general stock.
# of Volumes:	1,500
Specialties:	Americana; early voyages and travel; cartography, maritime.
Services:	Search service, accepts want lists.
Credit Cards:	No
Owner:	Bernard Zelanka
Year Estab:	1990

Biblion, Inc.
(718) 263-3910

PO Box 9 Forest Hills 11375

Collection:	Specialty
# of Volumes:	20,000
Specialties:	Science (history of); medicine.
Services:	Occasional catalog, accepts want lists.
Credit Cards:	No
Owner:	Ludwig Gottschalk
Year Estab:	1947

Black and White Books
(718) 855-2598

111 Hicks Street, Ste. 11-F Brooklyn 11201

Collection:	Specialty
# of Volumes:	3,500
Specialties:	Mystery; detective; science fiction; fantasy.
Services:	Catalog
Credit Cards:	No
Owner:	Rushton H. Potts
Year Estab:	1986

Frederick Blake, Bookseller
(516) 689-3754

1152 North Country Road Stony Brook 11790

Collection:	Specialty
# of Volumes:	4,000
Specialties:	Mineralogy; mining; geology; gemology.
Services:	Search service, catalog, accepts want lists.
Credit Cards:	No
Year Estab:	1985

C.J. Boardman
(315) 245-1950

Route 13, Box 26 Camden 13316

Collection:	General stock.
# of Volumes:	20,000+
Services:	Accepts want lists.
Credit Cards:	No
Owner:	Crager J. Boardman
Year Estab:	1978

The Book Corner   (716) 624-5079
7203 Meadowview Drive Lima 14485

Collection:	Specialty
# of Volumes:	2,000
Specialties:	Early Americana; New York State.
Services:	Catalog, accepts want lists.
Credit Cards:	No
Owner:	William Colangelo
Year Estab:	1990

Book Journeys   (516) 751-6089
15 Bowen Place Stony Brook 11790

Collection:	Specialty
# of Volumes:	4,000
Specialties:	Adventure; travel; nautical; mountainteering.
Services:	Irregular catalog, accepts want lists.
Credit Cards:	No
Owner:	Evert Volkersz
Year Estab:	1982

The Book Mark   (716) 662-9554
6212 Taylor Road Orchard Park 14127

Collection:	Specialty
Specialties:	Roycroft Press; music; cookbooks.
Services:	Search service, catalog, accepts want lists.
Credit Cards:	No
Owner:	Mark R. Tedeschi
Year Estab:	1990

Book Mark-It   (914) 473-0876
86 College Avenue Poughkeepsie 12603

Collection:	General stock.
# of Volumes:	5,000+
Specialties:	Lincoln; Civil War; presidential biographies.
Services:	Accepts want lists, catalog in planning stage.
Credit Cards:	No
Owner:	Edward D. Babcock
Year Estab:	1989

Book Search Service
GPO Box 168 Brooklyn 11202

Collection:	General stock.
# of Volumes:	7,500
Specialties:	Americana; belles lettres; scholarly; government publications; film; health, history, biography.
Services:	Search service, catalog, accepts want lists.

Credit Cards: No
Owner: H. Rosman
Year Estab: 1973

Book Treasures   (516) 922-3758
PO Box 121 East Norwich 11732

Collection: Specialty
# of Volumes: 1,500
Specialties: Children's; illustrated. Primarily from mid 1850's-1930.
Services: Accepts want lists.
Credit Cards: No
Owner: Rebecca Kaufman
Year Estab: 1979

Martin Breslauer, Inc.   (212) 794-2995
PO Box 607 New York 10028-0006   Fax: (212) 794-4913

Collection: Specialty
Specialties: Illuminated manuscripts; illustrated; early printing.
Services: Appraisals, catalog.
Credit Cards: No
Owner: B.H. Breslauer
Year Estab: 1898

Bridgman Books   (315) 337-7252
906 Roosevelt Avenue Rome 13440

Collection: General stock and ephemera.
# of Volumes: 20,000
Services: Catalog, accepts want lists.
Credit Cards: No
Owner: Patrick H. Bridgman
Year Estab: 1977

Elliott W. Brill   (212) 695-1996
249 West 34th Street, Ste. 70 New York 10001   Fax: (212) 967-4524

Collection: Specialty
# of Volumes: 10,000
Specialties: Judaica
Services: Appraisals, accepts want lists.
Credit Cards: No
Year Estab: 1972

Broadwater Books   (716) 754-8145
PO Box 278 Lewiston 14092

Collection: Specialty
# of Volumes: 10,000
Specialties: Natural history.

Services:	Search service, accepts want lists.
Credit Cards:	No
Owner:	Lyman W. Newlin
Year Estab:	1933

Warren F. Broderick-Books   (518) 235-4041
PO Box 124 Lansingburgh 12182

Collection:	Specialty
# of Volumes:	500-700
Specialties:	Gardening/horticulture, especially garden design, history, color plate books.
Services:	Search service, catalog, accepts want lists.
Credit Cards:	No
Year Estab:	1977

Calendula Horticultural Books   (607) 272-7364
425 North Cayuga Street Ithaca 14850

Collection:	Specialty
Specialties:	Gardening; horticulture; flower arrangements; landscape architecture; North American wildflowers.
Services:	Catalog, accepts want lists.
Credit Cards:	No
Year Estab:	1987

Camel Book Company   (212) 865-4093
PO Box 1936 New York 10025   Fax: (212) 865-4093

Collection:	Specialty
# of Volumes:	2,000-3,000
Specialties:	Islam; Middle East, Arabia; Iran; Turkey; Arabic literature; Judaica.
Services:	Catalog, accepts want lists. Also creators and distributors of Bibliofile software for antiquarian booksellers and collectors.
Credit Cards:	No
Owner:	Carl & Faith Wurtzel
Year Estab:	1986

H. Celnick   (718) 823-5731
2144 Muliner Avenue Bronx 10462

Collection:	General stock.
# of Volumes:	50,000
Specialties:	Natural healing, chiropractic; natural history; judaica; occult.
Services:	Search service, accepts want lists.
Credit Cards:	No
Year Estab:	1963

Certo Books   (914) 361-1190
PO Box 322 Circleville 10919

Collection:	Specialty
# of Volumes:	10,000
Specialties:	Mystery; detective; science fiction; fantasy; pulps; vintage paperbacks.
Services:	Catalog, accepts want lists.
Credit Cards:	No
Owner:	Nick Certo
Year Estab:	1987

B.Chamalian
PO Box 787 Crompond 10517

Collection:	General stock.
# of Volumes:	100,000-150,000
Specialties:	Mostly out of print fiction; plays; poetry, children's.
Credit Cards:	No
Owner:	G. Chamalian
Year Estab:	1960

Cicero's Books, Etc.   (716) 394-8453
115 Beal Street Canandaigua 14424

Collection:	General stock.
# of Volumes:	6,000
Specialties:	Cookbooks.
Services:	Search service, accepts want lists, occasional catalog.
Credit Cards:	No
Owner:	Ellen Cicero
Year Estab:	1990

J. M. Cohen, Rare Books   (718) 548-7160
PO Box 542 Bronx 10463   Fax: (212) 601-6593

Collection:	Specialty
# of Volumes:	5,000
Specialties:	Decorative arts; applied arts; antiques; design and decoration; fashion and costume; jewelry; ornaments; modern design.
Services:	Appraisals, catalog, accepts want lists.
Credit Cards:	No
Owner:	Judy M. Cohen
Year Estab:	1982
Comments:	Collection may also be viewed by appointment.

Continental Book Search   (212) 254-8719
PO Box 1163 New York 10009

Collection:	General stock.
# of Volumes:	10,000
Services:	Search service, catalog, accepts want lists.
Credit Cards:	No
Year Estab:	1977

Croton Book Service
PO Box 131 Croton-on-Hudson 10520

(914) 271-6575
Fax: (914) 271-6575

Collection:	Specialty
Specialties:	Hudson River; Croton Dam; military; West Point.
Services:	Search service, accepts want lists.
Credit Cards:	No
Owner:	Edith Scott
Year Estab:	1966

L.W. Currey
PO Box 187 Elizabethtown 12932

(518) 873-6477

Collection:	Specialty
# of Volumes:	50,000
Specialties:	American literature; modern first editions; horror; science fiction; fantasy.
Services:	Catalog, accepts want lists.
Credit Cards:	Yes
Year Estab:	1968

G. Curwen, Books
1 West 67th Street, #710 New York 10023

(212) 595-5904

Collection:	Specialty
# of Volumes:	2,000
Specialties:	Modern first editions; performing arts; magic; Punch & Judy; detective; cookbooks.
Services:	Accepts want lists.
Credit Cards:	No
Owner:	Ginger Curwen & Jack Nessel
Year Estab:	1992

Den of Antiquity
124 Sargent Lane Liverpool 13088

(315) 457-0925

Collection:	Specialty
# of Volumes:	800
Specialties:	Hunting; fishing; out of doors; history; military; children's.
Services:	Accepts want lists.
Credit Cards:	No
Owner:	Merle & Sherry Pratt
Year Estab:	1981

Denning House
Box 42 Salisbury Mills 12577

(914) 496-6771

Collection:	General stock.
# of Volumes:	15,000-20,000
Specialties:	Maps; autographs; manuscripts; rare; antiquarian.
Services:	Catalog, appraisals, accepts want lists.

Credit Cards:	No
Owner:	Denning McTague
Year Estab:	1963
Comments:	Plans to have an open shop in late 1993. Call for details.

Down Under Books (914) 693-9828
PO Box 144 Ardsley 10502

Collection:	Specialty
# of Volumes:	10,000
Specialties:	Literature; biography; art; Australia; New Zealand; South Pacific.
Services:	Search service, especially for libraries and publishers, accepts want lists.
Credit Cards:	No
Owner:	Jeanne R. Dolgin
Year Estab:	1987

Richard & Eileen Dubrow, Inc. (718) 767-9758
Box 128 Bayside 11361

Collection:	Specialty
Specialties:	Decorative arts; 19th century furniture.
Services:	Search service, accepts want lists.
Credit Cards:	No
Year Estab:	1975

Eastwood Products (315) 736-7232
5627 Lovers Lane Oriskany 13424

Collection:	Specialty
# of Volumes:	Several hundred.
Specialties:	Cookbooks
Services:	Occasional lists, accepts want lists.
Credit Cards:	No
Owner:	Robert LaSalle
Year Estab:	1988

Editions (914) 657-7000
Route 28 Boiceville 12412   Fax: (914) 657-8849

Collection:	General stock.
# of Volumes:	50,000
Services:	Catalog
Credit Cards:	Yes
Owner:	Norman & Joan Levine
Year Estab:	1948

Elgen Books (516) 536-6276
336 DeMott Avenue Rockville Centre 11570

Collection:	Specialty

# of Volumes:	10,000
Specialties:	Medicine; science; mathematics.
Services:	Appraisals, catalog, accepts want lists.
Credit Cards:	No
Owner:	Esther Geller
Year Estab:	1978
Comments:	Collection can also be viewed by appointment.

J.H. Faber, Antiquarian Books   (914) 762-2656
Box 24 Millwood 10546

Collection:	Specialty
# of Volumes:	4,000-5,000
Specialties:	Military; world history.
Services:	Catalog, accepts want lists.
Credit Cards:	No
Owner:	Jack & Jane Faber
Year Estab:	1981

The Footnote   (718) 858-4371
179 Washington Park Brooklyn 11205

Collection:	General stock.
# of Volumes:	200,000
Specialties:	Americana; music; dance; gardening, cookbooks; biography.
Services:	Search service, accepts want lists.
Credit Cards:	No
Owner:	David Frost & David Hovell
Year Estab:	1970

Roberta & Stuart Friedman   (914) 245-8642
Box 49 Granite Springs 10527

Collection:	Specialty
# of Volumes:	5,000
Specialties:	Art; photography; graphic design; decorative arts. (All from 1890-1960).
Services:	Search service, accepts want lists, occasional catalog.
Credit Cards:	No
Year Estab:	1983

Ronald B. Frodelius
c/o The Open Season, PO Box 12 Fayetteville 13066

Collection:	Specialty books and magazines.
# of Volumes:	500
Specialties:	Trapping; country living; hunting; fishing; fur trade; Gladys Taber; reprints of early U.S. fur trapping company catalogs.
Services:	Catalog
Credit Cards:	No
Year Estab:	1972

Robert Frost Books　　　　　(518) 477-7894
PO Box 719 Rensselaer 12144

Collection:	Specialty books and ephemera.
# of Volumes:	2,000
Specialties:	Robert Frost.
Services:	Search service, catalog, accepts want lists.
Credit Cards:	No
Owner:	Robert J. McCausland
Year Estab:	1991

Brandon A. Fullam
8 Wigwam Path Babylon 11702

Collection:	Specialty books and ephemera.
Specialties:	First editions (19th century American); autographs.
Credit Cards:	No
Year Estab:	1985

Shirley R. Gellis　　　　　(516) 666-8512
57 Seafield Lane Bay Shore 11706

Collection:	Specialty
# of Volumes:	A few thousand
Specialties:	Books by and about women, including diaries, letters, fiction, women's studies, suffrage, travel, poetry.
Services:	Search service, catalog, accepts want lists.
Credit Cards:	No
Year Estab:	1988

GFS Books　　　　　(516) 581-7076
PO Box 12 Great River 11739

Collection:	General stock.
# of Volumes:	10,000+
Services:	Search service, accepts want lists.
Credit Cards:	No
Owner:	G. Schwebish
Year Estab:	1979

Gordon Booksellers
PO Box 459 New York 10004

Collection:	General stock.
# of Volumes:	28,000
Specialties:	Americana; history; biography; holistic medicine; Judaica; Islam; social movements; economics; finance; ballroom dancing; propaganda; anthropology; film; law enforcement; military; library science; bibliography; theater; literary translation; mass communication; limited editions; scholarly.

Services:	Search service, catalog, accepts want lists.
Credit Cards:	No
Owner:	R. Gordon
Year Estab:	1972

Gorgon Books   (516) 472-3504
102 Joanne Drive Holbrook 11741   Fax: (516) 472-4235

Collection:	Specialty
# of Volumes:	40,000+
Specialties:	Mystery; science fiction; literature; collectible paperbacks; original artwork used for book cover illustrations.
Services:	Appraisals, search service, catalog, accepts want lists, auctions, publishes book of auction results from all paperback auctions.
Credit Cards:	Yes
Owner:	Joe Crifo & John Gargiso
Year Estab:	1980

M & M Halpern, Booksellers   (718) 544-3885
67-32 136th Street Flushing 11367

Collection:	General stock.
Specialties:	Illustrated; children's; first editions; film.
Services:	Accepts want lists.
Credit Cards:	No
Owner:	Michael & Mildred Halpern

Hayden & Fandetta   (212) 581-8520
PO Box 1549 New York 10101

Collection:	Specialty
# of Volumes:	9,500
Specialties:	Decorative arts (pottery, porcelain and ceramics).
Services:	Search service, accepts want lists, collection development.
Credit Cards:	No
Owner:	J.P. Hayen, Jr. & D. J. Fandetta
Year Estab:	1988

C.F. Heindl, Books   (716) 271-1423
PO Box 18345 Rochester 14618

Collection:	Specialty books and ephemera.
# of Volumes:	500
Specialties:	Charles Dickens.
Services:	Appraisals
Credit Cards:	No
Owner:	Charles F. Heindl
Year Estab:	1976

Claude Held Collectibles   (716) 634-4842
PO Box 515 Buffalo 14225

Collection:	Specialty
# of Volumes:	12,000+
Specialties:	Science fiction; mystery; advance books; pulps; comics, including Sunday comic sections; film memorabilia.
Services:	Catalog, accepts want lists.
Credit Cards:	No
Year Estab:	1948

Morris Heller   (914) 583-5879
PO Box 529 Monticello 12701

Collection:	Specialty
# of Volumes:	2,000
Specialties:	Hunting; fishing.
Services:	Accepts want lists.
Credit Cards:	No
Year Estab:	1963

Hemlock Books   (718) 318-0737
170 Beach 145 Street Neponsit 11694   Fax: (718) 318-5750

Collection:	Specialty
# of Volumes:	3,000-4,000
Specialties:	Medicine; medical history.
Services:	Catalog
Credit Cards:	No
Owner:	Norman & Sheila Shaftel
Year Estab:	1978

Herpetological Search Service & Exchange   (516) 957-3624
117 East Santa Barbara Road Lindenhurst 11757

Collection:	Specialty
Specialties:	Natural history.
Services:	Catalog
Credit Cards:	No
Owner:	Steven Weinkselbaum
Year Estab:	1978

Peter Hlinka Historical Americana
PO Box 310 New York 10028

Collection:	Specialty books and related items.
# of Volumes:	1,000+
Specialties:	Military; medallic reference; military uniforms and insignia.
Services:	Appraisals, catalog, accepts want lists.
Credit Cards:	No
Year Estab:	1963

Michael Huxley, Bookseller   (518) 449-7280
355 Loudon Road Loudonville 12211

Collection:	Specialty
# of Volumes:	2,000
Specialties:	Natural history.
Services:	Occasional catalog, accepts want lists.
Credit Cards:	No
Year Estab:	1986

I Love A Mystery   (518) 439-6782
1621 New Scotland Road Slingerlands 12159

Collection:	Specialty
# of Volumes:	5,000
Specialties:	Mystery; detective.
Services:	Appraisals, catalog, accept want lists.
Credit Cards:	No
Owner:	William L. Simmons
Year Estab:	1990

Island Books   (516) 759-0233
Box 19 Old Westbury 11568   Fax: (516) 759-7818

Collection:	Specialty hardcover and paperback.
# of Volumes:	20,000
Specialties:	Science fiction; mystery; pulps
Services:	Catalog, accepts want lists.
Credit Cards:	No
Owner:	Glen Vilchek
Year Estab:	1992

JMD-Enterprise   (607) 898-5114
PO Box 155 Groton 13073

Collection:	Specialty
# of Volumes:	10,000+
Specialties:	Science fiction; fantasy; mystery; westerns; romance.
Services:	Search service, catalog, accepts want lists.
Credit Cards:	No
Owner:	Jim Doty
Year Estab:	1985
Comments:	Collection can be viewed by appointment.

Philip Kalb Books   (516) 484-0885
P.O. Box 317 Roslyn 11576   Fax: (516) 228-3857

Collection:	Specialty
# of Volumes:	5,000
Specialties:	Art; graphic art; photography.

Services:	Catalog, accepts want lists.
Credit Cards:	No
Year Estab:	1962
Comments:	Collection can also be viewed by appointment.

David M. King Automotive Books   (516) 766-1561
5 Brouwer Lane Rockville Centre 11570

Collection:	Specialty
Specialties:	Automobiles, including travel narratives, racing, history and biography.
Services:	Search service, accepts want lists.
Credit Cards:	No
Year Estab:	1967

Yoshio Kishi
165 West 66th Street New York 10023

Collection:	Specialty
# of Volumes:	10,000
Specialties:	Asian Americana; modern first editions; poetry; film; theater.
Services:	Appraisals, catalog, accepts want lists.
Year Estab:	1970

Bella Kleinman   (212) 655-4689
Box 243 New York 10163

Collection:	Specialty
# of Volumes:	2,500
Specialties:	Antiques; fine art; first editions.
Services:	Accepts want lists.
Credit Cards:	No
Year Estab:	1978

Koster's Collectible Books   (516) 732-5216
35 Hanrahan Avenue Farmingville 11738

Collection:	General stock.
# of Volumes:	8,000
Specialties:	Military; modern first editions; children's.
Services:	Limited search service; accepts want lists; catalog planned.
Credit Cards:	No
Owner:	Kevin Koster
Year Estab:	1991

Liebling & Levitas   (914) 693-0400
489 Ashford Avenue Ardsley 10502   Fax: (914) 693-3824

Collection:	Specialty
# of Volumes:	1,000+
Specialties:	Early American imprints.
Services:	Accepts want lists.

Credit Cards: No
Owner: Michael Zinman
Year Estab: 1988

The Loon People   (716) 786-2319
6353 Burke Hill Road Perry 14530

Collection: General stock.
# of Volumes: 2,000
Specialties: Natural history; birds.
Services: Search service, accepts want lists.
Credit Cards: No
Owner: Charles Goetzinger
Year Estab: 1985

Lubrecht & Cramer, Ltd.   (914) 794-8539
38 County Route 48 Forestburgh 12777   Fax: (914) 791-7575

Collection: Specialty
Specialties: Botany; mycology; geology.
Services: Catalog
Credit Cards: Yes
Owner: Harry D. Lubrecht

Peter Luke-Antiques, Ephemera, Old & Rare Books   (518) 756-6492
PO Box 282 New Baltimore 12124

Collection: Specialty books and ephemera.
Specialties: Americana (19th century); trade catalogs; broadsides; medi-
                   cine; travel and hotel promotional literature.
Services: Accepts want lists.
Credit Cards: No
Year Estab: 1985

Charles L. Male, Used Books
39 Riverview Road Clifton Park 12065-6807

Collection: General stock of hardcover and paperbacks.
# of Volumes: 10,000
Specialties: Americana; local history; westerns; science fiction; mystery.
Services: Catalog
Credit Cards: No
Year Estab: 1984

Martin Buber-Revisionist-Mutualist Press, Booksellers
GPO Box 2009 Brooklyn 11202

Collection: Specialty
# of Volumes: 18,000
Specialties: Social movements; economic reform; land reform; film; World
                   War I & II; H.L. Mencken; historiography.
Services: Search service, catalog, accepts want lists.

Credit Cards: No
Owner: B. Chaim
Year Estab: 1971

Katherine M. Maye   (718) 745-3127
7406 Narrows Avenue Brooklyn 11209

Collection: General stock.
# of Volumes: 8,000-10,000
Specialties: Literature
Services: Search service, accepts want lists.
Credit Cards: No
Year Estab: 1983

Jeffrey Meyerson   (718) 833-8248
8801 Shore Road, #6A East Brooklyn 11209

Collection: Specialty
# of Volumes: 2,500+
Specialties: Mystery; detective (out-of-print British books).
Services: Catalog, accepts want lists.
Credit Cards: No
Year Estab: 1977

Walter Miller   (315) 432-2282
6710 Brooklawn Parkway Syracuse 13211   Fax: (315) 432-8256

Collection: Specialty
Specialties: Automobiles
Credit Cards: Yes
Year Estab: 1970

Moran Books
PO Box 1231 Rocky Point 11778

Collection: Specialty books, magazines and ephemera.
Specialties: Transportation; natural history.
Credit Cards: No
Owner: Ed Moran

S. M. Mossberg, Bookseller   (914) 937-6400
50 Talcott Road Rye Brook 10573   Fax: (914) 235-5210

Collection: Specialty
# of Volumes: 15,000
Specialties: Science fiction; fantasy; horror.
Services: Catalog, accepts want lists.
Credit Cards: No
Year Estab: 1991

Mountain View Books   (914) 386-9226
314 County Road 35 Port Jervis 12771

Collection:	Specialty
# of Volumes:	1,000
Specialties:	Classics; antiquarian; philosophy.
Services:	Appraisals, catalog, accepts want lists.
Credit Cards:	Yes
Owner:	Christopher P. Mooney
Year Estab:	1988

New Wireless Pioneers   (716) 681-3186
PO Box 398 Elma 14059   Fax: (716) 681-3186

Collection:	Specialty
# of Volumes:	6,000
Specialties:	Television; radio; electricity and telegraphy; x-ray.
Credit Cards:	No
Owner:	James Kreuzer
Year Estab:	1985

Next Best Friend   (518) 537-4689
RD 1, Box 100-1 Elizaville 12523

Collection:	General stock.
# of Volumes:	10,000
Specialties:	Literature; history; travel; exploration. (Primarily scholarly)
Services:	Appraisals, catalog, accepts want lists.
Owner:	J. & B. Salamon
Year Estab:	1992

Nipper   (914) 679-6982
Box 4 Woodstock 12498   Fax: (914) 679-6904

Collection:	Specialty books, autographs, records.
# of Volumes:	5,000
Specialties:	Music (classical).
Services:	Appraisals, search service, catalog, accepts want lists.
Credit Cards:	Yes
Owner:	J.R. Peters & David Norbeck
Year Estab:	1971

Pages Antiquarian Books & Prints   (914) 666-8281
16 Dakin Avenue Mt. Kisco 10549

Collection:	General stock.
Specialties:	Dance; art.
Owner:	Trudy & Lew Goldmann

Paths Untrodden   (212) 661-5997
PO Box 3245. Grand Central Station New York 10163

Collection:	Specialty out of print and new books.
# of Volumes:	3,000+
Specialties:	Homosexuality (male only); men's issues; gay liberation.

Services: Search service, catalog, accepts want lists.
Credit Cards: No
Owner: Walter J. Phillips
Year Estab: 1979

Albert J. Phiebig Inc.   (914) 948-0138
PO Box 352 White Plains 10602   Fax: (914) 948-0784

Collection: Specialty
Specialties: Foreign books and periodicals.
Services: Search service, accepts want lists.
Credit Cards: No
Year Estab: 1947

Pier Books Inc.   (914) 268-5845
PO Box 5 Piermont 10968

Collection: Specialty
# of Volumes: 5,000
Specialties: Nautical
Services: Appraisals, search service, accepts want lists, occasional cata-
                   log.
Credit Cards: No
Owner: Dave Roach
Year Estab: 1976

Thomas Plasko   (718) 631-1013
57-15 246 Crescent Douglaston 11362

Collection: General stock.
# of Volumes: 2,000
Specialties: Books before 1900.
Credit Cards: No
Year Estab: 1983

Polyanthos Park Avenue Books   (516) 271-5558
600 Park Avenue Huntington 11743

Collection: General stock.
# of Volumes: 30,000
Specialties: Modern first editions; German; French; scholarly.
Services: Catalog, accepts want lists.
Credit Cards: Yes
Owner: Phyllis Ruth Nottman
Year Estab: 1974

Pride and Prejudice - Books   (518) 877-5310
11 North Hill Road Ballston Lake 12019

Collection: Specialty
# of Volumes: 8,000
Specialties: Rhetoric; women's studies; literary first editions; antiquarian.

Services:	Catalog, accepts want lists.
Credit Cards:	No
Owner:	Diane & Merrill Whitburn
Year Estab:	1985

Quaker Hill Books   (914) 238-5457
1016 Hardscrabble Road Chappaqua 10514

Collection:	General stock.
# of Volumes:	3,500
Specialties:	Signed first editions; sets; fine bindings; Civil War; Americana.
Services:	Appraisals, catalog in planning stage.
Credit Cards:	No
Owner:	Anthony Freyberg
Year Estab:	1987

William Roberts Co.   (516) 741-0781
99 Seventh Street Garden City 11530

Collection:	General stock.
# of Volumes:	2,000
Specialties:	Science; horology; fine art; cartography.
Services:	Accepts want lists.
Credit Cards:	No
Owner:	Robert Stenard
Year Estab:	1975

Craig W. Ross, Books & Autographs   (716) 798-1493
217 East Center Street Medina 14103

Collection:	General stock, ephemera and autographs.
# of Volumes:	2,000
Specialties:	Early Americana.
Services:	Lists, accepts want lists.
Credit Cards:	No
Year Estab:	1963

Charlotte E. Safir
1349 Lexington Avenue, 9-B New York 10128

Collection:	General stock
Specialties:	Cookbooks (in all languages); children's.
Services:	Search service, accepts want lists.
Credit Cards:	No
Year Estab:	1982
Comments:	Collection may also be viewed by appointment.

H. & R. Salerno   (516) 265-3008
1 Given Court Hauppauge 11788

Collection:	General stock.

# of Volumes:	15,000
Specialties:	Fine art; applied art; decorative arts; architecture; archeology.
Services:	Accepts want lists.
Credit Cards:	No
Owner:	Hank & Rose Salerno
Year Estab:	1975

Sandys   (516) 484-4678
PO Box 181 Albertson 11507

Collection:	General stock.
# of Volumes:	5,000
Specialties:	Children's
Services:	Appraisals.
Credit Cards:	No
Owner:	Norman & Doris Sandys
Year Estab:	1981

C. J. Scheiner, Books   (718) 469-1089
275 Linden Boulevard, B2 Brooklyn 11226   Fax: (718) 469-1089

Collection:	Specialty
# of Volumes:	10,000
Specialties:	Erotica, curiosa, sexology.
Services:	Appraisals, search service, catalog, accepts want lists.
Credit Cards:	No
Year Estab:	1978

Scottish Enterprises   (518) 462-3015
PO Box 2 Rensselaer 12144

Collection:	Specialty new and used books, prints and ephemera.
# of Volumes:	1,500
Specialties:	Scotland; British Isles; limited general stock, primarily literature and travel.
Services:	Search service, lists; accepts want lists.
Credit Cards:	No
Owner:	Elizabeth Naismith
Year Estab:	1989

Sentry Box Booksellers   (315) 458-6615
PO Box 2854 Syracuse 13220

Collection:	Specialty
# of Volumes:	2,000
Specialties:	French & Indian War; American Revolution; military history prior to 1900.
Services:	Catalog, accepts want lists.
Credit Cards:	No
Owner:	Donald Stoetzel
Year Estab:	1987

Tom Shaw Books
(518) 456-5905

11 Albright Avenue Albany 12203

Collection:	Specialty
# of Volumes:	10,000
Specialties:	Mystery; detective.
Services:	Search service, accepts want lists, occasional catalog.
Credit Cards:	Yes
Year Estab:	1963

Jonathan Sheppard Books
(518) 766-2781

Box 2020 Albany 12220

Collection:	General stock and specialty.
# of Volumes:	10,000+
Specialties:	Genealogy (American and European); American history (regional and local); European history; maps; ethnic history.
Services:	Search service, catalog, accept want lists. Owner also publishes reprints of 18th and 19th century European and North American maps.
Credit Cards:	No
Owner:	Meldon J. Wolfgang, III
Year Estab:	1977

Myrna Shinbaum - Books and Book Themes
(212) 982-5749

PO Box 1170 New York 10159

Collection:	General stock and prints with reading and book themes.
Specialties:	Children's; New York State; Judaica; etiquette; cookbooks; illustrated; art; J.M. Barrie.
Services:	Accepts want lists.
Credit Cards:	No
Year Estab:	1982

Silver Fields
(315) 736-7258

3 Slaytonbush Lane Utica 13501

Collection:	General stock.
# of Volumes:	10,000-15,000
Services:	Catalog in planning stage, accepts want lists.
Credit Cards:	No
Owner:	Pam Tritten
Year Estab:	1983

Marvin Sommer Bookseller
(716) 354-9761

PO Box 442, Bridge Station Niagara Falls 14305

Collection:	General stock.
# of Volumes:	100,000
Specialties:	Detective; true crime; food and drink; vintage paperbacks, pulps.

Services: Catalog, accepts want lists.
Credit Cards: No
Year Estab: 1971

Lee Ann Stebbins-Books   (607) 775-0432
PO Box 53 Conklin 13748

Collection: General stock
# of Volumes: 1,000-2,000
Specialties: Fiction, primarily western, mysteries, children's.
Services: Search service, catalog, accepts want lists.
Credit Cards: No
Year Estab: 1986

Sumac Books   (518) 279-9638
RD 1, Box 197 Troy 12180

Collection: General stock.
# of Volumes: 25,000
Specialties: Russian royalty; Russia; communism; socialism; radicalism; biography; politics; university press.
Services: Search service, accepts want lists.
Credit Cards: No
Owner: Edward Conroy
Year Estab: 1987

Terra Firma Books   (716) 244-5546
PO Box 10307 Rochester 14610

Collection: Specialty books, records and phonograph ephemera.
# of Volumes: 1,000
Specialties: History of recorded sound; Edison; mechanical music.
Services: Appraisals, search service, accepts want lists.
Credit Cards: No
Year Estab: 1985

Tesseract   (914) 478-2594
Box 151A Hastings-on-Hudson 10706   Fax: (914) 478-5473

Collection: Specialty
# of Volumes: 2,000
Specialties: History of scientific and medical instruments. Also sells early scientific instruments.
Services: Appraisals, catalog, accepts want lists.
Credit Cards: No
Owner: David Coffen
Year Estab: 1980

Sid Theil   (212) 421-5447
320 East 57th Street New York 10022   Fax: (212) 421-5365

Collection: General stock.

# of Volumes:	2,000
Services:	Lists, accepts want lists.
Credit Cards:	No
Year Estab:	1980

Theoria Scholarly Books   (212) 532-2162
175 Fifth Avenue, Ste. 2456 New York 10010

Collection:	Specialty
# of Volumes:	50,000
Specialties:	Philosophy; philosophy of science; linguistics; social sciences.
Services:	Appraisals, search service, catalog, accepts want lists.
Credit Cards:	Yes
Owner:	Marvin Lipper
Year Estab:	1976

Thomolsen Books   (516) 628-8819
P.O. Box 24 Bayville 11709

Collection:	Specialty
# of Volumes:	2,000
Specialties:	Mystery; detective; true crime.
Services:	Catalog, accepts want lists.
Credit Cards:	No
Owner:	Joan O. Golder
Year Estab:	1977
Comments:	Collection can also be viewed by appointment.

Winifred Tillotson   (315) 637-3955
215 Hunt Drive Fayetteville 13066

Collection:	Specialty
# of Volumes:	1,500
Specialties:	Decorative bindings; natural history.
Services:	Appraisals, accepts want lists, catalog.
Credit Cards:	No
Year Estab:	1988

Meir Turner Books   (718) 263-4782
105-24 67th Avenue, Ste. 2E Forest Hills 11375   Fax: (718) 544-6834

Collection:	Judaica
# of Volumes:	30,000
Services:	Appraisals, search service, accepts want lists.
Credit Cards:	No
Year Estab:	1984

Robert E. Underhill, Bookseller   (914) 452-5986
85 Underhill Road Poughkeepsie 12603

Collection:	Specialty new and used.

# of Volumes:	2,000 (combined)
Specialties:	Natural history; agriculture; hunting; fishing.
Services:	Search service, accepts want lists.
Credit Cards:	No
Year Estab:	1950

The Union Booktrader   (518) 725-4133
20 Union Street Gloversville 12078

Collection:	Specialty
# of Volumes:	3,000
Specialties:	American political history; American military history.
Services:	Appraisals, search service, catalog, accepts want lists.
Credit Cards:	No
Owner:	Alan P. Hosbach
Year Estab:	1990

The Veatchs, Arts Of The Book   (516) 265-3357
20 Veronica Court Smithtown 11787   Fax: (516) 360-2296

Collection:	Specialty
# of Volumes:	5,000
Specialties:	Printing history and technique; papermaking; book binding; calligraphy; book illustration; books about books; private presses; fine printings.
Services:	Appraisals, search service, catalog, accepts want lists.
Credit Cards:	No
Owner:	Robert & Lynne Veatch
Year Estab:	1975

D. Vining - Fine Books   (716) 425-1808
PO Box 981 Pittsford 14534

Collection:	General stock.
# of Volumes:	10,000
Specialties:	P.G. Wodehouse; fantasy; horror; detective fiction; books about books.
Services:	Appraisals, accepts want lists, subject lists.
Credit Cards:	No
Owner:	Douglas Vining
Year Estab:	1976

Alfred F. Zambelli   (212) 734-2141
156 Fifth Avenue New York 10010

Collection:	Specialty
Specialties:	Middle Ages; renaissance; reformation; bibliography; paleography; philosophy; history.
Services:	Catalog
Credit Cards:	No
Year Estab:	1950's

Zita Books   (212) 866-4715
760 West End Avenue, 3E New York 10025

Collection:	Specialty
# of Volumes:	2,500
Specialties:	Americana; American literature; poetry; art; children's; American illustration; music; Japan; Judaica; mission and exotic imprints; Southeast Asia; satirical drawing in broadsides; illustration and satirical periodicals.
Services:	Catalog
Credit Cards:	No
Owner:	G. Laderman
Year Estab:	1970

Zobel Book Service   (914) 883-6532
PO Box 153 Clintondale 12515   Fax: (914) 883-9016

Collection:	General stock.
# of Volumes:	200,000+
Specialties:	Scholarly; limited editions; signed editions; art; architecture; economics; education; literature; medicine; history; philosophy; religion; psychology; science; sociology; technical.
Services:	Search service, catalog, accepts want lists.
Credit Cards:	Yes
Owner:	Miriam & Aaron Zobel
Year Estab:	1942

Pennsylvania

Alphabetical Listing By Dealer

Alphabetical Listing By Location

Richboro	T. W. Clemmer	337
Riddlesburg	Brandywine Books	335
Rillton	Hoffman Research Services	330
Saegertown	Richard J. Sheakley - Antique and Book Store	311
Scranton	D.B. Lasky	339
	Mostly Books	311
Selinsgrove	D. J. Ernst - Books	312
Shippensburg	Robert M. Wynne (Cloak And Dagger Books)	342
Shohola	Alan F. Innes - Books	339
Sinking Spring	Thomas S. DeLong	331
Skippack	The Book Place	313
Slatington	Meadowbrook Hollow Books & Bits	331
Somerset	The Book Shoppe	313
Soudersburg	Mr. 3 L Collectors & Antique Center	313
Spring City	Indian Path Books	314
Spring Run	Somewhere In Time	341
State College	Harvey Abrams	334
	Steve Deutsch	337
Stewartstown	Stone House Books	331
Strasburg	Robert M. Grabowski Rare Books & Art	331
	Moyer's Book Barn	314
Stroudsburg	Carroll & Carroll, Booksellers	315
Tire Hill	Tire Hill Books	315
Unionville	J & J House Booksellers	315
Warminster	Volume Control	342
Warren	Dr. Ernest C. Miller	332
Washington	Rosemary Sullivan Rare Books	332
Wayne	Beattie Book Company	332
	The Book Shelf	316
	Konigsmark Books	332
Waynesboro	Kenton H. Broyles	336
	By The Books	316
	On The Road Books	333
West Chester	Antiques	333
	Baldwin's Book Barn	316
	Second Reading Book Store	317
Wilkes Barre	Michael B. Libenson, Bookseller	333
Williamsport	Do Fisher Books	333
	Timothy Hughes Rare & Early Newspapers	339
	Last Hurrah Bookshop	317
Willow Street	Game Bag Books	333
Wyncote	David Lachman	334
Wyoming	The Hermit's Book House	318
Yardley	George C. Bullock Bookseller	336
York	First Capitol Antiquarian Book & Paper	318
	Lauchman's Book Shop	319
	McIlnay's Books	319
	RAC Books in York Antique Mall	319
Youngwood	Second Time Around Bookstore	320

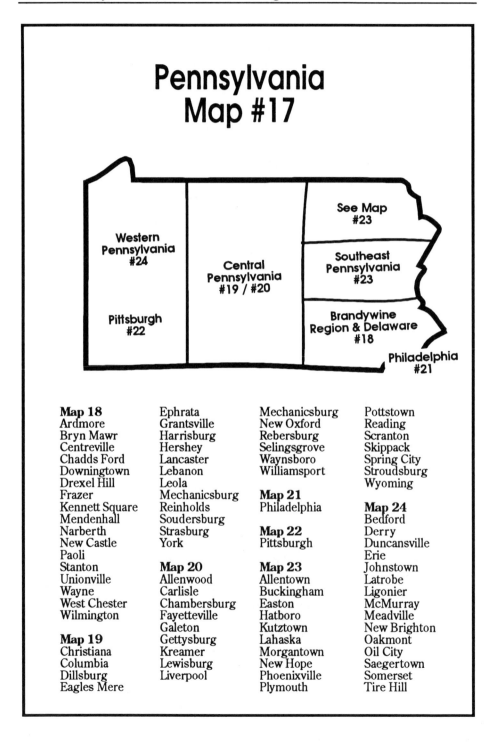

Pennsylvania
Map #17

See Map #23

Western Pennsylvania #24

Central Pennsylvania #19 / #20

Southeast Pennsylvania #23

Pittsburgh #22

Brandywine Region & Delaware #18

Philadelphia #21

Map 18
Ardmore
Bryn Mawr
Centreville
Chadds Ford
Downingtown
Drexel Hill
Frazer
Kennett Square
Mendenhall
Narberth
New Castle
Paoli
Stanton
Unionville
Wayne
West Chester
Wilmington

Map 19
Christiana
Columbia
Dillsburg
Eagles Mere

Ephrata
Grantsville
Harrisburg
Hershey
Lancaster
Lebanon
Leola
Mechanicsburg
Reinholds
Soudersburg
Strasburg
York

Map 20
Allenwood
Carlisle
Chambersburg
Fayetteville
Galeton
Gettysburg
Kreamer
Lewisburg
Liverpool

Mechanicsburg
New Oxford
Rebersburg
Selingsgrove
Waynsboro
Williamsport

Map 21
Philadelphia

Map 22
Pittsburgh

Map 23
Allentown
Buckingham
Easton
Hatboro
Kutztown
Lahaska
Morgantown
New Hope
Phoenixville
Plymouth

Pottstown
Reading
Scranton
Skippack
Spring City
Stroudsburg
Wyoming

Map 24
Bedford
Derry
Duncansville
Erie
Johnstown
Latrobe
Ligonier
McMurray
Meadville
New Brighton
Oakmont
Oil City
Saegertown
Somerset
Tire Hill

Allentown

Another Story (PA1)   *(215) 435-4433
100 North Ninth Street 18102

Collection:	General stock.
# of Volumes:	15,000-20,000
Hours:	Tue, Wed, Sat 10-5. Thu & Fri 10-9.
Services:	Accepts want lists.
Travel:	From I-78: Proceed on Rte. 222 North (Hamilton Blvd) to 10th St. Left on 10th and proceed 2 blocks. Right on next street for 1 block, then right on 9th. Shop is at end of block. Map 23.
Credit Cards:	No
Owner:	Bill Bascom
Year Estab:	1984
Comments:	A relatively small shop whose entrance is five steps up. The collection is somewhat limited with an emphasis on popular subjects such as entertainment, mystery, etc. Prices are quite reasonable.

Beachead Comics (PA2)   *(215) 437-6372
1601 Chew Street 18102

Collection:	Specialty
Specialties:	Science fiction; media; books about comics.
Hours:	Tue-Thu 12-8. Fri 12-9. Sat 10-6. Sun 12-5.
Services:	Appraisals, search service, accepts want lists.
Travel:	15th St. exit off Rte. 22. Proceed south on 15th St. to Chew. Right on Chew. Shop is one block ahead on right. Map 23.
Credit Cards:	No
Owner:	Jeff Rabkin & Biff Crossley
Year Estab:	1985

Books 'N More (PA3)   *(215) 435-4444
1409 North Cedar Crest Boulevard 18104

Collection:	General stock of paperback and hardcover.
# of Volumes:	10,000
Hours:	Mon-Fri 9-7. Sat 9-5.
Services:	Search service, accepts want lists.
Travel:	Cedar Crest Blvd. exit off Rte. 22. Proceed north on Cedar Crest. Shop is 500 feet ahead on right in shopping center. Map 23.
Credit Cards:	Yes
Owner:	Gwendolyn Allen

* Area code will change to 610 in January, 1994.

Year Estab:	1986
Comments:	The stock is 99% paperback and hardly worth a stop unless you're a paperback person or in the neighborhood.

The Occult Emporium (PA4)   *(215) 433-3610
102 North 9th Street 18102

Collection:	Specialty new and used books and related items.
# of Volumes:	1,000+
Specialties:	Occult
Hours:	Mon-Fri 1-7. Sat 1-5.
Services:	Catalog, mail order.
Travel:	See Another Story above. Map 23.
Credit Cards:	No
Owner:	Jay S. Solomon
Year Estab:	1977

Allenwood

The Last Hurrah Bookshop (PA5)   (717) 538-1886
At Bald Eagle Antique Center, Route 15
Mailing address: 937 Memorial Avenue Williamsport 17701

Collection:	General stock.
# of Volumes:	8,000-10,000
Hours:	Daily 10-5.
Travel:	On Rte. 15, 2 miles north of Allenwood, on the right. Map 20.
Credit Cards:	Yes
Owner:	Andy & Linda Winiarczyk
Year Estab:	1991
Comments:	See also Williamsport and Lewisburg.

Ardmore

Mystery Books (PA6)   *(215) 642-3565
42 Rittenhouse Place 19003   Fax: (215) 664-3899

Collection:	Specialty books and related items.
# of Volumes:	35,000
Specialties:	Mystery; horror; true crime; spy, adventure.
Hours:	Wed-Fri 11-6. Sat 11-5. Sun 11-4.
Services:	Accepts want lists, mail order.
Travel:	Exit 24 off PA Tpk. Proceed on I-476 south to Villanova exit, then east on Rte. 30 for about 5 miles into Ardmore. Right at Main Line Federal S &L building on Rittenhouse Pl. Map 18.
Credit Cards:	No
Owner:	Robert M. Nissenbaum & Norma R. Frank

Year Estab:	1990
Comments:	As its name implies, this shop is filled with mystery and detective fiction in mostly paperback but some hardcover. The condition of the books, however, leaves something to be desired. The fact that the books are very well organized so that whatever author you may be searching for can quickly be found is a plus. "Collectible" titles are shelved separately. If you don't see what you want on the shelves, ask, as the basement carries a back-up supply of titles as great as that which appears on the first floor shop area. The shop is roomy and neat with a comfortable seating area. The shop also carries a limited supply of new titles.

Athens

Franklin Book Shop   (717) 888-2616
224 South Main Street 18810

Collection:	General stock of new and used, paperback and hardcover.
Hours:	Mon-Fri 9-5, except Fri till 7. Sat 9-4.
Travel:	Exit 60 off Rte. 17. Follow signs to Athens business district.
Credit Cards:	Yes
Owner:	Janet Luft
Comments:	Primarily paperback with some hardcovers interspersed.

Bedford

Acorn Book Shop (PA8)   (814) 623-6824
200 East Pitt Street 15522

Collection:	General stock.
# of Volumes:	10,000
Hours:	Mon-Sat 10-5.
Services:	Appraisals, search service, accepts want lists, book binding.
Travel:	Exit 11 off PA Tpk. Proceed south for 2 miles on Business Rte. 220 (Richards St). Shop is in the basement of the building on corner of Pitt and Richards. Map 24.
Credit Cards:	No
Owner:	D & M Jones
Year Estab:	1959
Comments:	This basement level shop carries a modest sized collection of mostly older books bereft of dust jackets. We noted some interesting titles. While the books are neatly organized by subject, unfortunately, there are no labels on the shelves to direct the browser. The owner is knowledgeable with regard to local writers, including fantasy writer Dean Koontz.

Bryn Mawr

Avalon Books (PA9)   *(215) 525-3605
916 West Lancaster Avenue 19010   Fax: (215) 525-3605

Collection:	General stock.
# of Volumes:	15,000
Hours:	Tue-Sat 11-7.
Services:	Appraisals, search service.
Travel:	Exit 5 (St. Davids/Villanova) off Rte. 476. Bear right on Rte. 30 (Lancaster Ave). Proceed for about 2 miles. Shop is on the right. Look for a green neon sign in the window. Map 18.
Credit Cards:	Yes
Owner:	Anthony & Mirtha Amenta
Year Estab:	1992
Comments:	This is a group shop of 24 dealers. When displaying their books in a group shop, particularly one as clean and attractive as this one, dealers tend to put their best foot forward and the result is newer books that are in excellent condition, older books that are in the "hard to find" category and/or "interesting" titles. It is easy and pleasant to browse this shop, although you won't need a very long time to do so. The books are moderately priced.

The Owl Bookshop (PA10)   *(215) 525-6117
801 Yarrow Street 19010

Collection:	General stock.
# of Volumes:	50,000
Hours:	Tue, Thu, Fri 1-5. Sat 10-3. Closed Aug and 2 weeks at Xmas.
Travel:	From Lancaster Ave. (Rte. 30), turn at Elliot (look for 2 gas stations on corners), then left on Morris. Proceed under the railroad and twist to traffic light. Continue straight through light one short block and make left on Yarrow. Shop is in a house on right. Map 18.
Credit Cards:	No
Year Estab:	1971
Comments:	Owned and operated by Bryn Mawr volunteers for the benefit of the college's scholarship fund.

The Title Page (PA11)   *(215) 527-1772
24 Summit Grove Avenue 19010

Collection:	General stock.
# of Volumes:	15,000-20,000
Specialties:	Americana; art; architecture; scholarly.

Hours:	Tue & Thu 1-5. Sat 11-3. Other times by appointment.
Services:	Appraisals, search service, accepts want lists, mail order.
Travel:	Off Rte. 30, 1 block west of Bryn Mawr Trust Bank. Proceed 1/2 block. Shop is on right in the Wilson Building, a two story frame building. Map 18.
Credit Cards:	No
Owner:	Beverley Bond Potter
Year Estab:	1982
Comments:	The owner of this shop is both knowledgeable and "buyer friendly" and the shop is definitely worth a visit. Although the books are shelved in an organized manner, the browser must be sharp since the shelves are not labeled. The shop has more to offer than one might expect, including many titles of an unusual nature. There are bargains to be had. Rare items are kept in a locked bookcase.

Buckingham

Mainly Books (PA12)   (215) 794-8876
Buckingham Green, Route 202
Mailing address: PO Box 274   Holicong 18928

Collection:	General stock of paperback and hardcover and records.
# of Volumes:	8,000
Hours:	Mon-Fri, except Tue 10-6. Sat 10-5. Sun 1-5, except closed one Sun per month on a random basis.
Travel:	Located in a shopping plaza on Rte. 202, 1 mile south of Peddlers Village and 1/3 mile north of Rte. 413. Map 23.
Credit Cards:	No
Owner:	Tony & Carolyn Lemmo
Year Estab:	1990
Comments:	Approximately 85%-95% of the stock consists of paperbacks, mostly of the more popular variety. Hardcovers are scattered throughout the collection but few of them seemed to fall in the "uncommon" category. Unless you're in the neighborhood, we don't believe this shop requires a special trip.

Carlisle

Tarman's Friends of Man Books (PA13)   (717) 566-9843
At Northgate Antiques Mall   Fax: (717) 566-9843
Mailing address: 10 Dunover Court   Hummelstown 17036

Collection:	General stock and specialty (See Comments)
# of Volumes:	6,000

Specialties:	Dogs; cats.
Hours:	Daily 10-5.
Services:	Appraisals, catalog, accepts want lists.
Travel:	Map 19 or 20.
Credit Cards:	No
Owner:	Mary Ellen & James E. Tarman
Year Estab:	1989
Comments:	See also Kelley Court Antiques Mall in Grantsville. The dog and cat books are available by mail order only.

Chadds Ford

Doe Run Valley Books (PA14)   *(215) 388-2826
At Pennsbury-Chadds Ford Antique Mall
640 Baltimore Pike 19317

Collection:	General stock, maps and ephemera.
# of Volumes:	3,000
Specialties:	Brandywine illustrators.
Hours:	Thu-Sun 10-5. Mon by appointment.
Services:	Appraisals, accepts want lists, mail order.
Travel:	From Rte. 202, proceed south on Rte. 1 through Chadds Ford and up hill for about 2 miles. The antique mall is on left, in a red brick building. The book shop has a separate entrance on right side of the building. Look for a green awning. Map 18.
Credit Cards:	Yes
Owner:	Judith Shaw Helms
Year Estab:	1981
Comments:	An attractive shop with a modest collection of books in good condition. Little of what we saw was of an exceptional, i.e., rare, nature.

Elizabeth L. Matlat (PA15)   *(215) 358-0359
Route 202, Brandywine Summit Center
19317 Mailing address: PO Box 3511   West Chester 19381

Collection:	Specialty new and used.
Specialties:	Antiques, architecture.
Hours:	Mon-Sat 9-5. Sun 1-5 (except June-August).
Service:	Accepts want lists.
Travel:	1/4 mile south of intersection of Rtes. 1 & 202, or 5 miles north of I-95 on Rte. 202 proceeding north to West Chester. Map 18.
Credit Cards:	No
Owner:	Elizabeth L. Matlat

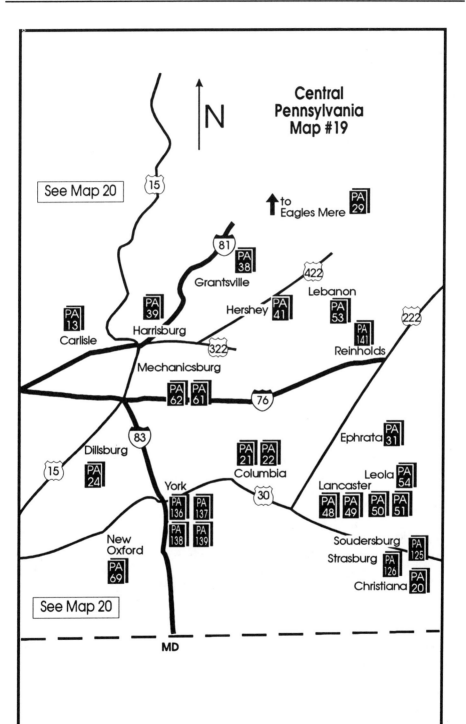

See Map 20

Central
Pennsylvania
Map #19

15

to
Eagles Mere

PA
29

81

PA
38

422

Grantsville

Lebanon

PA
13

PA
39

Hershey

PA
41

PA
53

222

Carlisle

Harrisburg

PA
141

322

Reinholds

Mechanicsburg

PA
62

PA
61

76

Ephrata

PA
31

83

Dillsburg

PA
21

PA
22

15

PA
24

Columbia

Leola

PA
54

York

30

Lancaster

PA
48

PA
49

PA
50

PA
51

PA
136

PA
137

PA
138

PA
139

New
Oxford

Soudersburg

PA
125

Strasburg

PA
126

PA
69

Christiana

PA
20

See Map 20

MD

Chambersburg

William B. Earley
On The Road Books
At Chambersburg Antique & Flea Market (PA16)   (717) 267-0886
868 Lincoln Way West 17201

Collection:	General stock.
Hours:	Daily 9-5.
Travel:	On Rte. 30, west of Chambersburg. Map 20.
Comments:	Multi dealer antique shop.

Light of Parnell Bookshop
At Famous Antique & Flea Market (PA17)   (717) 264-5916
1495 Lincoln Way East 17201

Collection:	General stock.
Hours:	Daily 9-5.
Travel:	On Rte. 30, east of Chambersburg. Map 20.
Comments:	Multi dealer antique shop.

Mason's Rare & Used Books (PA18)   (717) 261-0541
115 South Main Street 17201

Collection:	General stock.
# of Volumes:	22,000
Specialties:	Black history and literature; Civil War; Freemasonry; Pennsylvania; religion.
Hours:	Mon-Sat 10-5.
Services:	Appraisals, search service, catalog, accepts want lists.
Travel:	In downtown Chambersburg at intersection of Rtes. 11 & 30, just off I-81. Map 20.
Credit Cards:	Yes
Owner:	Jon D. & Susan L. Mason
Year Estab:	1975
Comments:	A real winner. A most hospitable owner will greet you and assist you in any way he can in this delightful shop located in the center of town. Almost all subject categories are represented and there are many bargains to be had if you happen to find titles of interest to you.

Northwood Books (PA19)   (717) 267-0606
59 North Main Street 17201

Collection:	General stock of hardcover and paperback.
# of Volumes	50,000
Specialties:	Children's; local history.

Hours:	Mon-Sat 10-5.
Services:	Appraisals, accepts want lists, mail order.
Travel:	See Mason's above. Map 20.
Credit Cards:	No
Owner:	Paula Rice
Year Estab:	1988
Comments:	While the stock in this storefront shop is at least 50% paper-back, the 50% that is hardcover is worth a quick run through. We would not normally consider this shop worth going out of the way for, but because it is only a few blocks from another used book store, we think it is worth the extra effort.

Christiana

Back Room Books (PA20)   *(215) 593-7021
2 South Bridge Street 17509   Fax: (215) 593-7021

Collection:	Specialty
# of Volumes:	5,000
Specialties:	Decorative arts.
Hours:	Wed-Sat 10-5. Sun 10-2. Other times by appointment.
Services:	Accepts want lists, catalog.
Travel:	Three miles south of intersection of Rtes. 41 & 30. Map 19.
Credit Cards:	No
Owner:	Charles & Michele Bender
Year Estab:	1986

Columbia

RAC Books (PA21)   (717) 684-5364
At Partner's Antique Center, 403 North Third Street
Mailing address: Box 296, RD 2   Seven Valleys 17360

Collection:	General stock.
# of Volumes:	3,000
Hours:	Daily 10-5.
Services:	Accepts want lists, mail order.
Travel:	Rte. 441 exit off Rte. 30. Shop is 1 block on left. Map 19.
Credit Cards:	Yes
Owner:	Anne P. Muren & Robin L. Smith
Year Estab:	1991
Comments:	See also York Antique Mall in York.

Antonio Raimo Fine Books (PA22)   (717) 684-4111
401 Chestnut Street 17512

Collection:	Specialty

# of Volumes:	10,000
Specialties:	Rare
Hours:	Mon-Fri 9-5 and other times by appointment.
Services:	Appraisals, search service, catalog, accepts want lists.
Travel:	Columbia exit off Rte. 30. Left at first light on Chestnut. Shop is one block ahead at corner of 4th & Chestnut. Map 19.
Credit Cards:	Yes
Owner:	Antonio Raimo
Year Estab:	1980
Comments:	"Mouth watering" are the words we would use to describe a visit to this establishment. Located in a stately mansion that is in the process of being renovated, a visit here is more like visiting a museum than a used, or even antiquarian, book shop. Book lovers may come and admire the books, kept behind glass in ornately carved book cases, but unless you have a fat checkbook and a taste for the truly rare (not merely scarce), this is not a place for the casual book buyer. Needless to say we were more than impressed.

Derry

The Used Book Store (PA23)   (412) 694-8600
Box 194A, RD 1 15627

Collection:	General stock of hardcover and paperback.
# of Volumes:	10,000
Hours:	Tue-Sat 10-5. Sun and Mon by appointment.
Services:	Accepts want lists.
Travel:	Blairsville exit off Rte. 22. Proceed on Rte. 217 south for about 7 miles. Call for additional directions. Map 24.
Credit Cards:	No
Owner:	Margaret B. Sell
Year Estab:	1982

Dillsburg

The Book House (PA24)   (717) 432-2770
Village Shops, Route 15 17019

Collection:	General stock new and used books.
# of Volumes:	25,000
Specialties:	Children's series; vintage paperbacks.
Hours:	Mon & Tue 10-4. Wed & Thu 10-6. Fri 10-7:30. Sat 10-4. First and third Sun 10-4.
Services:	Accepts want lists.

Travel:	Directly on Rte. 15 in a small shopping plaza. Map 19.
Credit Cards:	Yes
Owner:	Larry Klase
Year Estab:	1976

Downingtown

The Country Shepherd (PA25)   *(215) 873-0732
109 East Lancaster Avenue 19335

Collection:	General stock.
# of Volumes:	12,000+
Specialties:	Local history.
Hours:	Wed-Sat 10-6.
Services:	Search service, accepts want lists.
Travel:	Rte. 202 exit off Schuylkill Expy. (Rte. 76). Proceed south on Rte. 202 to Rte. 30. Stay on local road which becomes Bus. Rte. 30 or East Lancaster Ave. Shop is on the right, across from Downingtown National Bank. Map 18.
Credit Cards:	No
Owner:	Dorothy & Joseph Hirt
Year Estab:	1990
Comments:	A small, nicely decorated compact shop, offering books in generally good condition. The books are moderately priced and the owners go out of their way to please. Don't overlook the back room. The owners have an equal number of books in storage at home and are in the process of computerizing their collection.

Drexel Hill

Ron Lowden, Philadelphia's   Mall: *(215) 789-6622
Phoremost Ephemera File (PA26)
At Ardmart Antiques Mall, Landsdowne Ave. & State St. 19026

Collection:	General stock, ephemera and records.
# of Volumes:	Limited stock of books.
Specialties:	Musical theater (18th & 19th centuries).
Hours:	Thu-Sun 11-6, except Fri till 9. Closed Thu Jun-Aug.
Travel:	See below. Map 18.
Credit Cards:	No
Owner:	Ron Lowden
Comments:	In addition to the stock on display at the mall, the owner has a large collection in storage. If you call in advance, he can bring items you might be interested in to the shop.

Sottile's Books (PA27)   Mall: *(215)789-6622
At Ardmart Antiques Mall, Landsdowne Ave. & State St.
Mailing address: PO Box 528 Concordville 19331   Home: (215) 789-6742

Collection:	General stock and ephemera.
# of Volumes:	7,000-10,000
Specialties:	Local history; Philadelphia; southeastern Pennsylvania; New Jersey; Delaware; children's illustrated; antiques reference.
Hours:	Thu-Sun 11-6, except Fri till 9. Closed Thu Jun-Aug.
Services:	Appraisals, accepts want lists, mail order.
Travel:	From intersection of Rtes. 1 & 3, proceed for about 1 mile east on Landsdowne to State Rd. Mall is on right. Map 18.
Credit Cards:	No
Owner:	J. Robert Sottile
Year Estab:	1974
Comments:	Unlike other used book booths in antique malls, this "booth" is the size of a fair sized used book shop. The area is roomy, well lit and the books nicely displayed. We noted some older and interesting collectible items. Although the stall is technically closed when the owner is not there, access to the collection is available by asking one of the attendants.

Duncansville

Paper Americana (PA28)   (814) 696-4293
1314 Third Avenue 16635

Collection:	General stock and ephemera.
# of Volumes:	3,000
Specialties:	Local history; western Americana.
Hours:	Mon-Sat 11-5.
Services:	Appraisals, accepts want lists, mail order.
Travel:	Three miles south of intersection of Rtes. 220 & 22. Left at light in Duncansville. Shop is 4 blocks ahead on left. Map 24.
Credit Cards:	Yes
Owner:	Margaret Donnelly
Year Estab:	1973

Eagles Mere

Eagles Mere's Bookstore (PA29)
Route 42
Mailing address: RD #6, Box 40 Muncy 17756

Collection:	General stock.

# of Volumes:	Thousands
Hours:	Jul & Aug: Daily. Remainder of year: Sat & Sun.
Travel:	On Rte. 42 off Rte. 220 Map 19.
Credit Cards:	Yes
Owner:	Kathy A. Lyons
Year Estab:	1980
Comments:	The owner describes her stock as "mass market titles published within the last three years."

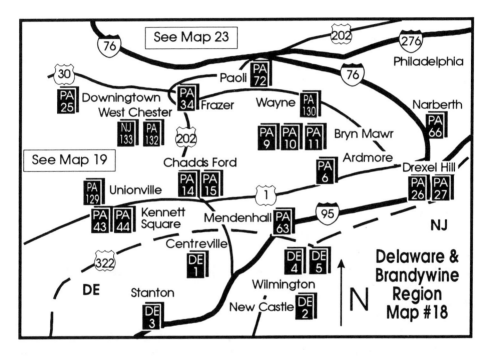

Easton

Quadrant Book Mart (PA30)   *(215) 252-1188
20 North Third Street 18042

Collection:	General stock.
# of Volumes:	60,000
Specialties:	Literature; film; music; performing arts; regional Americana; first editions.
Hours:	Mon-Sat 9:30-5:30, except Fri till 8.
Travel:	In downtown Easton, off the Centre Square. Map 23.
Credit Cards:	Yes
Owner:	Dick & Barbara Epstein
Year Estab:	1977

Comments: This bi-level shop offers a good selection of books, which for the most part, are quite reasonably priced. The books are in mixed condition. The majority of the collection consists of mostly vintage books, which in our judgement, is a plus.

Ephrata

Clay Book Store (PA31)   (717) 733-7253
2450 West Main Street 17522

Collection: General stock
# of Volumes: 50,000
Hours: Mon, Tue, Thu, Fri 8AM-9PM. Wed & Sat 8-5.
Travel: On Rte. 322 in village of Clay. Map 19.
Credit Cards: No
Owner: Lester Sauder
Year Estab: 1968

Erie

Erie Book Store (PA32)   (800) 252-3354
717 French Street 16501

Collection: General stock of new and used books.
# of Volumes: 20,000
Specialties: Pennsylvania petroleum history; Great Lakes; western Pennsylvania.
Hours: Mon-Sat 9-6.
Services: Accepts want lists.
Travel: Northbound on Rte. 79: Stay on Rte. 79 to the end when it becomes 12th St. Continue on 12th to Peach. Left on Peach, then right on 7th and right on French. Southbound on Rte. 79: Exit 6. Proceed on Peach and follow above directions. Map 24.
Credit Cards: No
Owner: Kathleen Cantrell
Year Estab: 1921
Comments: One of the few open shops offering used books in the northwestern corner of the state, the used books in this combination new and used book shop are of mixed vintage and are in various levels of condition.

Fayetteville

George Hall, Jr.
Somewhere In Time Books
At Fayetteville Antique & Flea Market (PA33)   (717) 352-8485
3653 Lincoln Way East 17222

Collection:	General stock.
Hours:	Daily 9-5.
Travel:	On Rte. 30, east of Chambersburg. Map 20.
Comments:	Multi dealer antique shop.

Frazer

Chester Valley Old Books (PA34)   *(215) 251-9500
489 Lancaster Avenue 19355

Collection:	General stock hardcover and paperbacks.
# of Volumes:	65,000
Specialties:	Children's; cookbooks; religion.
Hours:	Tue, Thu, Sat 11-6. Wed & Fri 11-8. Sun & hol 12-6.
Services:	Accepts want lists.
Travel:	Located on Rte. 30 (Lancaster Ave), 1 mile east of Rte. 202. Proceeding east, shop is on left. Map 18.
Credit Cards:	Yes
Owner:	Alicia W. Goodolf
Year Estab:	1986
Comments:	The first floor of this tightly packed bi-level roadside shop contains a mix of newer used books and older volumes. The basement is almost all paperback, except for some hardcover non fiction categories and science fiction. The shop offers few bargains but a nice variety of titles. The shop was formerly known as the Gwynedd Valley Book Store.

Galeton

Aaha! Books! (PA35)   (814) 435-3420
195 West Main Street 16922   (814) 628-5881

Collection:	General stock.
# of Volumes:	20,000
Specialties:	Religion
Hours:	Wed-Sat 11-5. Other times by appointment.
Services:	Appraisals, search service, accepts want lists, mail order.
Travel:	On Rte. 6, 1/4 mile east of Ox Yoke Motel. Map 20.
Credit Cards:	No

Owner: Gary R. Grah
Year Estab: 1992

Owner: Gary R. Grah
Year Estab: 1992

Gettysburg

Mel's Antiques (PA36)   (717) 334-9387
Rear 103 Carlisle Street 17325

Collection:	General stock.
Hours:	Fri-Sun 9-5.
Travel:	Eastbound: Go 3/4 round the circle in center of Gettysburg to Carlisle St. Shop is in alley behind first gas station on right. Go through the station. Map 20.
Comments:	Multi dealer antique mall.

Obsolescence (PA37)   (717) 334-8634
24 Chambersburg Street 17325

Collection:	Specialty
# of Volumes:	Small stock.
Specialties:	Religion
Hours:	Mon-Sat 9:30-5, except Fri till 8.
Travel:	On Rte. 30, in heart of downtown Gettysburg, 1/2 mile from square. Map 20.
Credit Cards:	No
Owner:	Donald & Joan Hinks
Comments:	Primarily a new book store with a small used book section.

Grantsville

Tarman's Friends of Man Books (PA38)   (717) 566-9843
At Kelley Court Antiques Mall   Fax: (717) 566-9843
Mailing address: 10 Dunover Court Hummelstown 17036

Collection:	General stock and specialty (See Comments)
# of Volumes:	6,000
Specialties:	Dogs; cats.
Hours:	Thu-Mon 10-5.
Services:	Appraisals, catalog, accepts want lists.
Travel:	Map 19.
Credit Cards:	No
Owner:	Mary Ellen & James E. Tarman
Year Estab:	1989
Comments:	See also Northgate Antiques Mall in Carlisle. The dog and cat books are available by mail order only.

Harrisburg

The Bookworm (PA39)   (717) 657-8563
At Silver Springs Antique & Flea Market, 6416 Carlisle Pike
Mailing address: 4335 Crestview Road Harrisburg 17112

Collection:	General stock.
# of Volumes:	50,000
Hours:	Sun 8-3. Other times by appointment at home location.
Services:	Appraisals, search service, accepts want lists, mail order.
Travel:	Exit 16 off PA Tpk. Proceed north on Rte. 11 for about 8 miles. Market is on left. Map 19 or 20.
Credit Cards:	No
Owner:	Sam Marcus
Year Estab:	1980

Hatboro

Abby's BookCase (PA40)   (215) 443-5799
291 County Line Road 19040

Collection:	General stock of hardcover and paperback and records.
# of Volumes:	20,000
Specialties:	Biography; history; mystery; science fiction; children's.
Hours:	Mon-Thu 11-8. Fri 11-7. Sat 11-6.
Services:	Search service, accepts want lists, mail order.
Travel:	Willow Grove/Jenkintown exit off PA Tpk. Proceed north on Rte. 611 for a few yards. Right on Mill Rd. which becomes Warminster Rd. Right at dead end on County Line. Shop is just ahead on left in County Line Shopping Center. Map 23.
Credit Cards:	Yes
Owner:	Abby Fern Cohen
Year Estab:	1988
Comments:	When we visited, the owner had recently relocated and was still in the process of stocking her shelves.

Hershey

Canal Collectibles (PA41)   (717) 566-6940
22 West Canal Street 17033

Collection:	General stock.
# of Volumes:	4,000
Hours:	Tue-Thu 10-6. Sat 10-6. Other times by appointment. Also, Apr 1-Labor Day only: Fri 10-4.

Services:	Appraisals, limited search service, accepts want lists, mail order.
Travel:	Exit 27 off I-81. Proceed on Rte. 39 towards Hershey for about 5 miles. Right at "Y" and proceed to bottom of hill. Right on West Canal. Shop is next to third house on left. Alternate directions: Shop is 1/2 mile off Hershey Park Drive in village of Union Deposit. Map 19.
Credit Cards:	No
Owner:	Kathleen Armstrong
Year Estab:	1990
Comments:	This attractively decorated stand alone building adjacent to the owner's home houses a modest collection of hardcover titles, paperbacks, ephemera and collectibles. You're not likely to find any truly rare items here but you might locate something of nostalgic interest.

Johnstown

Griffin Bookshop (PA42)   (814) 535-2322
430 Main Street 15901

Collection:	General stock of new and used hardcover and paperback.
# of Volumes:	4,000-5,000
Specialties:	Primarily fiction.
Hours:	Mon-Sat 9-5.
Services:	Search service, accepts want lists, mail order.
Travel:	Somerset exit off PA Tpk. Proceed north on Rte. 219 to Rte. 56 West (Johnstown Expy). Take Walnut St. exit off Rte. 56. Right at gas station and proceed 2 lights to Main. Right on Main. Shop is 1½ blocks ahead on right, across from Park. Map 24.
Owner:	Carolyn Walker
Year Estab:	1993 (See Comments)
Comments:	Primarily a new book store that has been in business for 11 years, the relatively new used book section is about evenly divided between paperbacks and more recent vintage previously owned hardcover titles. The books are in good condition and almost all the hardcover volumes are in dust jackets.

Kennett Square

Kennett Square Area Senior Center Bookstore (PA4)   *(215) 444-6069
202 East State Street 19348

Collection:	General stock.
# of Volumes:	Varies
Hours:	Daily 10-4.
Travel:	Located next to post office. Map 18.

Comments: If your interest is inexpensive reading copies of popular fiction, you're likely to pick up some bargains in this shop. Book hunters searching for more scholarly volumes, may, if they're lucky and/or have patience, find an item or two of interest. Operated by and for the benefit of the community's senior citizens, the stock comes entirely from donations.

Thomas Macaluso Rare & Fine Books (PA44)   *(215) 444-1063
130 South Union Street
Mailing address: PO Box 133   Kennett Square 19348

Collection: General stock, maps and prints.
# of Volumes: 20,000
Specialties: Children's; illustrated; literature; fine art; decorative arts; architecture; Americana.
Hours: Tue-Fri 1-5. Sat 11-5. Other times by appointment.
Services: Appraisals, catalog, accepts want lists, book binding and repair.
Travel: From Rte. 1, proceed to downtown Kennett Square. Union St. is Rte. 82. Shop is one block south of State. Map 18.
Owner: Thomas P. Macaluso
Year Estab: 1973
Comments: You'll find good books and good titles in this bi-level shop, as well as some unusual titles certainly in the rare and/or scarce category, if not antiquarian. The shop's better books and first editions are located on the first floor while the second floor is set aside for books in the $5-$15 price range. Few bargains.

Kreamer

Graybill's Old & Used Books (PA45)   (717) 374-1085
PO Box 157   17833

Collection: General stock and ephemera.
# of Volumes: 7,500+
Specialties: Pennsylvania history; history; medical; military; science fiction; mystery.
Hours: Tue, Fri & Sat 9-5. Wed & Thu 9-1. Other times by chance or appointment. Best to call ahead.
Services: Accepts want lists, mail order.
Travel: From Selinsgrove, proceed west on Rte. 522 for about 5 miles. Left at Freeburg Rd. (the second left after the bridge and opposite the red brick Wood Mode building on right). Shop is in center of town. Look for a large white house with green shutters. The shop is in a barn behind the house. Map 20.

Credit Cards:	No
Owner:	Eric & Diane Graybill
Year Estab:	1980
Comments:	While this collection, located on the second floor of a barn, is relatively small, we noted some period pieces worth examining. Prices were reasonable. The entire stock is computerized, although the computer is located in the house, not the barn.

Kutztown

The Used Book Store (PA46)   *(215) 683-9055
474 West Main Street 19530

Collection:	General stock.
# of Volumes:	35,000
Specialties:	Detective; mystery; science fiction; fantasy; vintage paperbacks.
Hours:	Tue-Fri 12-6. Sat 10-5. Closed first 3 weeks in Jan.
Travel:	Located on Main St. (Business Rte. 222) at west end of Kutztown. From US Rte. 78, proceed south at Krumsville/Kutztown exit on Rte. 737 to Kutztown. Then west (left) on Main and proceed to top of hill just before university. Look for a 2 story white house on left with a porch with pillars. Map 23.
Credit Cards:	No
Owner:	James H. Tinsman
Year Estab:	1979
Comments:	If you're a mystery or science fiction aficionado, you should enjoy browsing the many shelves of both hardcover and paperback titles this shop has to offer. In addition to the standard issue, there are lots of older and harder to find titles available. The rest of the collection is a mixed bag of fairly ordinary used and out-of-print books (few of which are rare) and typical of what one might find directly across from a university campus. The shop's second floor is devoted almost entirely to back issues of National Geographic.

Lahaska

Bucks County Bookshop (PA47)   (215) 794-3911
Hollyberry Square, Routes 202 & 263
Mailing address: PO Box 522 18931

Collection:	General stock.
# of Volumes:	8,000
Specialties:	Literature; scholarly.
Hours:	Thu-Sun 11-6.

Services:	Catalog (modern first editions and world literature only).
Travel:	Approximately 6 miles east of Doylestown, opposite the Friends Meeting House. Proceeding eastbound, shop is on right in a small shopping center. Map 23.
Credit Cards:	No
Owner:	Stephen Powell
Year Estab:	1979
Comments:	This is a relatively new location for an experienced used book dealer who takes well deserved pride in his stock. We noted a nice first editions section in addition to other traditional general stock categories. The shop is spacious and inviting.

Lancaster

The Book Bin Bookstore (PA48)   (717) 392-6434
14 West Orange Street 17603

Collection:	General stock and ephemera.
# of Volumes:	30,000
Specialties:	20th century fiction (including criticism and literary biographies); science fiction (paperbacks).
Hours:	Mon-Sat 10-6, except Wed & Fri till 9. Sun 12-5.
Services:	Accepts want lists, catalog.
Travel:	From Rte. 30 eastbound, take Fruitville Pike exit and proceed south into town on Prince St. From Rte. 30 westbound, take Rte. 501 south. Exit over railroad bridge at stockyards, then forced right on McGovern Ave. to Prince and left into town. The municipal parking lot on Prince, 1/2 block south of Orange, is within walking distance of all Lancaster shops. Map 19.
Credit Cards:	Yes
Owner:	Jane E. Shull
Year Estab:	1988
Comments:	A well organized, well labeled attractive shop with an interesting selection of hardcover and paperback books in good condition. The majority of the titles are of more recent vintage. Comfortable chairs encourage leisurely browsing.

Book Haven (PA49)   (717) 393-0920
146 North Prince Street 17603

Collection:	General stock, prints, maps and ephemera.
# of Volumes:	100,000
Specialties:	Pennsylvania Dutch/German/Amish; Pennsylvania imprints; children's illustrated; local history; Pennsylvania; magazines.

Hours:	Mon-Fri 10-5, except Wed till 9. Sat 10-4.
Services:	Appraisals, search service, accepts want lists, mail order.
Travel:	See above. Map 19.
Credit Cards:	Yes
Owner:	Kinsey Baker
Year Estab:	1978
Comments:	An absolutely delightful bi-level shop because a) it has a large selection of books which are almost all consistently in very good condition, b) the shelves are well organized and labeled, c) the books are reasonably priced, and, d) the shop is spacious, well lit, clean as a whistle and easy to browse.

Chestnut Street Books (PA50)   (717) 393-3773
11 West Chestnut Street
Mailing address: PO Box 846 17608-0846

Collection:	General stock.
# of Volumes:	12,500
Specialties:	Baseball; religion; Abraham Lincoln
Hours:	Mon-Sat 10-6, except Wed till 8.
Services:	Search service, catalog.
Travel:	See The Book Bin above. Map 19.
Credit Cards:	Yes
Owner:	Warren Anderson
Year Estab:	1991
Comments:	A most pleasant shop located within easy walking distance of three other shops. The books are well cared for and in almost pristine condition. Few if any older volumes.

Mosher Books (PA51)   (717) 293-1310
28 North Water Street
Mailing address: PO Box 111   Millersville 17551-0111

Collection:	Specialty
# of Volumes:	500-700
Specialties:	Antiquarian; fine bindings; early imprints; private presses; fine printing.
Hours:	Tue-Thu 10-6 and other times by chance or appointment.
Services:	Appraisals, accepts want lists, mail order, lists.
Travel:	See The Book Bin above. Map 19.
Credit Cards:	Yes
Owner:	Philip R. Bishop
Year Estab:	1991

Latrobe

Second Time Around Bookstore (PA52)   (412) 539-2062
Latrobe Plaza, Route 30 15650

Collection:	General stock of paperback and hardcover.
Hours:	Mon-Sat 1-8. Sun 12-5.
Services:	Accepts want lists.
Travel:	On Rte. 30 by airport. Map 24.
Credit Cards:	No
Owner:	Pat Selinger
Year Estab:	1989
Comments:	Primarily a paperback shop.

Lebanon

Johnson & Roth Used Books (PA53)   (717) 272-2511
121 East Cumberland Street 17042

Collection:	General stock.
# of Volumes:	20,000
Specialties:	Pennsylvania; military; theology; music
Hours:	Mon-Sat 10-5, except Fri till 9. Other times by appointment.
Services:	Appraisals, search service, catalog, accept want lists.
Travel:	East of Lebanon, on Rte. 422 West, between the traffic lights at 5th & Lincoln Aves. Note: The numbered streets are repeated to the east and west of Lincoln and Rte. 422 East and West are one way streets. Rte. 422 East is Walnut St. Map 19.
Credit Cards:	No
Owner:	James F. Johnson
Year Estab:	1981
Comments:	We found the stock in this storefront shop to be plentiful, in mixed condition, reasonably priced and well organized. Although there was some general disarray, such as books piled on the floor and in many of the aisles, we think the shop is worth a visit as there may well be some real finds here. The owner lives above the shop and is most gracious about accommodating visitors who may arrive a bit early or late.

Leola

Greg's Book Mart (PA54)   (717) 299-4734
At Meadowbrook Farmers Market, 345 West Main Street
Mailing address: 2721 Royal Road Lancaster 17603

Collection:	General stock.

# of Volumes:	50,000
Hours:	Fri 9-7. Sat 8-5.
Services:	Accepts want lists, mail order.
Travel:	Morgantown exit off PA Tpk. Take Rte. 10 to Rte. 23, which becomes West Main St. Map 19.
Credit Cards:	Yes
Owner:	Billie Dommell
Year Estab:	1981
Comments:	"New" stock is acquired by trade only.

Lewisburg

The Last Hurrah Bookshop (PA55)   (717) 327-9338
Route 15 Flea Market
Mailing address: 939 Memorial Avenue Williamsport 17701

Collection:	General stock.
# of Volumes:	4,000-5,000
Hours:	Sun only 8-4.
Travel:	Map 20.
Credit Cards:	No
Owner:	Andrew & Linda Winiarczyk
Year Estab:	1982
Comments:	See also Allenwood and Williamsport.

Otzinachson Book Shop
Carol's Paper Collectibles
Quill and Scroll
At Lewisburg Antique Center (PA56)   (717) 524-5733
Roller Mills Marketplace, 517 St. Mary Street 17837

Collection:	General stock and ephemera.
Hours:	Daily 10-5.
Travel:	North on Rte. 15 past intersection of Rtes. 45 & 25. Right on St. Mary St. Look for a large red building about 1 block ahead on right. Map 20.
Credit Cards:	No
Comments:	Multi dealer antique mall.

Ligonier

Drummer Boy Books (PA57)   (412) 238-7933
212 East Main Street 15658

Collection:	General stock of used and new.

# of Volumes:	15,000 (used)
Hours:	Mon-Sat 10-5. Also Sun 1-5 (May-Dec only).
Travel:	Donegal exit off PA Tpk. Proceed north on Rte. 711 for about 12 miles into Ligonier. Right at circle. Shop is about 2 blocks ahead on left. Map24.
Credit Cards:	Yes
Owner:	Wyatt & Nancy Young
Year Estab:	1983
Comments:	Located in what was once a private residence, most of the used books in this very pleasant shop are located in the basement (appropriately labeled "Best Cellars") and on the second floor where the browser will also find some comfortable chairs. Most of the books are older and very reasonably priced. We found the owners most helpful.

Liverpool

Alice's Book Shop (PA58)   (717) 444-7673
Routes 15/11
Mailing address: RD 2, Box 318   17045

Collection:	General stock.
# of Volumes:	20,000
Hours:	Dec 1-Mar 31: Mon, Tue, Thu-Sat. 10-5. Apr 1-Nov 30: Mon-Sat 10-5. Sun 12-5.
Services:	Accepts want lists, mail order.
Travel:	On Rtes. 11/15, about 2 miles south of Liverpool. Map 20.
Credit Cards:	Yes
Owner:	Henry & Alice Shaffer
Year Estab:	1975
Comments:	This roadside shop gives one the impression of what a country book store would have looked like many years ago. The shop has mostly older books, not always in the best condition. The owner is most pleasant and helpful. The books are inexpensive and there is a separate bargain book room (one step down) where the book hunter can walk away with lots of books (again not in the greatest condition) for very little money. The owner has plans to expand the shop which was formerly known as Bob's Books.

McMurray

Nancy Fireside's Book Exchange (PA59)   (412) 941-8146
226 East McMurray Road 15317

Collection:	General stock.

# of Volumes:	30,000
Hours:	Tue-Sat 10-5, except Thu till 8.
Travel:	Rte. 79 south to Canonsberg exit. Right off ramp and first right to bottom of hill. Bear right to fork in road. Bear right to light at Rte. 19. Proceed through light and onto East McMurray Rd. Shop is ahead on right. Map 24.
Credit Cards:	No
Owner:	Nancy Christiana
Year Estab:	1981
Comments:	Primarily a paperback shop.

Meadville

Leprechaun's Lair (PA60)   (814) 333-6527
926 Diamond Park 16335

Collection:	General stock.
# of Volumes:	25,000
Specialties:	Celtic history, biography and music; military; American history; world history.
Hours:	Mon-Fri 10-5 (closed for lunch). Sat: Opens at 10. Closing times varies.
Services:	Appraisals, search service, mail order.
Travel:	Diamond Park is in the center hub of the city. Map 24.
Credit Cards:	No
Owner:	John Delaney Hadden
Year Estab:	1989
Comments:	This small basement level shop stocks more books than it can reasonably shelve. While the owner's solution to his space problem is to pile books on top of each other on tables in a back room, browsers must lift the books in each pile separately to read the individual titles. We did see some first editions and the owner indicates that his rare titles and fine bindings are stored elsewhere. If you plan to visit this shop and your interest is fiction, leave yourself ample time to be able to browse the collection; the books are not necessarily shelved alphabetically. Moderately priced.

Mechanicsburg

Cloak and Dagger Books (PA61)   (717) 795-7470
219 East Main Street 17055

Collection:	Specialty new and used.
# of Volumes:	Several hundred.

Specialties:	Mystery
Hours:	Mon-Fri 10-8. Sat 10-5.
Services:	Accepts want lists.
Travel:	Located in Frankenberger Place, a 2 story red brick office building, on Rte. 641. Map 19 or 20.
Credit Cards:	Yes
Owner:	Deborah Beamer
Comments:	Primarily a new book store, this shop carries a very modest sized collection of used hardcover and a few paperback titles. What the store lacks in depth, it makes up for by carrying other non book mystery items such as games and puzzles.

Windsor Park Books & News (PA62)   (717) 795-8262
5252 Simpson Ferry Road 17055

Collection:	General stock of new and used, hardcover and paperback.
# of Volumes:	3,000-5,000
Hours:	Mon-Sat 7AM-9PM. Sun 7AM-5 PM.
Services:	Search service, accepts want lists, mail order.
Travel:	Rossmoyne/Wesley Drive exit off Rte. 15. Proceed 1 mile north on Wesley. Left at Simpson Ferry Rd. Shop is 200 yards ahead on left in shopping center. Map 19 or 20.
Credit Cards:	Yes
Owner:	John Kelley & Nick Marshall
Year Estab:	1989
Comments:	The rear section of this combination new/used book shop contains several bookcases filled with a variety of used books, some of more recent vintage and some a great deal older, with a bit of ephemera thrown in.

Mendenhall

William Hutchinson (PA63)   *(215) 388-0195
330 Kennett Pike
Mailing address: PO Box 909   19357

Collection:	General stock.
# of Volumes:	12,000+
Hours:	Most days 12-5, except Sun 1-5. Best to call ahead.
Services:	Appraisals, accepts want lists.
Travel:	On Rte. 52, 3 miles south of Rte. 1 or 8 miles north of I-95 in a one story, stand alone building. Map 18.
Credit Cards:	No
Owner:	William Hutchinson
Year Estab:	1978

Comments: If you're looking for recent best sellers, skip this shop. But, if you're looking for older books, this may be just the place for you. Located in a former general store, the shop has a fine collection of older (many turn of the century) books. A second building adjacent to the shop houses less expensive volumes and over-stock. For mystery aficionados, we saw several copies of "Queen's Quorum" titles at most reasonable prices. We also saw several "Oz" titles.

Morgantown

Walter Amos, Bookseller (PA64)   *(215) 286-0510
The Marketplace, Routes 10 & 23, RD 1, Box 205 19543

Collection:	General stock.
# of Volumes:	65,000
Specialties:	Religion; history; biography; fiction.
Hours:	Mon-Tue & Thu-Sat 10-5, except Fri till 8.
Travel:	On Rtes. 10 & 23, 1½ miles south and west of exit 22 off PA Tpk. Map 23.
Credit Cards:	Yes
Owner:	Walter L. Amos, Jr.
Year Estab:	1980
Comments:	Plan to spend a reasonable amount of time browsing this large collection located on the site of a weekend Farmer's Market. Most of the books are reading copies ranging from recent editions to some volumes well over 50 years old. Truly rare (or should we say "scarce"?) items are displayed in glass cases close to the cashier's counter. There's also a large New Arrivals section in the front of the shop. One rather large back room (which could easily constitute a shop of its own) contains paperbacks and large size hardcover titles. Prices are very reasonable. A visit here provides the browser with a double benefit as the shop is located two doors away from another fine used book store.

CML Books (PA65)   *(215) 286-7297
The Market Place, Routes 23 & 10 19543

Collection:	General stock of hardcover and paperback.
# of Volumes:	7,500
Specialties:	Military; religion; literature.
Hours:	Mon, Wed, Thu 10-5. Fri & Sat 10-6.
Travel:	See above. Map 23.
Credit Cards:	No

Owner:	Carolanne Lulves
Year Estab:	1990
Comments:	This is a very neat, spacious shop stocks a modest and meticulously organized collection. Most of the books are in excellent condition and reasonably priced.

Narberth

Narberth Books (PA66)   *(215) 664-5899
235 Haverford Avenue 19072

Collection:	General stock of new and used, hardcover and paperback.
# of Volumes:	20,000 (combined)
Specialties:	Metaphysical; eastern religions; astrology.
Hours:	Mon-Sat 11-7. Sun 12-5.
Services:	Accepts want lists.
Travel:	Rte. 1 exit off Schuylkill Expy. (Rte. 76). South on Rte. 1 to Presidential Blvd. Right on Presidential which leads into Montgomery. Left on Haverford. Map 18.
Credit Cards:	Yes
Owner:	Art Hochberg
Year Estab:	1991
Comments:	Most of the used stock in this combination new/used shop consists of fairly recent vintage books in pretty good condition and at prices a bit higher than in other used book shops. Perhaps this is a reflection of the upscale community in which the shop is located. According to the owner, the majority of his used stock comes from trades.

New Brighton

Book Trade (PA67)   (412) 847-3282
1008 Third Avenue 15066

Collection:	General stock of used and new, paperback and hardcover.
# of Volumes:	15,000 (used)
Hours:	Mon-Sat 10-5.
Services:	Accepts want lists.
Travel:	From Pittsburgh, proceed north on Rte. 65 which becomes Rte. 18 which leads into Third Ave. which is the main thoroughfare. Shop is across from Brighton Music Center. Map 24.
Credit Cards:	No
Owner:	Chris Dessler
Year Estab:	1986
Comments:	Primarily a paperback shop.

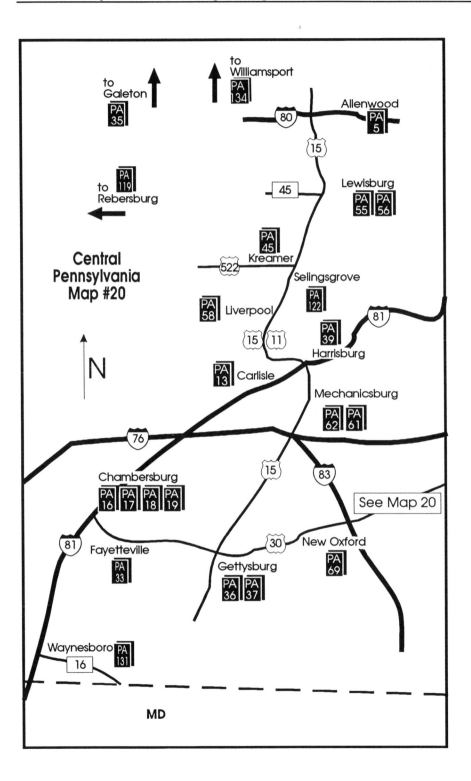

to Galeton
PA 35

to Williamsport
PA 134

80

Allenwood
PA 5

15

to Rebersburg
PA 119

45

Lewisburg
PA 55 PA 56

PA 45
Kreamer

522

Selingsgrove
PA 122

Central Pennsylvania Map #20

PA 58 Liverpool

N

15 11

PA 39

81

Harrisburg

PA 13 Carlisle

Mechanicsburg
PA 62 PA 61

76

Chambersburg
PA 16 PA 17 PA 18 PA 19

15

83

See Map 20

81 Fayetteville
PA 33

30 New Oxford
PA 69

Gettysburg
PA 36 PA 37

Waynesboro PA 131
16

MD

New Hope

Bridge Street Old Books (PA68)   (215) 862-0615
129 West Bridge Street 18938

Collection:	General stock.
# of Volumes:	6,000
Specialties:	First editions; illustrated; fine bindings; local history; art; performing arts.
Hours:	Sat & Sun 11-6 and other times by appointment.
Services:	Appraisals, accepts want lists, mail order.
Travel:	New Hope exit off Rte. 95. Proceed north on Taylorville Rd. and Rte. 32 (River Rd.) to New Hope. Left at the light (Main and Bridge Sts). Proceed 1/8 of a mile past the Wedgwood Inn. The shop is on the left. Map 23.
Credit Cards:	Yes
Owner:	Diane & Merritt Whitman
Year Estab:	1985

New Oxford

The Scott Family's Bookstore (PA69)   (717) 624-4142
5 Center Circle 17350   Fax: (717) 624-4142

Collection:	General stock.
# of Volumes:	20,000
Specialties:	World War II; scouting; antiques; coins; stamps; presidents; John F. Kennedy; hobbies.
Hours:	Sun 12-4. Mon 3:30-5. Tue 9-5. Wed 3:30-5. Thu 12-5. Fri 9-8. Sat 9-5.
Services:	Accepts want lists, mail order.
Travel:	On Rte. 30 in center of New Oxford hamlet. Map 19 or 20.
Credit Cards:	No
Owner:	John Vernon Scott
Year Estab:	1987

Oakmont

Mystery Lovers Bookshop (PA70)   (412) 828-4877
514 Allegheny River Blvd. 15139

Collection:	Specialty new and used.
# of Volumes:	A few hundred used.
Specialties:	Mystery
Hours:	Mon-Fri 10-7. Sat & Sun 9-5.

Services:	Newsletter, mail order.
Travel:	Exit 5 off PA Tpk. Follow signs to Oakmont. After crossing Hulton bridge, first right after railroad tracks on Allegheny. Shop is 5 blocks ahead on left. Map 24.
Credit Cards:	Yes
Owner:	Mary Alice Gorman
Year Estab:	1991

Oil City

Oil Region Book & Exchange (PA71)   (814) 677-4368
15 Central Avenue 16301

Collection:	General stock, records and ephemera.
# of Volumes:	8,000-10,000
Specialties:	Local history; early oil and petroleum maps; the oil region.
Hours:	Tue-Fri 10-6. Sat 11-4. Mon by chance or appointment.
Services:	Appraisals, search service, accepts want lists, mail order.
Travel:	Exit 3 off I-80. Proceed north on Rte. 8 for 24 miles. Map 24.
Credit Cards:	No
Owner:	Roxanne Hitchcock & R.E. Bowman
Year Estab:	1992
Comments:	A relatively small shop with a limited collection of mostly reading copies. Some interesting titles in the shop's areas of specialization, but few, if any, items of a truly rare nature. The owner has plans to expand the shop.

Paoil

Paoli Book Exchange (PA72)   *(215) 647-7150
11 Paoli Village Shoppes 19301

Collection:	General stock of paperback and hardcover.
# of Volumes:	25,000
Hours:	Mon-Sat 10-7. Sun 12-7.
Services:	Accepts want lists.
Travel:	1 block north of Rte. 30 (Lancaster Ave), behind Mellon Bank building in a shopping plaza. Proceeding west, turn right just after railroad station. Map 18.
Credit Cards:	No
Owner:	Sally Blaufuss
Year Estab:	1978
Comments:	The first floor of this bi-level shop is almost exclusively paperback. The basement, however, contains an even mix of paperback and older hardcovers not always in good condition. If you're

looking for inexpensive books, you'll find them here. But, if you're looking for books that are scarce and/or in very good condition, this is not a shop for you.

Philadelphia

William H. Allen, Bookseller (PA73)   (215) 563-3398
2031 Walnut Street 19103

Collection:	Specialty
# of Volumes:	30,000
Specialties:	Scholarly books with an emphasis on literature; history; philosophy; classical and medieval history.
Hours:	Mon-Fri 8-5. Sat 8:30-1.
Services:	Appraisals, catalog, accepts want lists.
Travel:	Between 20th & 21st Streets. Map 21.
Credit Cards:	No
Owner:	George R. Allen
Year Estab:	1917
Comments:	This absolutely wonderful shop is a scholar's dream. The three story shop is filled with serious works in a wide range of fields, with many fields represented in great depth. Considering the vintage and condition of the books, prices are most reasonable.

W. Graham Arader III (PA74)   (215) 735-8811
1308 Walnut Street 19107

Collection:	Specialty books, prints and maps.
Specialties:	Antiquarian (16th-19th centuries).
Hours:	Mon-Fri 10-6. Sat 10-5. Other times by appointment.
Services:	Catalog, appraisals, accepts want lists.
Travel:	Between 12th & 13th Streets. Map 21.
Credit Cards:	Yes
Owner:	W. Graham Arader, III
Year Estab:	1972
Comments:	Like its sister store in New York, this is a shop for serious book collectors with large pocketbooks, not a shop for browsers.

Bauman Rare Books (PA75)   (215) 546-6466
1215 Locust Street 19107   Fax: (215) 546-9064

Collection:	Specialty
Specialties:	Antiquarian; rare.
Hours:	Mon-Fri 10-5.
Services:	Catalog
Travel:	Between 12th & 13th Streets. Map 21.

Credit Cards:	Yes
Owner:	David L. Bauman
Comments:	This is not your typical walk-in used book store. Visitors need to be buzzed in before they can view and/or examine the shop's mouth watering volumes, all in pristine condition and displayed on open shelves. We suggest that anyone with a deep interest in the types of books likely to be seen here, write ahead for a catalog and then visit the shop to examine the books described therein.

Bob's Books, Record & Magazine Shop   (215) 755-7334
212 Ritner Street 19148

Collection:	General stock.
# of Volumes:	20,000 (See Comments)
Specialties:	Magazines
Hours:	Tue, Wed & Fri 10-8. Other times by appointment.
Services:	Search service, accepts want lists, mail order.
Travel:	Packer Avenue exit from Rte. 95. Left on Front St. and proceed to Oregon Ave. Left on Oregon, then second right on Ritner. Shop is in southern part of the city.
Credit Cards:	No
Year Estab:	1983
Comments:	The owner estimates he has an additional 80,000 books in storage. The shop also sells video games.

Book Mark (PA77)   (215) 735-5546
2049 Rittenhouse Square West 19103

Collection:	General stock, ephemera and prints.
# of Volumes:	5,000
Specialties:	Architecture
Hours:	Mon-Fri 10-5. Sat 12-5. Other times by appointment.
Services:	Appraisals, catalog (architecture only), accepts want lists.
Travel:	Between 20th & 21st and Locust & Spruce Sts. Map 21.
Credit Cards:	No
Owner:	Robert Langmuir Valerie Polin
Year Estab:	1978
Comments:	A charming shop with mostly older volumes, circa 1920's-40's, in good condition. While visitors will not find a large selection, the shop does offer many interesting titles and some classics.

The Book Shop   (215) 632-7835
3828 Morrell Avenue 19114

Collection:	General stock of paperback and hardcover.
# of Volumes:	50,000

Hours:	Mon-Wed & Fri & Sat 10-4:30.
Services:	Accepts want lists, mail order.
Travel:	Off 9900 Frankford Avenue (Rte. 13).
Credit Cards:	No
Owner:	Kathleen Schlarp
Year Estab:	1974
Comments:	The overwhelming majority of the stock is paperback.

The Book Trader (PA79)   (215) 925-0219
501 South Street 19147

Collection:	General stock.
# of Volumes:	250,000
Hours:	Daily 10-midnight.
Travel:	Corner of 5th St. in South Side neighborhood. Map 21.
Credit Cards:	Yes
Owner:	Peter C. Hiler
Year Estab:	1976
Comments:	Probably the largest, and certainly one of the most attractive, used book shops in Philadelphia, book lovers planning to visit this shop should leave lots of time for browsing. The books, most of which are in very good condition, are shelved in the most meticulous manner, and the shop's upstairs area is almost library-like in comfort and ambience. While the shop does carry paperbacks, mostly in the mystery and science fiction genres, a majority of the books are hardcover.

Bookhaven (PA80)   (215) 235-3226
2202 Fairmount Avenue 19130

Collection:	General stock.
# of Volumes:	50,000
Specialties:	Literary fiction; history; drama; poetry.
Hours:	Tue, Thu & Fri 11-7. Wed 11-9. Sat 10:30-5:30. Sun 12-5:30.
Services:	Accepts want lists, mail order.
Travel:	I-95 or I-76 to I-676 (Vine Street Expy). Take 22nd St. exit and proceed north on 22nd St. to Fairmount Ave. Turn left. Shop is second building on south side of street. Map 21.
Credit Cards:	No
Owner:	Rolf & Ricci Andeer
Year Estab:	1987
Comments:	If you're looking for a particular work of fiction that might have eluded you elsewhere, give this unpretentious storefront shop a try. The shop carries an excellent selection of both classic and semi classic fiction and literature, plus other scholarly subjects.

There's also a large section of paperback mysteries and science fiction. The books are reasonably priced.

BOOKS, etc. (PA81)   (215) 923-4640
609 South 3rd Street 19147

Collection:	General stock of paperback, hardcover, magazines and records.
# of Volumes:	20,000
Specialties:	Magazines
Hours:	Mon-Thu, except Tue 12-8. Fri & Sat 12-11. Sun 12-7.
Services:	Accepts want lists, mail order.
Travel:	South Street neighborhood, between Bainbridge & South Sts. Map 21.
Credit Cards:	No
Owner:	Joe Russakoff
Year Estab:	1990
Comments:	This small shop utilizes every inch of its limited space by using bookcases to partition off a maze of narrow alcoves. The books, more paperback than hardcover, are plentiful but not unusual. At least one third of the store's stock consists of records.

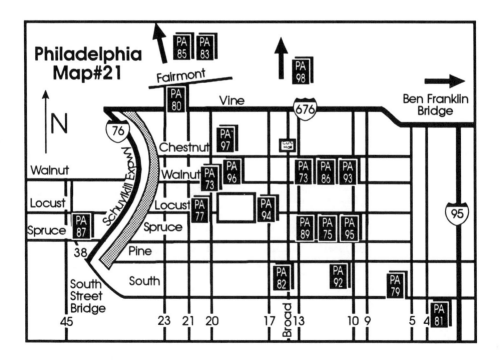

Factotum (PA82)   (215) 985-1929
1709 South Street 19146-1528

Collection:	Specialty
# of Volumes:	10,000
Specialties:	Art, including fine art, monographs; reference; catalogues raisonne; decorative arts; scholarly.
Hours:	Tue-Sun 12-6.
Services:	Appraisals, search service, catalog, accept want lists, estate consultation.
Travel:	South St. exit off Rte. 76. Proceed east on South to 17th. Map 21.
Credit Cards:	No
Owner:	Paul Reuther
Year Estab:	1983

Fran's Bookhouse (PA83)   (215) 438-2729
6601 Greene Street 19119   Fax: (215) 438-8997

Collection:	General stock.
# of Volumes:	40,000
Specialties:	Black studies; children's; multi cultural.
Hours:	Tue-Fri 11-6:30. Sat 12-6.
Travel:	Exit 32 (Lincoln Dr.) off Rte. 76. Proceed on Lincoln for 6 lights. Right on Hortter and proceed 1 block. Shop is at corner of Hortter and Greene in West Mt. Airy neighborhood near Wissahickon Park. Map 21.
Credit Cards:	Yes
Owner:	Francenia Emeru
Year Estab:	1978
Comments:	Fran treats her customers well. In addition to the coffee pot that greets one at the door, there are also plates of candy scattered through this neat, well organized and attractive shop. In addition to a strong collection in the specialty areas listed above, there are books representing most other general areas of interest. The books are in the "collectible" category. We were delighted to have been able to visit this shop and hope our readers will be able to share this experience. Don't miss the basement, several side rooms, and the display of "Contemptible Collectibles."

Friends of the Free Library   (215) 567-0527
Corner of 20th & Wood Streets 19103

Collection:	General stock.
# of Volumes:	6,000
Hours:	Mon-Fri 10:30-5:30. Sat 11-3:30.
Travel:	In Logan Square, behind Main Library, off Ben Franklin Pkwy.

Credit Cards:	No
Comments:	Operated by volunteers for the benefit of the public library. All books are donated.

George's Books of Manayunk (PA85)   (215) 482-2040
110 East Cotton Street 19127

Collection:	General stock.
# of Volumes:	20,000
Specialties:	Literature; history; metaphysical.
Hours:	Daily. Call for hours.
Services:	Search service, accepts want lists, mail order.
Travel:	Green Lane exit off Schuylkill Expy. Right on Main St. and proceed to Cotton. Map 21.
Credit Cards:	Yes
Owner:	George Miehle
Year Estab:	1992

Hibberd's Books (PA86)   (215) 546-8811
1310 Walnut Street 19107

Collection:	General stock of used, new and remainders.
# of Volumes:	5,000-10,000 (used)
Specialties:	Fine bindings; art; literature.
Hours:	Mon-Fri 10-6. Sat 10-5. Sun 1-6.
Services:	Search service, accepts want lists, mail order.
Travel:	At 13th Street. Map 21.
Credit Cards:	Yes
Owner:	Vail & Hayes Hibberd
Year Estab:	1986
Comments:	One should not be mislead by the appearance of this shop into thinking that it may not offer the fare of a true used book shop. This just isn't so. While the center of the store is devoted to new books and remainders, all attractively displayed, the side walls and rear portion of the store are devoted to used titles, with rare books displayed behind locked bookcases. Few bargains.

House Of Our Own (PA87)   (215) 222-1576
3920 Spruce Street 19104

Collection:	General stock of new and used books.
# of Volumes:	20,000
Hours:	Mon-Thu 10-6:30. Fri & Sat 10-6.
Travel:	South St. exit off I-76 (Schuylkill Expy). Proceed west on South which becomes Spruce to 38th St. Shop is on left between 38th & 40th Sts, across from the Univ. of Pennsylvania. Map 21.

Credit Cards:	Yes
Owner:	Deborah Sanford
Year Estab:	1971
Comments:	This bi-level shop carries a mix of scholarly new trade paperbacks on the first floor and used volumes, also of a scholarly nature, plus a strong literature section, on the second floor. The books are in generally good condition and are moderately priced.

George S. MacManus Company (PA89)   (215) 735-4456
1317 Irving Street 19107

Collection:	Specialty
Specialties:	Americana (18th & 19th century); English and American literature (19th & 20th century first editions).
Hours:	Mon-Fri 9-5.
Services:	Catalog, accepts want lists.
Travel:	Between Locust & Spruce, Juniper & 13th Sts, behind Historical Society of Pennsylvania building. Map 21.
Credit Cards:	No
Owner:	Clarence Wolf
Year Estab:	1930's
Comments:	Once the door is unlocked, you will have an opportunity to walk down three long aisles of books, all focusing on American history and culture. The books are in excellent condition and are moderately priced considering that these volumes are not generally available in typical used book stores.

Marlo Book Store   (215) 331-4469
2339 Cottman Avenue 19149

Collection:	General stock of new and used, hardcover and paperback.
Hours:	Mon-Sat 10-9:30. Sun 12-5.
Travel:	Cottman Ave. exit off Rte. 1. Shop is in Roosevelt Mall, just off exit.
Credit Cards:	Yes
Owner:	Rita Broad
Year Estab:	1963
Comments:	Primarily a new book store, the limited used collection is about evenly divided between hardcover and paperback titles.

Ninth Street Books & Records   (215) 922-2352
1022 South 9th Street 19147

Collection:	General stock and records.
# of Volumes:	5,000
Specialties:	Cookbooks

Hours:	Tue-Fri 10:30-5:30. Sat 9:30-5:30. Sun 9:30-2:30.
Travel:	Washington Ave. exit off I-95. Proceed on Washington to 9th St. Right on 9th. Shop is 1/2 block ahead on left.
Credit Cards:	No
Owner:	Molly Russakoff & Bob Dickie
Year Estab:	1989
Comments:	Located in the midst of a busy outdoor food market, even if you're not interested in books, you might find a walk through the market an experience. While we can't promise that the reader will discover any truly rare of esoteric volumes here, the book lover will get a taste of a less than traditional used book store atmosphere.

Old Original Bookfinders (PA92)   (215) 238-1262
1018 Pine Street 19107

Collection:	General stock of hardcover and paperback.
# of Volumes:	25,000-30,000
Hours:	Daily 12-7.
Services:	Accepts want lists, mail order.
Travel:	Between 10th & 11th Streets. Map 21.
Credit Cards:	No
Owner:	Bill Epler
Year Estab:	1984
Comments:	The books in this fairly crowded shop are mostly reading copies with the stock about evenly divided between hardcover and paperback. Book lovers are not likely to find anything rare or extremely unusual here.

Reedmor Magazine Company (PA93)   (215) 922-6643
1229 Walnut Street, 2nd Fl. 19107

Collection:	Specialty and some general stock.
# of Volumes:	2,000,000+
Specialties:	Magazines back to 1760; science fiction; horror; fantasy.
Hours:	Mon-Fri 11-5.
Services:	Search service, accepts want lists, mail order.
Travel:	Between 12th & 13th Streets. Map 21.
Credit Cards:	No
Owner:	David & Elaine Bagelman
Year Estab:	1935

Rittenhouse Medical Book Store (PA94)   (215) 545-6072
1706 Rittenhouse Square 19103   Fax: (215) 735-5633

Collection:	Specialty

# of Volumes:	5,000
Specialties:	Medicine
Hours:	Mon-Fri 9-5. Sat 10-5. Appointments preferred.
Services:	Catalog
Travel:	Map 21.
Credit Cards:	Yes
Owner:	Richard W. Foster
Year Estab:	1946

Russakoff Bookstore (PA95)   (215) 592-8380
259 South 10th Street 19107

Collection:	General stock of hardcover and paperback and records.
# of Volumes:	30,000
Hours:	Mon-Sat 11-7. Sun by chance.
Travel:	Between Spruce & Locust Streets. Map 21.
Credit Cards:	No
Owner:	Shassy & Jerry Russakoff
Year Estab:	1982
Comments:	We found it somewhat difficult to maneuver around the bookcases in this small, extremely crowded shop. Paperbacks seemed to outnumber hardcover titles, and in our opinion, most of the older books on the shop's "antiquarian" shelves lacked any true antiquarian value. The collection could be better organized.

John F. Warren, Bookseller (PA96)   (215) 561-6422
116 South 20th Street 19103

Collection:	Specialty new and used.
# of Volumes:	6,000
Specialties:	Art; art history; graphic arts.
Hours:	Mon-Fri 10-5.
Services:	Appraisals, accepts want lists, catalog.
Travel:	Between Chestnut & Walnut Streets. Map 21.
Credit Cards:	No
Owner:	John F. Warren
Year Estab:	1979

Whodunit? (PA97)   (215) 567-1478
1931 Chestnut Street 19103

Collection:	Specialty used and new, hardcover and paperback.
Specialties:	Mystery; espionage; suspense
Hours:	Mon-Sat 11-6:30.
Services:	Accepts want lists, catalog.
Travel:	Between 19th & 20th Streets. Map 21.

Credit Cards:	Yes
Owner:	Art Bourgeau
Year Estab:	1976
Comments:	The majority of the books are used and somewhat more than half the used collection is paperback.

Zavelle Book Store (PA98)   (215) 763-1514
1700 North Broad Street 19121

Collection:	General stock of new and used, hardcover and paperback.
Hours:	Mon-Thu 9-6. Fri 9-5. Sat 11-4.
Services:	Accepts want lists.
Travel:	At corner of North Broad and C.B. Moore Sts, approximately 1½ miles north of Vine St, on campus of Temple University. Shop is located in the Pizza Hut complex. Map 21.
Credit Cards:	Yes
Owner:	Angelo Bergonzi
Year Estab:	1908
Comments:	The majority of the used stock, divided about equally between hardcover and paperback, reflects the shop's location near a major university.

Phoenixville

The Book Bin Inc. (PA99)   *(215) 933-8450
Valley Forge Mall, Route 23 19460

Collection:	General stock of new and used, hardcover and paperback.
# of Volumes:	2,000 (used).
Hours:	Mon-Sat 10-9. Sun 12-5.
Services:	Search service, accepts want lists.
Travel:	Just west of intersection of Rtes. 113 & 23 in an indoor shopping mall. Map 23.
Credit Cards:	Yes
Owner:	Dot Mandell
Year Estab:	1976
Comments:	The used collection is about 60% paperback. The shop offers little that is special and for the true used book lover is generally not worth going out of one's way to visit.

The Bookworm (PA100)   *(215) 983-1490
742 Main Street 19460

Collection:	General stock.
Hours:	Tue 12:4:30. Wed 7-9PM. Thu 12-4:30. Sat 12-4:30.
Travel:	At corner of Main St. and Rtes. 23 & 29. Map 23.

Comments: This bi-level shop is operated by volunteers for the benefit of the
                local hospital. All books are donated.

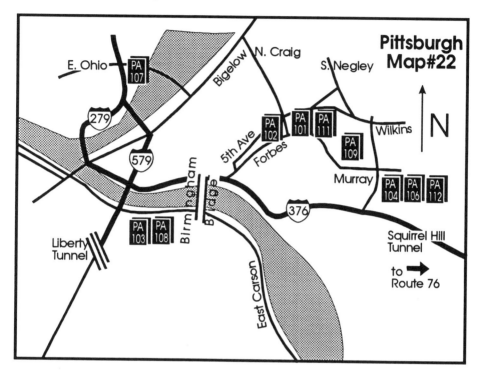

Pittsburgh

Bryn Mawr-Vassar Book Store (PA101)   (412) 687-3433
4612 Winthrop Street 15213

Collection: General stock and magazines.
# of Volumes: 20,000
Hours: Tue-Sat 10-4. Call ahead for reduced schedule of summer hours.
Travel: Oakland exit off Rte. 376. Proceed to Forbes Avenue. Make left
                  on South Craig and right on Winthrop. Map 22.
Credit Cards: No
Year Estab: 1973
Comments: In our travels we have visited several Bryn Mawr shops and
                  we're pleased to report that this is one of the best organized and
                  neatest of those visited to date. The books are in generally good
                  condition and cover most areas of interest. Needless to say, the
                  books are very reasonably priced. The shop is operated by vol-
                  unteers for the benefit of the college's scholarship fund and all
                  books are donated.

Caliban Book Shop (PA102)   (412) 681-9111
416 South Craig Street 15213

Collection:	General stock.
# of Volumes:	15,000
Specialties:	Poetry; humanities; scholarly; travel.
Hours:	Mon-Sat 11-5:30. Sun 12-5.
Services:	Appraisals, catalog, mail order.
Travel:	See above. Shop is on left immediately after turn on S. Craig. Map 22.
Credit Cards:	Yes
Owner:	John Schulman
Year Estab:	1986
Comments:	Located within easy walking distance of two other used book shops, this very neat and well organized shop is certainly worth a visit. The comfortable chairs are a sure sign that the owner welcomes browsers.

City Books, Inc. (PA103)   (412) 481-7555
1111 East Carson Street 15203

Collection:	General stock.
# of Volumes:	20,000
Specialties:	Philosophy; scholarly; literature; poetry; humanities.
Hours:	Mon & Sat 11-6. Tue, Wed, Thu 11-9. Fri 11-11. Sun 1-6.
Services:	Accepts want lists, mail order.
Travel:	On south side of city. Exit 6 off Rte. 376. Proceed on Blvd. of the Allies for 2 blocks, then make left and proceed to Forbes Ave. Right on Forbes and proceed 2 blocks to Birmingham Bridge. Right on East Carson at end of bridge. Shop is about 10-12 blocks ahead on right. Map 22.
Credit Cards:	Yes
Owner:	Ed Gelblum
Year Estab:	1986
Comments:	This bi-level shop features a rich collection of used and some rare books well displayed in a reader friendly environment. In addition to a first floor packed with "good stuff," browsers willing to climb a flight of stairs will find a second collection large enough to house a separate book shop, plus a selection of comfortable chairs. The prices are right and the store, in this writer's opinion, is a winner.

Crown Antiques & Collectibles (PA104)   (412) 422-7995
2301 Murray Avenue 15217

Collection:	General stock.

Hours:	Mon & Wed 12-7. Tue & Thu 12-9. Fri 12-5. Sun 12-5.
Travel:	See Mandala Books below. Map 22.
Owner:	Baruch Hyman
Comments:	Located a few doors away from another used book shop, this mostly antique and collectibles shop is worth a drop in visit when you're in the neighborhood.

Handy Andy   (412) 884-8400
3501 Saw Mill Run Blvd. 15227

Collection:	General stock of paperback and hardcover.
Hours:	Sat 10-5.
Travel:	Saw Mill Run Blvd. is Rte. 51. About 3 miles after Liberty Tubes.
Credit Cards:	No
Owner:	Andrew Levitske
Year Estab:	1993
Comments:	Primarily paperback.

Mandala Books (PA106)
2022 Murray Avenue 15217

Collection:	General stock.
# of Volumes:	15,000
Specialties:	Literature; scholarly; esoterica.
Hours:	Mon-Fri 10-9. Sat 10-7. Sun 10-6.
Services:	Accepts want lists.
Travel:	Rte. 376 to Squirrel Hill exit. Follow signs to Squirrel Hill. Left on Murray Avenue. Map 22.
Credit Cards:	Yes
Owner:	Frank Carroll
Year Estab:	1993

Pittsburgh Camera Exchange (PA107)   (412) 422-6372 (800) 722-6372
529 East Ohio Street 15212   Fax: (412) 231-1217

Collection:	Specialty books, magazines and images.
# of Volumes:	1,000
Specialties:	Photography
Hours:	Mon-Thu 9-5:30. Fri 9-7. Sat 9:30-5.
Services:	Appraisals, accepts want lists, mail order.
Travel:	Rte. 279 north through tunnel to downtown. After tunnel, take exit 13. Left at light at end of ramp on East Ohio. Shop is 2 blocks ahead on left. Map 22.
Credit Cards:	Yes
Owner:	Bruce Klein & Frank Watters
Year Estab:	1988

Riverrun Books (PA108)   (412) 481-9060
1113 East Carson Street, 2nd Floor 15203

Collection:	General stock.
# of Volumes:	25,000
Specialties:	Modern first editions; poetry; literature; art; vintage paper-backs.
Hours:	Mon-Thu 11-7. Fri 11-11. Sat 11-6. Sun 11-5.
Services:	Appraisals, search service, catalog, accepts want lists.
Travel:	On south side of city, two doors from City Books. Map 22.
Owner:	Maggy Aston & Robert Richards
Year Estab:	1985
Comments:	This roomy shop carries a selection of more recent used titles in addition to several bookcases of first editions. While there are no obvious signs to that effect, one suspects that this shop is likely to attract more of the "offbeat" crowd. See also By Appointment section in Greensboro.

Schoyer's Books (PA109)   (412) 521-8464
1404 South Negley Avenue 15217   Fax: (412) 521-8410

Collection:	General stock (primarily non fiction).
# of Volumes:	20,000
Specialties:	Pennsylvania history; American history; travel; history; women's studies; science; technology; oil; WPA.
Hours:	Sat 1-5 and other times by chance or appointment.
Services:	Appraisals, accepts want lists, catalogs (subject specific) .
Travel:	Pittsburgh exit off PA Tpk. Proceed south on Rte. 376 to Squirrel Hill exit. Follow signs for Squirrel Hill. Left on Murray, left on Solway and left on South Negley. Shop is on right. Map 22.
Credit Cards:	Yes
Owner:	Donnis deCamp & Marc Selvaggio
Year Estab:	1952

Seerveld's Books & Emporium   (412) 471-7793
400 Stanwix Street 15214

Collection:	General stock of remainders and used books.
Hours:	Mon-Fri 10-6. Sat 11-5.
Travel:	Downtown, near Gateway 3 building.
Credit Cards:	No
Owner:	Wesley C. Seerveld
Comments:	About 15% of the stock is used with a mix of hardcover and paperback.

Townsend Booksellers (PA111)   (412) 682-8030
4612 Henry Street 15213

Collection:	General stock.
# of Volumes:	20,000
Specialties:	Scholarly
Hours:	Mon-Sat 11-6. Sun 1-5. Other times by appointment.
Services:	Appraisals, search service, catalog, accepts want lists.
Travel:	Rte. 376 to Oakland exit. Proceed to Forbes Ave. Right on South Craig St. and right on Henry. Map 22.
Credit Cards:	Yes
Owner:	Neil & Beverly Townsend
Year Estab:	1984
Comments:	This shop, though modest in square feet, contains a wealth of good titles in equally good condition. We bought more than we anticipated here and after leaving regretted not having purchased some additional titles. The books are well cared for and selectively chosen by the owner. Don't overlook the recent arrivals section at the door. The entrance is up a few steps.

The Tuckers (PA112)   (412) 521-0249
2236 Murray Avenue 15217

Collection:	General stock.
# of Volumes:	10,000
Specialties:	Western Pennsylvania; medieval and Renaissance history.
Hours:	Mon-Fri 1-5. Sat 10-5. Other times by chance or appointment.
Services:	Appraisals, search service, accepts want lists, mail order.
Travel:	From Pittsburgh, take Rte. 376 east to Squirrel Hill exit. Follow signs to Squirrel Hill. Left on Murray. Map 22.
Owner:	Esther J. Tucker
Year Estab:	1972
Comments:	This is a moderate sized storefront shop with a collection displayed in an unpretentious manner. The subject areas are clearly identified and the books vary in age with the majority falling into the "older" category. We noted some interesting titles. The books are moderately priced and we consider the shop definitely worth a visit.

Writ & Wisdom   (412) 369-0689
9625 Perry Highway 15237

Collection:	General stock.
# of Volumes:	2,000
Specialties:	Religion; fiction.
Hours:	Mon-Sat 9-5.

Services:	Accepts want lists.
Travel:	Southbound on I-79, exit at Rte. 19 (Perry Hgwy) and proceed south. Northbound on I-79, exit at Yellow Belt and proceed east.
Credit Cards:	Yes
Owner:	Jane & Paul Sampsell
Year Estab:	1989
Comments:	The used books are in a section of a large religious book/church supply store.

Plymouth

Today's Treasures (PA114)   (717) 779-2929
10 East Main Street 18651

Collection:	General stock.
Hours:	Mon-Sun, except Tue, 12-5.
Services:	Accepts want lists, search service, mail order.
Travel:	Nanticoke (Rte. 29) exit off Rte. 81. After the bridge, make right on Rte. 11 North. Shop is on right, after 2nd light. Map 23.
Credit Cards:	No
Owner:	Donna Michak
Year Estab:	1968

Pottstown

The Americanist (PA115)   *(215) 323-5289
1525 Shenkel Road 19464   Fax: (215) 323-0885

Collection:	General stock.
# of Volumes:	10,000
Specialties:	Americana (literary and historical); literature.
Hours:	Mar 15-Dec 15: Mon-Sat 9:30-5:30. Sun by chance or appointment. Dec 15-Mar 15: by chance or appointment.
Services:	Appraisals, catalog.
Travel:	Rte. 100 to Rte. 724. Proceed west on Rte. 724 to Catfish Lane (3rd left after the shopping center). Left on Catfish and proceed to "T." Right at "T" on Valleyview Rd. Go .8 of a mile to 2nd left (Shenkel). Shop is first long driveway (gravel) on right. There are no signs indicating a book shop. Map 23.
Credit Cards:	Yes
Owner:	Norman & Michal Kane
Year Estab:	1954
Comments:	Somewhat out of the way but not hard to find, this book barn has room for far more books than were actually displayed when

we visited. The books we did see were an interesting assort-
ment of older titles in mixed condition. Although the owner
considers the collection a "general stock," not all areas are necessarily represented. The owners also conduct auctions from a
separate building on the site and many of the books in a recent
catalog were certainly in the antiquarian category.

John's Book Store (PA116)
125 North Charlotte Street 19464

Collection:	General stock.
# of Volumes:	20,000
Specialties:	Science fiction; Grace Livingston Hill.
Hours:	Mon-Sat 9-5.
Services:	Accepts want lists.
Travel:	Rte. 724 exit off Rte. 100. Proceed east to 3rd light (Hanover). Left at light, right on King and right on Charlotte. Map 23.
Credit Cards:	No
Owner:	John Sprague
Year Estab:	1991
Comments:	This two room corner shop, located in a residential neighborhood a block or two away from downtown Pottstown, carries a good general collection of used books in average to slightly below average condition. The back room is devoted strictly to fiction. While the books are shelved by category, there are no labels on the shelves to guide the browser.

Reading

Dell's Flea Market (PA117)   *(215) 376-7957
1018 Windsor Street
Mailing address: PO Box 13156   19612-3156

Collection:	General stock.
# of Volumes:	5,000
Hours:	Tue-Sat 11-5.
Travel:	Warren St. bypass off Rte. 222. Proceed to 11th St. exit. Proceed for about 2½ blocks. Right on 10th St. and proceed for about 8-10 blocks. Left on Windsor. Map 23.
Credit Cards:	No
Comments:	This establishment gives new meaning to the term "flea market." There are some books, both hardcover and paperback, and lots of old magazines. However, organization is non existent and access to some of the bookcases is blocked. Unless you have lots of patience and aren't fussy about ambience, your time could better be used traveling to a "real" used book store.

Whale of a Bookstore (PA118)   *(215) 373-3660
1001 Oley Street 19604

Collection:	General stock.
# of Volumes:	10,000
Hours:	Tue-Sat 10-5:30 and by chance on Mon.
Services:	Search service, accepts want lists, catalog.
Travel:	5th St. exit off Rte. 422. Map 23.
Credit Cards:	No
Owner:	Bob Smith
Year Estab:	1989
Comments:	Sadly, our advice is to visit this shop only if you or your spouse are interested in spending time in Reading's famous outlet shops located one block from the book shop. The shop is small, haphazardly organized and the books are not in the best condition. If, however, you do plan to visit, we suggest a call ahead as the owner may be relocating in the near future.

Rebersburg

Lamplight Bookshop (PA119)   (814) 349-8160
105 East Main Street   Fax: (814) 349-5933
Mailing address: PO Box 165   16872

Collection:	General stock.
# of Volumes:	5,000
Hours:	Mon-Sat 10-1.
Services:	Search service.
Travel:	On Rte. 192, 2 doors west of post office. Map 20.
Credit Cards:	No
Owner:	Carole M. Vetter
Year Estab:	1986

Reinholds

Heritage Antique Center (PA141)   *(215) 484-4646
RD #2, Box 225 17569

Collection:	General stock.
Hours:	Daily 10-5.
Travel:	Exit 21 off PA Tpk. Proceed north on Rte. 272 for about 1½ miles. Shop is on left. Map 19.
Year Estab:	1993
Comments:	A 40 dealer group shop.

Saegertown

Richard J. Sheakley - Antique and Book Store (PA120)
Mook Road   (814) 763-3399
Mailing address: RD 3, Box 8E 16433

Collection:	General stock.
# of Volumes:	3,000+
Specialties:	Antiques
Hours:	Mon-Fri 11-5 but best to verify. Sat & Sun 10-5.
Travel:	Exit 37 off I-79. Proceed on Rte. 198 east for about 2 miles. Turn right at shop sign. Map 24.
Credit Cards:	Yes
Owner:	Richard J. Sheakley
Year Estab:	1991
Comments:	During our visit, we saw some very old volumes which legitimately could be identified as antiquarian, as well as some more modern titles. The books were in mixed condition and were reasonably priced. Even though the collection is small, the shop is worth a visit if you're in the area. The owner also sells new reference books and price guides dealing with collectibles and antiques.

Scranton

Mostly Books (PA121)   (717) 343-2075
309 Adams Avenue 18503

Collection:	General stock of hardcover and paperback.
# of Volumes:	250,000
Specialties:	Guns; hunting; World War II, cookbooks; needlework; home repair; auto repair.
Hours:	Mon-Sat 10-5, and other times by appointment for serious buyers.
Travel:	Exit 53 off I-81. Continue straight to 2nd light at Adams Ave. Right on Adams and continue for one block and cross the intersection. Shop is first store on left. Map 23.
Credit Cards:	No
Owner:	Mary G. Scioscia
Year Estab:	1974
Comments:	A shop offering a large variety of mostly reading copies with few books priced in excess of $20. Also some remainders.

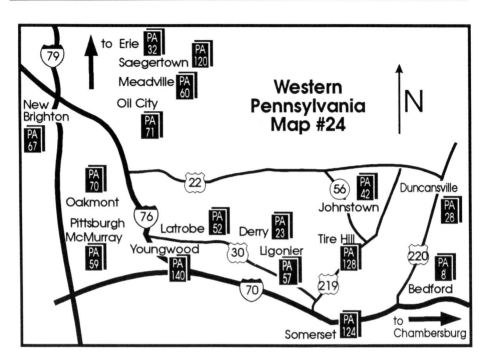

to Erie PA 32
Saegertown PA 120
79
Meadville PA 60
Oil City
New Brighton
PA 67
PA 71

Western Pennsylvania Map #24

N

PA 70
Oakmont
22
56 PA 42
Johnstown
Duncansville
PA 28

Pittsburgh
McMurray
76
Latrobe PA 52
Derry PA 23
Tire Hill
219
PA 128
220
PA 8

PA 59
Youngwood
30
Ligonier
PA 140
70
PA 57
Bedford

Somerset PA 124
to Chambersburg

Selinsgrove

D. J. Ernst - Books (PA122)   (717) 374-9461
27 North Market Street 17870

Collection:	General stock.
# of Volumes:	10,000
Specialties:	Central Pennsylvania history; Americana.
Hours:	Mon, Tue, Thu & Sat 9-4. Wed 9-12 noon. Fri 9-5:30.
Services:	Appraisals, search service, accepts want lists, mail order.
Travel:	In center of town, off Routes 11 & 15. Map 20.
Credit Cards:	No
Owner:	Donald Johnston Ernst
Year Estab:	1975
Comments:	Located on the main street of a small university town, this rather modest sized shop has a fine but limited collection of books in generally very good condition. The titles are older and some of the books would most legitimately be classified as antiquarian. While we saw several reading copies, there were also books that were of a more scholarly nature. A true book lover would enjoy visiting, but would not find it necessary to remain too long.

Skippack

The Book Place (PA123)   *(215) 584-6966
Routes 113 & 73
Mailing address: PO Box 236 19474

Collection:	General stock of hardcover and paperback and ephemera.
# of Volumes:	15,000
Specialties:	Children's series; military; fiction; science fiction; detective.
Hours:	Tue-Sun 11-5.
Services:	Accepts want lists, mail order.
Travel:	Proceed south on Rte. 113 to Rte. 73. Shop is located in a red barn on the southwest corner of Rtes. 73 & 113. Book shop shares barn with other businesses. Map 23.
Credit Cards:	No
Owner:	Bannie M. Stewart & Lt. Col. Lane Rogers, Ret.
Year Estab:	1984
Comments:	This bi-level book barn, offering some interesting titles and older volumes, is worth driving a few miles out of your way for.

Somerset

The Book Shoppe (PA124)   (814) 445-6052
212 West Main Street 15501

Collection:	General stock.
# of Volumes:	13,000
Hours:	Mon-Fri 9-6. Sat 9-5. Sun 1-4.
Services:	Accepts want lists, mail order.
Travel:	Exit 10 off PA Tpk. Turn right and take North Center Ave. to West Main St. Right on West Main. Map 24.
Credit Cards:	Yes
Owner:	Henrietta S. Spangler
Year Estab:	1990
Comments:	Despite the sign at the entrance, we almost overlooked the back room when visiting this modest sized storefront shop. The books are moderately priced and offer an interesting, but not mouth watering, general collection. At the time of our visit, there was a strong collection of cookbooks.

Soudersburg

Mr. 3 L Collectors & Antique Center (PA125)   (717) 687-6165
2931 Lincoln Highway East 17577

Collection:	General stock.

Hours:	Mon-Sat 10-9. Sun 7PM-10PM. Best to call ahead as shop closes one day a week every two weeks on a changing basis.
Travel:	On Rte. 30, 7 miles east of Lancaster. Map 19.
Owner:	Leonard Lasko

Spring City

Indian Path Books (PA125)   *(215) 495-3001
Route 23 & Bethel Church Road
Mailing address: 1010 Mowere Road   Phoenixville 19460

Collection:	General stock.
# of Volumes:	25,000
Specialties:	Philosophy; religion; science fiction; American Indian.
Hours:	Mon-Sat 9-9. Sun 9-5.
Travel:	Exit 23 off PA Tpk. Proceed north on Rte. 100 to Rte. 23, then east on Rte. 23 for 2½ miles to the shop. Map 23.
Credit Cards:	No
Owner:	Joyce Watson & William Hornikel
Year Estab:	1990
Comments:	This roadside shop has a surprisingly good collection of books, most in relatively good condition. The collection is well organized and well labeled, although there is not much depth.

Strasburg

Moyer's Book Barn (PA126)   (717) 687-7459
Route 741 West
Mailing address: 1419 Village Road   17579-9625

Collection:	General stock.
# of Volumes:	60,000
Specialties:	Local history; Pennsylvania history; railroad; magazines.
Hours:	Mon-Fri 10-5 (except 12-5 in Jan & Feb). Sat 10-3.
Services:	Search service, accepts want lists, mail order.
Travel:	On Rte. 741, about 2 miles west of Strasburg. Map 19.
Credit Cards:	No
Owner:	David G. Moyer
Year Estab:	1985
Comments:	An easy to find, spacious old fashioned bi-level barn. Most of the books are older editions in mixed condition. Much of the second floor is devoted to fiction consisting of titles popular in the 1930's-50's. One pleasant plus for the browser is the manner in which the shelves are labeled: virtually every shelf has several labels, clearly indicating subcategories, or in the case of fiction, the name of the author.

Stroudsburg

Carroll & Carroll, Booksellers (PA127)   (717) 420-1516
740 Main Street 18360

Collection:	General stock used and new books.
# of Volumes:	6,000-7,000
Specialties:	Science fiction; fantasy; history; Pennsylvania; philosophy.
Hours:	Mon-Thu 10-7. Fri 10-9. Sat 10-7. Sun 1-5 during Jun-Aug, Nov & Dec. and by appointment in off season.
Services:	Search service, accepts want lists, mail order.
Travel:	Park Ave. exit off I-80. Left off ramp on Park and proceed 3 blocks to Main. Left on Main. Shop is 3/4 of a block ahead. Map 23.
Credit Cards:	No
Owner:	George & Lisa Carroll
Year Estab:	1991
Comments:	More than half the stock is used.

Tire Hill

Tire Hill Books (PA128)   (814) 288-4109
Route 403   Fax: (814) 288-5201
Mailing address: PO Box 358 15959

Collection:	General stock.
# of Volumes:	8,000
Specialties:	Pennsylvania
Hours:	Wed-Sat 10-6. Sun 12-5. Other times by appointment.
Services:	Search service, catalog, accepts want lists.
Travel:	Somerset exit off PA Tpk. Proceed north on Rte. 219 to Davidsville exit. Left on Rte. 403 North. Map 24.
Credit Cards:	No
Owner:	Patrick Caroff, Manager
Year Estab:	1993

Unionville

J & J House Booksellers (PA129)   *(215) 444-0490
731 Unionville Road 19375

Collection:	General stock.
# of Volumes:	7,500
Specialties:	Color plates; travel; exploration; hunting; ancient civilizations; literature; philosophy; science; medicine; western Americana; fine printing.
Hours:	Mon-Sat 10-5.
Services:	Appraisals, catalog, accepts want lists.

Travel:	Rte. 1 to Rte. 82 North. Proceed on Rte. 82 for about 3 miles. Shop is just before intersection of Rtes. 82 and 926. Map 18.
Credit Cards:	Yes
Owner:	Jonathan & Joann House
Year Estab:	1978

Wayne

The Book Shelf (PA130)   *(215) 688-1446
4 Louella Court 19087

Collection:	General stock.
# of Volumes:	5,000
Specialties:	Pennsylvania
Hours:	Wed-Sat 10-4:30 but best to call ahead. Closed Jul & Aug.
Travel:	Just off Rte. 30, across from a stone church. Map 18.
Owner:	Lee DeWitt
Year Estab:	1992
Comments:	A small bi-level storefront shop. We noted a well stocked children's corner that should help occupy the younger set while their parents are busy browsing.

Waynesboro

By The Books (PA131)   (717) 762-3668
38 East Main Street 17268

Collection:	General stock of hardcover and paperback.
# of Volumes:	30,000
Hours:	Mon-Sat 10-5.
Travel:	Exit 3 off Rte. 81. Proceed east on Rte. 16 to town. Map 20.
Credit Cards:	Yes
Owner:	M. Albert Morningstar
Year Estab:	1990
Comments:	We found this shop to be a rather pleasant surprise as the sight of so many paperbacks when one enters the shop can be misleading. The store carries almost as many hardcovers as paperbacks in what seems like a never ending series of tiny rooms one discovers as one keeps walking further and further and further back. Very reasonably priced.

West Chester

Baldwin's Book Barn (PA132)   *(215) 696-0816
865 Lenape Road 19382   Fax: (215) 696-0672

Collection:	General stock, prints and maps.

# of Volumes:	300,000+
Specialties:	Americana; golf; sports; fine bindings.
Hours:	Mon-Fri 9-9. Sat & Sun 10-5.
Services:	Appraisals, accepts want lists, mail order.
Travel:	On Rtes. 52 & 100, south of West Chester. Map 18.
Credit Cards:	Yes
Owner:	Thomas M. Baldwin
Year Estab:	1934
Comments:	This is one place we don't think any true book lover would want to miss. In fact, although the shop remains open till 9PM, our advice is to arrive early in order to be able to spend unhurried time exploring the many nooks and crannies of this five story stone barn. The shop offers an extremely wide assortment of books covering virtually all areas of interest and in every category of collectibility. Most subjects are covered in depth. Better books ($75 or more) are kept in the front room and a New Arrivals table can be found on the second level. If you're interested in seeing the fine bindings collection, which for obvious reasons is kept in a locked room, we suggest you visit between 9-5.

Second Reading Book Store (PA133)   *(215) 692-6756
124 South High Street 19380

Collection:	General stock.
Hours:	Mon-Fri 10-4.
Travel:	In center of town. Map 18.
Comments:	Operated by and for the benefit of the area's senior citizens.

Williamsport

Last Hurrah Bookshop (PA134)   (717) 327-9338
937 Memorial Avenue 17701

Collection:	General stock and specialty.
# of Volumes:	30,000
Specialties:	Americana (20th century political); political assassinations; Kennedys; conspiracies; espionage; intelligence agencies.
Hours:	Wed & Fri 9-6. Other times by chance or appointment.
Services:	Appraisals, search service, catalog, accepts want lists.
Travel:	Rte. 15 to Maynard St. exit. Turn towards town (away from bridge) and proceed to end of street (about 5 blocks). Turn left and then take second right on Fifth Ave. Proceed to stop sign and turn right. Shop is third house on right. Map 20.
Credit Cards:	Yes
Owner:	Andrew & Linda Winiarczyk
Year Estab:	1982

Comments: In addition to a modest sized but interesting general stock, this
                  collection, located in a three story private house, probably has
                  one of the most exhaustive collections of printed resources, in-
                  cluding hardcover and paperback books, magazines and jour-
                  nals, related to the assassination of John F. Kennedy as well as
                  that historical period. Even if you're not a zealot on the JFK
                  assassination, you should still find the shop's other books worth
                  a visit if you're in the area. The owners also have booths at
                  antique malls in Allenwood and Lewisburg.

Wyoming

The Hermit's Book House (PA135)   (717) 696-1474
34 Mt. Zion Road 18644

Collection: General stock.
# of Volumes: 20,000
Hours: Mar 15-Dec 15: Fri-Sun 12:30-5. Other times by appointment.
Services: Search service, accepts want lists, mail order.
Travel: Rte. 309 North exit off Rte. 81. Proceed on Rte. 309 for about 4
                  miles to first light. Right on Carverton Rd. and proceed for
                  about 5 miles to stop sign. Left on West 8th St. Then first right
                  on Mt. Zion Rd. Map 23.
Credit Cards: No
Owner: Stephen Casterlin
Year Estab: 1980

York

First Capitol Antiquarian Book & Paper (PA136)   (717) 846-2866
343 West Market Street 17401

Collection: General stock, ephemera and collectibles.
# of Volumes: 200,000+
Hours: Wed-Sat 10-5. Sun 12-5. Open to dealers by appointment at
                  other times.
Services: Accepts want lists, mail order.
Travel: In the center of York. Map 19.
Credit Cards: No
Owner: Gwyn L. Irwin & Gary L. Robey, Jr.
Year Estab: 1984
Comments: With apologies to Filene's Basement, one enters this rather large
                  almost warehouse like group shop and views books in every
                  direction and in every state of condition. So many dealers exhibit
                  here (approximately 18) that it is unfair to generalize in terms of
                  the books to be found. There are bargains galore if you don't mind

purchasing books that are not in top notch condition. There are also, if you have the patience to walk in and out of the many many aisles, titles not generally seen elsewhere. As long as you're not looking for books in pristine condition, a visit to this multi dealer shop is an experience you will not soon forget.

Lauchman's Book Shop (PA137)   (717) 854-8915
355 West Market Street 17401

Collection:	General stock.
# of Volumes:	5,000-10,000
Specialties:	Americana
Hours:	Wed & Thu 10-6. Fri & Sat 10-8. Sun 12-5.
Services:	Appraisals, search service, accepts want lists, mail order.
Travel:	In center of York. Map 19.
Credit Cards:	No
Owner:	Dennis E. Lauchman
Year Estab:	1993

McIlnay's Books (PA138)   (717) 846-0315
306 West Market Street 17401

Collection:	General stock.
# of Volumes:	5,000
Specialties:	History; literature.
Hours:	Wed-Sat 10-4.
Services:	Search service, mail order.
Travel:	In center of York. Map 19.
Credit Cards:	No
Owner:	Mary Ann McIlnay
Year Estab:	1983
Comments:	The titles in this modest sized shop deal with more serious rather than frivolous subjects which is quite appropriate for a shop identifying itself as an "antiquarian book shop." Most of the books were in good condition. Some were clearly library discards. If you are a serious collector interested in scholarly works, we think you would enjoy a visit here.

RAC Books in York Antique Mall (PA139)   (717) 845-7760
236 North George Street 17401
Mailing address: Box 296, RD 2 Seven Valleys 17360

Collection:	General stock.
# of Volumes:	6,000
Hours:	Daily 10-5.
Services:	Accepts want lists, mail order.

Travel: In center of York. Map 19.
Credit Cards: Yes
Owner: Robin Smith & Anne Muren
Year Estab: 1990
Comments: See also Columbia.

Youngwood

Second Time Around Bookstore (PA140)   (412) 925-7202
Route 119 North 15697

Collection: General stock of paperback and hardcover.
Hours: Mon-Sat 10-7. Sun 12-5.
Services: Accepts want lists.
Travel: Map 24.
Credit Cards: No
Owner: Pat Selinger
Comments: Primarily a paperback shop.

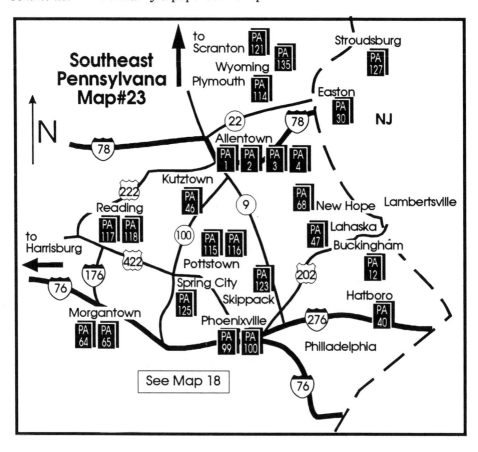

Ardmore

Tom Felicetti, Bookseller   *(215) 642-7961
606 Woodcrest Avenue 19003

Collection:	General stock.
Specialties:	Sports; horses; first editions; phrenology; film; nature; stage.
Services:	Accepts want lists, mail order.
Credit Cards:	No
Year Estab:	1992

Bethlehem

Dale Weiss   *(215) 868-7729
1411 Lorain Avenue 18018

Collection:	Specialty
# of Volumes:	500-1,000
Specialties:	Flintlock rifles; early military; mountainmen; fur trappers; western exploration; Indians; maps of the west and old forts.
Services:	Appraisals, search service, accepts want lists, mail order.
Credit Cards:	No
Year Estab:	1974

Bryn Mawr

Epistemolgist, Scholarly Books   *(215) 527-1065
PO Box 63 19010

Collection:	Specialty
Specialties:	Psychology; psychiatry; philosophy and related areas including mesmerism and pre 1840 phrenology.
Services:	Appraisals, catalog, accepts want lists.
Credit Cards:	Yes
Owner:	N.L. Wozniak
Year Estab:	1972

Carlisle

The Antiquarians   (717) 249-0922
885 West Old York Road 17013

Collection:	Specialty and ephemera.
# of Volumes:	1,000
Specialties:	Pennsylvania Germanica; early imprints (pre 1860); G.S. Peters Press; children's (early American).
Services:	Appraisals, accepts want lists.
Credit Cards:	No
Owner:	Edward L. & Linda K. Rosenberry
Year Estab:	1985

* *Area code will change to 610 in January, 1994.*

Blue Ridge Books   (717) 258-4408
PO Box 890 17013

Collection:	General stock.
# of Volumes:	5,000
Specialties:	Philosophy; history.
Services:	Search service, accepts want lists, mail order.
Credit Cards:	No
Owner:	Paul Drumheiser
Year Estab:	1992

Castanea

John J. McMann, Bookseller   (717) 748-8328
2 Collegewood Avenue 17745

Collection:	General stock.
# of Volumes:	6,000+
Services:	Search service, occasional catalog, accepts want lists, mail order.
Credit Cards:	No
Year Estab:	1986

Chambersburg

William Earley Books   (717) 263-8338
165 East Washington Street 17201

Collection:	General stock.
# of Volumes:	3,000
Specialties:	Beat generation; counter culture; modern literature; modern poetry; radical studies.
Services:	Search service, accepts want lists, mail order.
Credit Cards:	No
Comments:	See also Chambersburg in Open Shop section.

George Hall Jr. Books   (717) 263-4388
1441 Lincoln Way East 17201

Collection:	General stock
# of Volumes:	3,000
Specialties:	Non fiction.
Credit Cards:	No
Year Estab:	1975
Comments:	See also Fayetteville in Open Shop section.

Cesi Kellinger, Bookseller   (717) 263-4474
735 Philadelphia Avenue 17201

Collection:	Specialty
# of Volumes:	10,000
Specialties:	American art; women artists.
Services:	Catalog

Credit Cards: No
Year Estab: 1975

Doylestown

Oldhand Bindery   (215) 345-1553
14 Shady Spring Drive 18901   Fax: (215) 345-6224

Collection: General stock.
# of Volumes: 2,000+
Services: Search service, accepts want lists, mail order, book repair and
                   rebinding, slip cases.
Credit Cards: No
Owner: Theo B. & William Antheil, Jr.
Year Estab: 1991

Dresher

Myrna Bloom, The East West Room   (215) 657-0178
3139 Alpin Drive 19025   Fax: (215) 657-0178

Collection: Specialty
# of Volumes: 3,200
Specialties: Oriental rugs; textiles; Islamic art; travel history (Islamic World).
Services: Appraisals, catalog, accepts want lists.
Credit Cards: Yes (on orders over $200).
Year Estab: 1981

Glen Rock

The Family Album   (717) 235-2134
RD 1, Box 42 17327   Fax: (717) 235-8042

Collection: Specialty
# of Volumes: 20,000
Specialties: Antiquarian
Services: Appraisals, search service, catalog, accepts want lists.
Credit Cards: Yes
Owner: Ron Lieberman
Year Estab: 1969

Greencastle

Michael T. Shilling Bookseller   (717) 597-8007
152 South Washington Street 17225

Collection: General stock.
# of Volumes: 4,000-5,000
Specialties: Children's illustrated.
Services: Appraisals, search service, accepts want lists, mail order.
Credit Cards: No
Year Estab: 1981

Greensboro

Riverrun Books   (412) 943-3921
County Street 15338

Collection: General stock.
Owner: Maggy Aston & Robert Richards
Comments: Owners also maintain an open shop in Pittsburgh.

Hatfield

Jean's Book Service   (215) 362-0732
Box 264 19440

Collection: Specialty
# of Volumes: 8,000
Specialties: Americana; western Americana; children's; diaries.
Services: Appraisals, search service
Credit Cards: No
Owner: Roy & Jean Kulp
Year Estab: 1975

Havertown

Tamerlane Antiquarian Books and Prints   *(215) 449-4400
516 Katherine Road   Fax: (215) 449-7420
Mailing address: PO Box C Havertown 19083

Collection: General stock and ephemera.
# of Volumes: 500
Specialties: Illustrated; art; travel; sporting.
Services: Appraisals, catalog, accepts want lists.
Credit Cards: No
Owner: John Freas
Year Estab: 970

Hershey

Rebecca of Sunny Brook Farm   (717) 533-3039
PO Box 209 17033

Collection: Specialty
# of Volumes: 10,000+
Specialties: 20th century children's; illustrated; Golden books.
Services: Appraisals, catalog, accepts want lists.
Credit Cards: Yes
Owner: Rebecca Greason
Year Estab: 1981
Comments: The owner is writing a book about Golden Book collectibles.

Honesdale

Denis McDonnell, Bookseller
653 Park Street 18431

(717) 253-6416
Fax: (717) 253-6786

Collection:	Specialty
# of Volumes:	600-700
Specialties:	T.E. Lawrence (Lawrence of Arabia).
Services:	Appraisals, search service, lists, accepts want lists, mail order.
Credit Cards:	No
Year Estab:	1986

William Roos, Antiquarian Books
7 Hillcrest Circle
Mailing address: PO Box 247 Honesdale 18431-0247

(717) 253-4866
Fax: (717) 253-4866

Collection:	Specialty
Specialties:	E.A. Robinson; T.S. Eliot; private presses.
Services:	Appraisals, search service.
Credit Cards:	No
Year Estab:	1965

Jenkintown

Palinurus Antiquarian Books
101 Greenwood Avenue 19046

(215) 884-2297
Fax: (215) 884-2531

Collection:	Specialty
# of Volumes:	2,500
Specialties:	Technology; science; medicine; engineering; math; economics; early Americana; early literature.
Credit Cards:	No
Owner:	J. Hellebrand
Year Estab:	977

Landenberg

Rosamond L. duPont - Books
RD 1, Box 4 (Landenberg & Saw Mill Roads) 19350

*(215) 274-8436

Collection:	General stock.
Specialties:	Travel; children's; poetry; modern literature.
Services:	Mail order, accepts want lists.
Credit Cards:	No
Owner:	Rosamond L. duPont
Year Estab:	1987

Lititz

Antiquarian Maps & Book Den
217 East New Street
Mailing address: PO Box 412 Lititz 17543

(717) 626-5002
Fax: (717) 626-5002

Collection:	Specialty
# of Volumes:	3,000
Specialties:	Maps: 16th-19th centuries, including American and world.
Services:	Appraisals, search service, catalog, accepts want lists.
Credit Cards:	Yes
Owner:	James E. Hess
Year Estab:	1883

McSherrystown

Moog's Emporium   (717) 632-8157
155 North Second Street 17344

Collection:	General stock.
Services:	Accepts want lists, mail order.
Credit Cards:	No
Owner:	Blanch L. Moog
Year Estab:	1978

Mechanicsburg

William Thomas, Bookseller   (717) 766-7778
Box 331 17055

Collection:	General stock.
# of Volumes:	10,000
Specialties:	Pennsylvania history and imprints.
Services:	Appraisals, search service, occasional lists, accepts want lists, mail order.
Credit Cards:	No
Year Estab:	1960's

Mercersburg

Light Of Parnell Bookshop   (717) 328-3478
3362 Mercersburg Road 17236

Collection:	General stock.
# of Volumes:	10,000
Specialties:	Americana; Civil War; Pennsylvania; fiction.
Services:	Appraisals, search service, accepts want lists, mail order.
Credit Cards:	No
Owner:	Nathan O. Heckman
Year Estab:	1972
Comments:	See also Chambersburg in Open Shop section.

Mertztown

Charles Agvent Fine Books   *(215) 682-4750
RD 2, Box 377A 19539

Collection:	General stock.

# of Volumes:	3,000
Specialties:	Signed; fine bindings; private presses; handcolored plates; literary first editions (17th-20th centuries).
Services:	Appraisals, search service, catalog, accepts want lists, collection development.
Credit Cards:	Yes
Comments:	Owner also has books on display at the Kutztown Antique Gallery on Main Street in Kutztown.

Narberth

Bruce McKittrick Rare Books *(215) 660-0132
43 Sabine Avenue 19072 Fax: (215) 660-0133

Collection:	Specialty
Specialties:	15th & 16th century books.
Services:	Appraisals, catalog, accepts want lists.
Credit Cards:	No
Year Estab:	1980

New Brighton

Brighton Books (412) 847-2211
321 12th Avenue 15066

Collection:	Specialty new and used books.
# of Volumes:	2,000+
Specialties:	Civil War.
Services:	Appraisals, search service, catalog, accepts want lists.
Credit Cards:	No
Owner:	Jeffrey D. Wood
Year Estab:	1990

New Freedom

Miscellaneous Man (717) 235-4766
Box 1776 17349 Fax: (717) 235-2853

Collection:	Specialty
# of Volumes:	500-1,000
Specialties:	19th and 20th century graphic design.
Services:	Catalog, accepts want lists.
Credit Cards:	Yes
Owner:	George Theofiles
Year Estab:	1970

Newtown Square

S & C Najarian *(215) 353-5165
852 Milmar Road 19073

Collection:	Specialty
# of Volumes:	2,000-3,000
Specialties:	Americana; Harper's Weekly; 19th century sheet music.
Services:	Search service, accepts want lists, mail order.
Credit Cards:	No
Owner:	Chris & Steve Najarian
Year Estab:	1973

Philadelphia

Catherine Barnes   (215) 854-0175
2031 Walnut Street, 3rd Fl. 19103   Fax: (215) 854-0831

Collection:	Specialty books and autographs.
Specialties:	Signed; presidents; American history; European history; science; medicine; the arts.
Hours:	Mon-Fri 9-4.
Services:	Catalog, accepts want lists.
Credit Cards:	No
Year Estab:	985

Booksearch   (215) 843-6071
6228 Greene Street
Mailing address: PO Box 4197 Philadelphia 19144

Collection:	General stock.
# of Volumes:	25,000 .
Services:	Search service, catalog, accepts want lists.
Credit Cards:	No
Owner:	Art Carduner
Year Estab:	1980

David J. Holmes, Autographs   (215) 735-1083
230 South Broad Street, 3rd Fl. 19102   Fax: (215) 732-8151

Collection:	Specialty with some general stock.
# of Volumes:	2,000 (books)
Specialties:	Autographs; manuscripts, rare; first editions; presentation copies; original drawings of literary figures and artists.
Services:	Appraisals, catalog, accepts want lists.
Credit Cards:	No
Year Estab:	1982

Philadelphia Rare Books & Manuscripts Co.   (215) 744-6734
Box 9536 19124

Collection:	Specialty books and manuscripts.
Specialties:	Rare; Hispanica. (All books in collection printed prior to 1820).
Services:	Appraisals, catalog, accepts want lists.
Credit Cards:	Yes
Owner:	Cynthia Davis Buffington & David Szewczyk
Year Estab:	1985

Carmen D. Valentino, Rare Books & Manuscripts   (215) 739-6056
2956 Richmond Street 19134

Collection:	General stock and ephemera.
Specialties:	Americana; trade catalogues; local history; ledgers; diaries, broadsides, manuscripts.
Services:	Appraisals, accepts want lists, mail order.
Credit Cards:	No
Year Estab:	1977

Walk A Crooked Mile Books   (215) 242-0854
22 East McPherson Street 19119

Collection:	General stock.
# of Volumes:	5,000
Specialties:	Natural history; children's; children's illustrated; children's science; humor; detective; Americana; baseball; golf; classic automobiles.
Services:	Search service, catalog, accepts want lists. Will also make sales calls with stock to libraries and museums.
Credit Cards:	No
Owner:	Greg Williams
Year Estab:	1991

Phoenixville

Kathleen Rais & Co.   *(215) 933-1388
Rais Place Cottage, 211 Carolina Avenue 19460

Collection:	Specialty
# of Volumes:	500+
Specialties:	Dogs; Albert Payson Terhune.
Services:	Appraisals, search service, catalog, accepts want lists.
Credit Cards:	Yes
Year Estab:	1978

Pittsburgh

George Arent Fine Books   (412) 322-4362
3731 East Street 15214

Collection:	Specialty
# of Volumes:	10,000
Specialties:	Vintage paperbacks; pulps; science fiction; horror; fantasy.
Services:	Appraisals, accepts want lists, mail order.
Credit Cards:	No
Year Estab:	1983

Pignoli's   (412) 351-3365
965 Greensburg Pike 15221

Collection:	General stock.

# of Volumes:	10,000
Specialties:	Performing arts; golf autographs.
Services:	Accepts want lists, mail order.
Credit Cards:	No
Owner:	Christopher R. Pignoli
Year Estab:	1984

D. Richards Bookman   (412) 531-0531
314 Belle Isle Avenue 15226

Collection:	General stock.
# of Volumes:	8,000
Specialties:	Western Pennsylvania.
Services:	Accepts want lists, mail order.
Credit Cards:	Yes
Owner:	David Richards
Year Estab:	1977

Pottstown

S.F. Collins' Bookcellar   *(215) 323-2495
266 Concord Drive 19464

Collection:	Specialty
# of Volumes:	3,000
Specialties:	Children's; illustrated.
Services:	Accepts want lists, mail order, catalog in planning stage.
Owner:	Sue Collins
Year Estab:	1979

Revere

J. Howard Woolmer - Rare Books   *(215) 847-5074
577 Marienstein Road 18953

Collection:	Specialty
# of Volumes:	1,500
Specialties:	20th century literature.
Services:	Appraisals, catalog, accepts want lists.
Credit Cards:	No
Year Estab:	1960

Rillton

Hoffman Research Services   (412) 446-3374
PO Box 342, 243 Howell Road 15678

Collection:	General stock and specialty
# of Volumes:	15,000
Specialties:	Science; technical; sports.
Services:	Appraisals, search service, catalog, accepts want lists, research on any subject.

Credit Cards: No
Owner: Ralph Hoffman
Year Estab: 1966

Sinking Spring

Thomas S. DeLong   *(215) 777-7001
RD 6, Box 336 19608

Collection: General stock
# of Volumes: 3,500
Specialties: Western novels; western history.
Credit Cards: No
Year Estab: 1973

Slatington

Meadowbrook Hollow Books & Bits   (215) 767-7542
8842 Furnace Road 18080

Collection: General stock.
# of Volumes: 25,000
Hours: Owners are usually available by chance.
Services: Search service, mail order, accepts want lists.
Credit Cards: No
Owner: Margaret Anthony & Gail Haldeman
Year Estab: 1982

Stewartstown

Stone House Books   (717) 993-3927
RD 4, Box 4082, Webb Road 17363

Collection: General stock.
# of Volumes: 5,000
Specialties: Americana; native North American history; travel; gardening;
                 outdoor life.
Services: Search service, accepts want lists, mail order. Catalog planned.
Credit Cards: No
Owner: Jane M. Martin
Year Estab: 1991

Strasburg

Robert M. Grabowski Rare Books & Art   (717) 687-0924
PO Box 82 17579

Collection: Specialty books and historical prints and paintings.
# of Volumes: 200-500
Specialties: Early Americana (18th and early 19th centuries).
Services: Appraisals, catalog, accepts want lists.

Credit Cards: No
Year Estab: 1983

Warren

Dr. Ernest C. Miller   (814) 723-8335
PO Box 1 16365

Collection: Specialty
Specialties: Petroleum; natural gas.
Services: Appraisals
Credit Cards: No
Year Estab: 1946

Washington

Rosemary Sullivan Rare Books   (412) 225-1964
52 South Wade Avenue
Mailing address: PO Box 1596   15301

Collection: General stock.
# of Volumes: 20,000+
Specialties: Americana; genealogy; atlases; French and Indian War; Civil
                   War.
Services: Search service, catalog, accepts want lists.
Credit Cards: No
Year Estab: 1977

Wayne

Beattie Book Company   *(215) 687-3347
105 North Wayne Avenue 19087   Fax: (215) 687-5495

Collection: Specialty
# of Volumes: 1,000
Specialties: Architecture & allied arts; medicine; archaeology; fine bindings.
Services: Appraisals, catalog, collection development.
Credit Cards: Yes
Owner: Jim Beattie
Year Estab: 1975

Konigsmark Books   *(215) 687-5965
309 Midland Avenue, Box 543 19087

Collection: General stock.
# of Volumes: 15,000
Specialties: Literature; art; fine bindings.
Services: Appraisals, search service, lists, mail order.
Credit Cards: No
Owner: Jocelyn Konigsmark
Year Estab: 1980

Waynesboro

On The Road Books   (717) 762-4948
529 Green Street 17268

Collection:	General stock.
Specialties:	Hunting; fishing; first editions; natural history.
Services:	Appraisals, search service, lists, accepts want lists.
Credit Cards:	No
Owner:	Michael M. Kohler
Year Estab:	1984
Comments:	See also Chambersburg Open Shop section.

West Chester

Antiques   *(215) 436-4160
531 North High Street 19380

Collection:	Specialty
Specialties:	Children's illustrated.
Owner:	Bonnie & David Keyser

Wilkes Barre

Michael B. Libenson, Bookseller   (717) 779-3853
PO Box 83 18703

Collection:	General stock.
# of Volumes:	10,000+
Services:	Search service, accepts want lists, mail order.
Credit Cards:	No
Year Estab:	1992

Williamsport

Do Fisher Books   (717) 323-3573
1631 Sheridan Street 17701

Collection:	General stock, autographs and prints.
Specialties:	Pennsylvania; sports; illustrated; book plates; limited editions; first editions; children's; cookbooks.
Services:	Appraisals, search service, catalog, accepts want lists.
Credit Cards:	No
Owner:	Robert & Dolores Fisher
Year Estab:	1960

Willow Street

Game Bag Books   (717) 464-2941
2704 Ship Rock Road 17584

Collection:	Specialty

# of Volumes:	3,000
Specialties:	Hunting; fishing; outdoors.
Services:	Appraisals, search service, catalog, accepts want lists.
Credit Cards:	No
Owner:	Henry S. Saul
Year Estab:	1976

Wyncote

David Lachman   (215) 887-0228
127 Woodland Road 19095   Fax: (215) 887-0228

Collection:	Specialty
# of Volumes:	3,000-5,000
Specialties:	Theology; bibles; early printings; scholarly. (Secondhand to rare and valuable.)
Services:	Appraisals, search service, catalog, accepts want lists.
Credit Cards:	No
Year Estab:	1979

Mail Order Dealers

Harvey Abrams   (814) 237-8331
PO Box 732 State College 16804   Fax: (814) 237-8332

Collection:	Specialty
# of Volumes:	5,000+
Specialties:	Sports; olympic games; physical education; sports medicine; expositions and world fairs.
Services:	Appraisals, search service, catalog, accepts want lists, research, writing and consulting in areas of olympic games and sports history.
Credit Cards:	Yes
Year Estab:	1979

The Anglers Art Books For Fly Fisherman   (717) 243-9721
854 Opossum Lake Road Carlisle 17013

Collection:	Specialty new and used.
Specialties:	Fishing (fly).
Services:	Appraisals, search service, catalog, accepts want lists.
Credit Cards:	Yes
Owner:	Barry Serviente
Year Estab:	1973

Arnecliffe Books   (215) 527-2626
PO Box 292 Gladwyne 19035

Collection:	General stock.
# of Volumes:	2,000
Specialties:	Children's; New England.
Services:	Appraisals, search service, catalog, accepts want lists.
Credit Cards:	No
Owner:	Robert E. Trumbull
Year Estab:	1990

Thomas & Mary Jo Barron Books   (215) 572-6293
PO Box 232 Glenside 19038

Collection:	Specialty
# of Volumes:	2,500
Specialties:	Children's; illustrated; literature; private press.
Services:	Search service, accepts want lists.
Credit Cards:	No
Year Estab:	1987

Bookcell Books   *(215) 649-4933
                                              Fax: *(215) 658-0107
PO Box 506 Haverford 19041

Collection:	Specialty
# of Volumes:	8,000
Specialties:	History of science; medicine (history); mathematics; technology; physics; chemistry; biology.
Services:	Catalog, accepts want lists.
Credit Cards:	Yes
Owner:	George Lemmon
Year Estab:	1977

Booksearch   (215) 843-6071
6228 Greene Street Philadelphia 19144

Collection:	General stock.
Services:	Search service, accepts want lists.
Credit Cards:	No
Owner:	Arthur Carduner

Brandywine Books   (814) 928-5238
PO Box 127 Riddlesburg 16678

Collection:	General stock
# of Volumes:	40,000
Specialties:	Primarily non fiction.
Services:	Appraisals, search service, catalog, accepts want lists.
Credit Cards:	No
Owner:	Tim Shea
Year Estab:	1991

* Area code will change to 610 in January, 1994.

Kenton H. Broyles
(717) 762-3068
PO Box 42 Waynesboro 17268

Collection:	Specialty books and ephemera.
Specialties:	Ku Klux Klan.
Services:	Catalog, accepts want lists.
Credit Cards:	No
Year Estab:	1959

Buckingham Books
(717) 597-5657
8058 Stone Bridge Road Greencastle 17225   Fax: (717) 597-1003

Collection:	Specialty
# of Volumes:	6,000-7,000
Specialties:	Mystery; detective; espionage; bibliomysteries. First editions only.
Services:	Appraisals, search service, catalog, accepts want lists.
Credit Cards:	Yes
Owner:	Lewis J. Buckingham
Year Estab:	1989
Comments:	Collection can be viewed by appointment.

George C. Bullock Bookseller
(215) 493-2047
940 Queens Drive Yardley 19067

Collection:	Specialty
# of Volumes:	1,000
Specialties:	Americana; history; military.
Services:	Accepts want lists.
Credit Cards:	No
Year Estab:	1984

Harlow Chapman
*(215) 868-3362
1821 Homestead Avenue Bethlehem 18018

Collection:	Specialty
Specialties:	Black studies; history; Egypt.
Services:	Appraisals; lists; accepts want lists.
Credit Cards:	No
Year Estab:	1978

Stan Clark Military Books
(717) 337-1728
915 Fairview Avenue Gettysburg 17325

Collection:	Specialty
# of Volumes:	10,000
Specialties:	Military, especially Marine Corps; Civil War.
Services:	Appraisals, search service, catalog, accepts want lists.
Credit Cards:	No
Year Estab:	1985

T. W. Clemmer   (215) 355-1627
236 Manor Drive Richboro 18954

Collection:	Specialty
# of Volumes:	15,000
Specialties:	Children's; American literature.
Services:	Catalog (occasional), accepts want lists.
Credit Cards:	No
Year Estab:	1987

Miriam I. & William H. Crawford Books
PO Box 42587 Philadelphia 19101

Collection:	General stock and ephemera.
Specialties:	Black studies; radical; Marxism.
Services:	Accepts want lists.
Credit Cards:	No
Year Estab:	1986

Detecto Mysterioso   (215) 923-0211
c/o SHP, 507 South 8th Street Philadelphia 19147   Fax: (215) 923-1789

Collection:	Specialty
# of Volumes:	30,000
Specialties:	Mystery; thriller; suspense.
Services:	Accepts want lists.
Credit Cards:	Yes
Owner:	Jay Kogan
Year Estab:	1981

Steve Deutsch   (814) 238-1603
511 West Fairmount Avenue State College 16801

Collection:	General stock.
# of Volumes:	5,000-10,000
Specialties:	Modern first editions.
Services:	Search service, accepts want lists.
Credit Cards:	No
Year Estab:	1990

Esoterica Book Gallery   *(215) 527-1260
734 Waverly Road Bryn Mawr 19010

Collection:	General stock.
# of Volumes:	50,000
Specialties:	Science fiction; mystery; modern first editions; signed; proof copies; limited editions.
Services:	Appraisals, search service, accepts want lists, catalog.
Credit Cards:	Yes
Owner:	Judith Cutler
Year Estab:	1985

Gateway Booksellers
*(215) 847-5644

PO Box 163 Ferndale 18921

Collection:	Specialty
# of Volumes:	10,000
Specialties:	Occult; mysticism; eastern religions.
Services:	Appraisals (specialties only); accepts want lists, search service.
Credit Cards:	No
Owner:	Jeanne Gorham
Year Estab:	1931

Gravesend Books
(717) 646-3317

Box 235 Pocono Pines 18350

Collection:	Specialty
# of Volumes:	20,000
Specialties:	Mystery; crime fiction; Sherlock Holmes.
Services:	Appraisals, search service, catalog, accepts want lists.
Credit Cards:	No
Owner:	Enola Stewart
Year Estab:	1971

Gwyn's Collectibles
(717) 957-4669

211 Front Street Marysville 17053

Collection:	General stock.
# of Volumes:	10,000
Specialties:	Pennsylvania; Civil War; architecture.
Services:	Catalog, accepts wants lists.
Credit Cards:	No
Owner:	Gwyn L. Irwin
Year Estab:	1975
Comments:	Also displays at First Capitol Books & Antiques in York, PA.

Hectic Enterprises
(215) 923-2226

510 Pine Street Philadelphia 19106-4111

Collection:	Specialty books and prints.
# of Volumes:	2,000
Specialties:	First editions; American literature; English literature; art.
Services:	Accepts want lists.
Credit Cards:	No
Owner:	Barry J. Hecht
Year Estab:	1981

M. Martin Hinkle "Seeking Mysteries"
(215) 592-1178
Fax: (215) 592-1521

609 Addison Street Philadelphia 19147

Collection:	Specialty
# of Volumes:	1,000
Specialties:	Mystery; detective, signed first editions.

Services: Catalog, accepts want lists.
Credit Cards: No
Year Estab: 1992

Hobson's Choice   (215) 884-4853
511 Runnymede Avenue Jenkintown 19046

Collection: Specialty
# of Volumes: 5,000
Specialties: Philadelphia; first editions; literature; music; poetry; art.
Services: Search service.
Credit Cards: No
Owner: Jane Walker
Year Estab: 1980

Timothy Hughes Rare & Early Newspapers   (717) 326-1045
PO Box 3636 Williamsport 17701   Fax: (717) 326-7606

Collection: Specialty
Specialties: Newspapers, from 1620-1960.
Services: Appraisals, catalog.
Credit Cards: Yes
Year Estab: 1976

Alan F. Innes - Books   (717) 559-7873
PO Box 123 Shohola 18458

Collection: General stock.
# of Volumes: 2,500
Specialties: Early travel; voyages; exploration; maritime, H.D. Thoreau.
Services: Search service, accepts want lists.
Year Estab: 1989

D.B. Lasky   (717) 969-0241
314 Linden Street Scranton 18503

Collection: General stock.
# of Volumes: 12,000
Specialties: Americana
Services: Appraisals, accepts want lists.
Credit Cards: No
Year Estab: 1954

Legacy Books   (215) 675-6762
PO Box 494 Hatboro 19040

Collection: Specialty new and used.
# of Volumes: 2,000 (used)
Specialties: Folklore; American studies; related subjects.
Services: Subject catalogs (occasional), accepts want lists.
Credit Cards: Yes

Owner:	Lillian Krelove & Richard K. Burns
Year Estab:	1958

Ann W. McCreary   (717) 564-3291
PO Box 4043 Harrisburg 17111

Collection:	Specialty
# of Volumes:	1,000
Specialties:	Dogs
Services:	Accepts want lists.
Credit Cards:	No
Year Estab:	1981

Dave Ondulick   (412) 929-5923
615 Vernon Street Belle Vernon 15012

Collection:	General stock.
# of Volumes:	1,400
Services:	Accepts want lists.
Credit Cards:	No
Year Estab:	1981

Rebellion Numismatics   (412) 361-2722
1810 Antietam Street Pittsburgh 15206

Collection:	Specialty books, periodicals and catalogs.
Specialties:	Numismatics, including coins, medals, tokens, paper, engraving, counterfeiting, bank history and lotteries.
Credit Cards:	No
Owner:	Wayne K. Homren
Year Estab:	1989

Revere Books   *(215) 847-2709
PO Box 420 Revere 18953

Collection:	Specialty
# of Volumes:	3,000
Specialties:	Modern first editions; signed books; literary collectibles including proofs, review copies and letters.
Services:	Catalog, accepts want lists.
Credit Cards:	No
Owner:	Kenn Varane
Year Estab:	1992

Richard T. Rosenthal   (215) 726-5493
4718 Springfield Avenue Philadelphia 19143

Collection:	Specialty
# of Volumes:	1,000
Specialties:	Photography
Services:	Appraisals, search service, accepts want lists.

Credit Cards: No
Year Estab: 1980

Betty Schmid, Circusiana   (412) 341-4597
485 Sleepy Hollow Pittsburgh 15228

Collection:	Specialty books and ephemera.
# of Volumes:	2,000
Specialties:	Circus and carnivals in fact and fiction.
Services:	Appraisals, search service, catalog, accepts want lists.
Credit Cards:	No
Year Estab:	1958

Eileen Serxner   *(215) 664-7960
Box 2544 Bala Cynwyd 19004

Collection:	General stock.
# of Volumes:	10,000
Specialties:	Modern first editions; children's; sports.
Services:	Search service, accepts want lists.
Credit Cards:	No
Year Estab:	1991

Larry W. Soltys   *(215) 372-7670
330 South 17½ Street Reading 19602

Collection:	Specialty
Specialties:	Southeastern Pennsylvania history and local authors.
Services:	Accepts want lists.
Credit Cards:	No

Somewhere In Time   (717) 349-7003
PO Box 158 Spring Run 17262

Collection:	Specialty
# of Volumes:	25,000
Specialties:	First editions; Americana; Civil War.
Services:	Lists, accepts want lists.
Credit Cards:	No
Owner:	George H. & Adele P. Foreman
Year Estab:	1989
Comments:	See also Fayetteville Open Shop section.

Summerhouse Books   (215) 438-1230
Box 29593 Philadelphia 19144

Collection:	General stock.
# of Volumes:	2,000-3,000
Services:	Appraisals, accepts want lists, search service.
Credit Cards:	Yes
Owner:	Eugene Okamoto
Year Estab:	1989

T-P Antiques & Collectibles
192 Wilson Drive Hazleton 18201

(717) 459-0993
Fax: (717) 459-6090

Collection:	Specialty
# of Volumes:	2,500+
Specialties:	Signed; first editions; children's.
Credit Cards:	No
Owner:	Trudy Gutterman
Year Estab:	1985
Comments:	Collection can be viewed by appointment.

Volume Control
955 Sandy Lane Warminster 18974

(215) 674-0217

Collection:	Specialty
# of Volumes:	4,000+
Specialties:	World War II.
Services:	Search service, catalog, accepts want lists.
Credit Cards:	No
Owner:	Jack Hatter
Year Estab:	1984

Ernest Webb Books
Star Route Box 137 Huntingdon 16652

(814) 643-3197

Collection:	General stock.
# of Volumes:	7,000
Specialties:	Pennsylvania; hunting.
Services:	Search service, accepts want lists.
Credit Cards:	No
Year Estab:	1950's

Robert M. Wynne (Cloak And Dagger Books)
227 Lurgan Avenue Shippensburg 17257

(717) 532-8213

Collection:	General stock.
# of Volumes:	5,000
Specialties:	Mystery; detective.
Services:	Search service, catalog, accepts want lists.
Credit Cards:	No
Year Estab:	1987

Specialty Index

Children's illustrated

Children's series